COUNSELOR

NATIONAL CERTIFICATION
AND
STATE LICENSING PREPARATION

CRC and NCC

Leona H. Liberty, Ed.D., CRC, NCC

ARCO
NEW YORK

First Edition

Copyright © 1990 by Leona H. Liberty

 ARCO

Simon & Schuster, Inc.
15 Columbus Circle
New York, NY 10023

DISTRIBUTED BY PRENTICE HALL TRADE SALES

Text Design by Peter Katucki

Manufactured in the United States of America

1   2   3   4   5   6   7   8   9   10

Library of Congress Cataloging-in-Publication Data

Liberty, Leona H.
      Counselor : national certification and state licensing preparation
  / Leona H. Liberty.—1st ed.
          p.   cm.
      Includes bibliographical references.
      ISBN 0-13-183260-3
      1. Counselors—Certification—United States.   2. Rehabilitation
  counselors—Certification—United States.   3. Counselors—Licenses—
  United States.   4. Rehabilitation counselors—Licenses—United
  States.   5. Counseling—Examinations—Study guides.
  6. Rehabilitation counseling—Examinations—Study guides.
  7. National Counselor Examination—Study guides.   8. Certified
  Rehabilitation Counselor Examination—Study guide.   I. Title.
  BF637.C6L46   1989   89-28095
  361.3′23′076—dc20   CIP

CONTENTS

Section III

Career Counseling Theories, Occupational Resources and Tests, and Ability to Interpret Test Results

Section IV

Psychosocial and Medical Aspects of Common Disorders

Section V

Test Bank

PREFACE

This study skills guide has been written to assist candidates in their preparation for the *National Counselor Certification* (NCC) and the *Certified Rehabilitation Counselor* (CRC) examinations.

This book has been organized to address major content areas found on the NCC and CRC examinations. All material has been excerpted and summarized according to topical information found in major counseling textbooks.

No attempt is made to present this guide as a comprehensive resource. Rather, readers are directed to major textbooks found at the end of each section to aid in their examination preparation. In addition, to better prepare you as a test taker, each section is prefaced by a list of "Key Concepts," described in the respective chapter, and ten preview questions. A "Quick Quiz" at the end of each chapter reinforces pertinent concepts.

Section I reviews the guidelines required for certification eligibility for both examinations. The ethical guidelines are identified and discussed. As the CRC candidate must be familiar with major legislation that serves as the historical base for the profession of rehabilitation counseling, a chronology is presented. Service delivery, a required topic for both the CRC and NCC, completes Section I.

Section II presents an overview of major counseling theories and other theories of human behavior, material relevant to both the NCC and CRC candidate.

Section III presents an overview of career counseling theories and information, tests, and test-giving information. Both NCC and CRC candidates must know this information.

Section IV contains medical and psychosocial aspects of disabilities. The CRC candidate may find this section especially helpful. The NCC candidate may find a review of some of the disorders helpful in heightening counselor awareness of the multifaceted problems and needs of clients.

Section V contains a Test Bank. A concerted attempt has been made to develop test items covering all major topics, hypotheses, and tenets. The reader is reminded that test questions are not actual samples from earlier NCC or CRC examinations, as items from past examinations are reused and therefore not made public.

In addition to NCC and CRC candidates, other students of counseling may find this book helpful. One example may be students reviewing for their Master's degree comprehensive examination.

My intention in writing this book was to provide a helpful resource for professional counselors. Any comments or questions will be welcomed and appreciated.

Leona H. Liberty

This book is dedicated to the ones I love:

To Tom, my husband, for his support, encouragement,
and valuable assistance
To my children, for their uniqueness
To Jim, for his worldliness
To Chris, for his persistence
To Donna, for her graciousness
To Tomie, for his challenging nature
To Lee, for his unconditional positive regard

Section

I

History, Legal and Professional Ethics, and Service Delivery

Section I

History, Legal and Professional Ethics, and Service Delivery

KEY CONCEPTS

American Association for Counseling and Development
American Rehabilitation Counseling Association
Certification
Certified Rehabilitation Counselor
Code of Ethics
Competence
Confidentiality
Licensure
National Certified Counselor
Private Practitioner

REHABILITATION CONCEPTS

Civilian Rehabilitation Act
Disability
Education for All Handicapped Children
Handicapping Condition
Javits-Wagner-O'Day Act
Job Training Partnership Act
Office of Vocational Rehabilitation
Primitive Practices
Randolph-Shepperd Act
Rehabilitation Act and Amendments
Smith-Hughes Act
Smith-Sears Act
Social Security Disability
Soldier's Rehabilitation Act
Supplemental Security Income
Title V: Sections 501–508
Wagner-O'Day Act

5

PREVIEW QUESTIONS

1. What is the major reason that certification examinations were developed?

2. What is a code of ethics?

3. Is certification synonymous with state licensure?

4. Why must the counselor keep the contents of the counseling session confidential?

5. Is it professionally unethical to have a casual date with a client?

6. What should the counselor do if progress is not being made after a reasonable time?

7. What influence does politics play in the availability of human service programs?

8. For what length of time does the NBCC or the CRCC certify a candidate who passes the examination?

9. What do the letters NCC and CRC stand for, and in what ways are these credentials similar and different?

10. Why do certified counselors need to participate in continuing education courses?

NATIONAL BOARD FOR CERTIFIED COUNSELORS

The National Board for Certified Counselors (NBCC) was established in 1982 as an independent agency for the primary purpose of providing a national standard that could be used as a measure of generic counseling professionalism. As of May 1988, the NBCC has certified more than 17,500 counselors. Currently, thirteen states have adopted the NBCC examination as part of their licensure process. (*National Counselor Certification Information & Application Booklet, 1989*).

Once an individual is certified, he or she is entitled to use the designation of National Certified Counselor (NCC) for a period of five years, after which time the counselor must be recertified by either completing one hundred contact hours of continuing education, or by re-examination. NBCC also offers a specialty examination for career counselors. Eligibility includes and exceeds requirements beyond the NCC.

CODE OF ETHICS FOR THE NCC

A *Code of Ethics*, developed by the NBCC, guides the behavior of the professional counselor seeking the National Certified Counselor recognition (1987). The code is divided into six sections, which are summarized as follows:

Section A: General

This section emphasizes accountability to the profession and to the client. Certified counselors must neither claim nor imply professional qualities that exceed those possessed. Certified counselors are reminded that they not only have a responsibility to the clients they serve, but also to the agency or institutions by which they are employed. If there is a discrepancy between the counselor's job and the client's needs, the certified counselor must rectify this by either referring the client to another professional agency or by terminating his or her affiliation with the particular agency. Certified counselors must guard individual rights and become aware of stereotyping, discriminating, and/or condoning or engaging in sexual harassment either by repeated comments or gestures.

Section B: Counseling Relationship

This section addresses the belief that the client's integrity and welfare must be respected by the certified counselor at all times. Client- and counselor-shared information must be kept confidential, yet within the legal obligation of the law. That is, if a client's condition indicates a clear and imminent danger to either the client or others, the counselor must take *reasonable* personal action and inform the appropriate authorities. Clients must be informed of this obligation.

Counselors must make every effort to keep confidential information stored properly. This includes electronically stored information.

In the event that cooperation with other agencies is needed, the certified counselor must provide records that describe accurate, unbiased, and factual information and share only appropriate and needed information. The counselor is obligated to know referral sources and to recognize his or her limitations as a counselor and agency representative, as well as the limitations of other agencies.

There can be no dual relationships with clients. If the client and the counselor have established a personal relationship, the counselor must refer the client to another counselor, so that objectivity and professional judgment will remain intact.

Section C: Measurement and Evaluation

The purpose of testing and evaluation must be made known to the client. Certified counselors are responsible for selecting appropriate tests, recognizing psychometric limitations, and acting responsibly when evaluating test results. The certified counselor is cautioned against the overreliance of computer-assisted test administration and scoring.

Section D: Research and Publication

In planning research activities involving human subjects, the certified counselor must be aware of and responsive to all pertinent ethical principles as identified in the following resources:

Ethical Principles in the Conduct of Research with Human Participants, Washington, D.C., American Psychological Association, Inc., 1982; *Code of Federal Regulations, Title 45, Subtitle A, Part 46*, as currently issued; *Ethical Principles of Psychologists*, American Psychological Association, Principle #9: Research with Human Participants; *Buckley Amendment*; and current federal regulations and various state rights privacy acts.

The counselor must take all reasonable precautions to avoid causing injurious psychological, physical, or social effects on subjects by explaining experimental procedures, describing discomfort and risks, describing benefits expected, disclosing appropriate alternative procedures that would be advantageous, and instructing subjects that they are free to withdraw their consent and discontinue participation in the counseling at any time.

Original research data must be made available to others who may wish to replicate a study. Full credit must be given to all those who are so deserving.

Section E: Consulting

Certified counselors must be aware of their own values and limits of expertise. The counselor and the client must understand and agree upon problems, goals, and consequences of selected intervention.

Section F: Private Practice

Counselors engaged in private practice must adhere to the same professional guidelines that guide counselors who are employed by a not-for-profit or non-profit agency. Certified counselors must accurately present their credentials and not present any misleading information regarding their competencies or mission.

Appendix: Certification Examination

All applicants are responsible for the accuracy of information submitted to the National Board of Certified Counselors so that the Board may determine an applicant eligible to sit for the examination.

During the examination, the applicant may not use notes or communicate with others regarding questions or answers. After completing the examination, participants must not disclose to others items that appeared on the examination form.

THE NATIONAL COUNSELOR EXAMINATION

The National Counselor Examination (NCE) is comprised of 200 multiple-choice questions. Items are drawn from an existing pool. Of the 200 questions, only 160 items are used to determine a passing score; the remaining 40 items are being field tested to determine their appropriateness for future use. Test takers are not informed which questions are being field tested.

The content areas for the NCE were adopted from the standards used by the Council for Accreditation of Counseling and Related Educational Programs (CACREP). Only generic preparation areas are included in the test; these "common-core" areas are described below:

Section I: Human Growth and Development

This section addresses the nature and needs of individuals throughout their life span. Major theories of personality and of normal and abnormal human behaviors from historical, psychological, and sociological factors are covered. (*This information is addressed in Sections I, II, and IV of this book.*)

Section II: Social and Cultural Foundations

Information in this section includes socioeconomic, multicultural, and pluralistic trends. (*This information is addressed in Section I of this book.*)

Section III: The Helping Relationship

This section includes major counseling and consultation theories as well as research factors. (*This information is addressed in Sections II and III of this book.*)

Section IV: Group Dynamics, Processes, and Counseling

Information in this area is related to group dynamics, leadership, style, and counseling theories. (*This information is addressed in Section II of this book.*)

Section V: Life Span and Career Development

This section covers information related to career development and occupational information. (*This information is addressed in Section III of this book.*)

Section VI: Appraisal of Individuals

Information in this section reviews methods of interpretation, validity, reliability, and other psychometric information as well as ethical and legal considerations in the use of test data. (*This information is addressed in Section III of this book.*)

Section VII: Research and Evaluation

This section covers statistics, principles of needs assessment, and ethical and legal considerations. (*This information is addressed in Sections I and III of this book.*)

Section VIII: Professional Orientation

Information in this section reviews professional roles and functions, goals, objectives of professional organizations and associations, professional preparation standards, and credentialing. (*This information is addressed in Section I of this book.*)

The National Certified Counselor is a more generic counseling certification than the Certified Rehabilitation Counselor (CRC), a description of which follows. Many CRCs have dual certification as both a CRC and NCC.

REHABILITATION COUNSELOR CERTIFICATION

The following information is derived from the *Guide to Rehabilitation Counselor Certification* (1987). This guide describes professional requirements that determine eligibility to apply and sit for the Certified Rehabilitation Counselor (CRC) examination. In addition to this examination, the Certification Insurance Rehabilitation Specialists Commission (CIRSC) was established in 1984 to certify insurance professionals who serve clients who receive insurance disability monies. Eligibility to sit for the CIRS exam includes and exceeds requirements beyond those of the CRC.

The requirements for Rehabilitation Counselor Certification are divided into 17 sections, which are summarized as follows:

Section 1: The Certification Program

The establishment of the Commission on Rehabilitation Counselor Certification (CRCC) took place in 1974. It was a combined effort of the National Rehabilitation Counseling Association (NRCA) and the American Rehabilitation Counselor Association (ARCA). As of January 1989, there were 8,954 Certified Rehabilitation Counselors in the United States and 12 outside the United States.

Section 2: The Certification Calendar

The Certified Rehabilitation Counselor examination is given twice a year, typically once in the spring and once in the fall. Application deadlines are indentified in the most recent "Guide."

Section 3: Criteria for Eligibility

This section identifies requirements needed to sit for the CRC examination. There are nine categories, some of which are to be phased out by the end of 1992. If a candidate's degree was not a Master's degree in Rehabilitation

Counseling, or from a Rehabilitation Counselor Education Program that was not fully accredited by the Commission of Rehabilitation Education at the time the degree was granted (which included an approved internship under the supervision of a Certified Rehabilitation Counselor), applicants need to demonstrate they have acceptable employment experience.

Section 4: Criteria for Relatedness of Degree

This section describes required courses that determine whether a candidate's degree is related to a Master's degree in Rehabilitation Counseling. An applicant must have one course in the area of Theories and Techniques of Counseling. Three courses are required that address the following areas: Occupational Information and the World of Work; Job Placement and Development; Medical Aspects of Disabilities; Principles of Rehabilitation; Psychological Aspects of Disabilities; and/or Personal and Vocational Adjustment. Two courses are required that have as a primary focus the following areas: Psychological Assessment; Research Methodology; Work Evaluation; Community Resources; Career Development; and/or Delivery of Rehabilitation Services.

CRCC urges applicants who are interested in the certification process to send transcripts and course information to them. In turn, they will help determine eligibility.

Section 5: Criteria for Acceptable Employment Experience

Only full-time paid employment or its equivalent is considered acceptable employment criteria. At least 50 percent of an applicant's time must be spent working as a rehabilitation counselor in a rehabilitation setting, providing rehabilitation services to a disabled population, as defined by CRCC. Each place of employment must provide job activities with minimal acceptable percentages of time allowed for particular activities.

Section 6: Provisional Certification

An individual may apply for Provisional Certification and thereby be eligible to sit for the examination. This category is available only to an applicant who meets educational and employment criteria, but lacks supervision under a CRC.

Section 7: Instructions for Completing the Application

This section is self-explanatory. Applicants are urged to complete the application properly to expedite the evaluation process.

Section 8: Standards and Credentials: Purpose and Process

A Standards and Credentials Committee was established to ensure fairness. This committee reviews each application for approval or rejection and notifies the applicant accordingly.

Section 9: Appeals Committee: Purpose and Procedures

Section 9 describes the Appeals Process whereby an applicant may question the above committee's decision.

THE CRC EXAMINATION

Section 10: The Certification Examination

The Certification Examination consists of 400 multiple-choice questions drawn from an item pool. There are two sections to the examination. Section I is administered in the morning. A lunch break precedes Section II, which is administered in the afternoon. Three and one-half hours are allowed for the completion of each section. If necessary, special testing arrangements may be arranged.

A candidate who fails to achieve a minimum passing score on the first attempt is permitted to retake the examination within twelve months of the original examination date, without going through the re-application process in its entirety.

Section 11: Content Classification Chart

According to the CRC board, a candidate is required to demonstrate knowledge in the following five areas:

I. Foundations of Rehabilitation Counseling

This area includes principles, history, philosophy, legislation, and ethics of rehabilitation, and disability conditions. (*This information is addressed in Sections I and IV of this book.*)

II. Client Assessment

This area includes assessment techniques, interpretation, and resources for assessment. (*This information is addressed in Section III of this book.*)

III. Planning and Service Delivery

This area includes synthesis of client information, plan development, service delivery, case management, and community resources. (*This information is addressed in Section I of this book.*)

IV. Counseling and Interviewing

This area includes theories and techniques in vocational and affective counseling, foundations of interviewing, and principles of human behavior. (*This information is addressed in Sections II and III of this book.*)

V. Job Development and Placement

This area includes occupational and labor market information, job development, and placement. (*This information is addressed in Section III of this book.*)

Section 12: Sample Examination Questions

Eight questions and answers are presented.

Section 13: Reading List

Selected textbooks are identified in this section.

Section 14: Examination Scores, Profiles, and Certificates

Information regarding scoring procedures and the issuing of certificates is presented in this section.

Section 15: Use of the CRC Designation

The designations of CRC, CRC/P (Provisional) and the CRC/R (Retired) are described in this section.

Section 16: Certification and Maintenance

Certification is valid for five years. A Certification Maintenance Plan requires CRCs to demonstrate their continuous professional development. At the end of the five-year period, the CRC must have completed 100 contact hours of acceptable continuing education courses or programs or retake the examination. An Alternate Certification Maintenance Plan is also available (Wolfe, 1988).

Section 17: Fees

All fees affiliated with the examination and credential are identified in this section.

CODE OF ETHICS FOR THE CRC

The *Code of Ethics* that guides rehabilitation counselors is organized in ten canons, summarized as follows (1987):

Canon 1: Moral and Legal Standards

Rehabilitation counselors shall behave in a legal, ethical, and moral manner, in accordance with their profession.

Canon 2: Counselor-Client Relationship

The integrity of people and groups with whom rehabilitation counselors work shall at all times be placed in interest above their own.

Canon 3: Client Advocacy

Rehabilitation counselors shall serve as advocates for persons with disabilities.

Canon 4: Professional Relationships

Rehabilitation counselors shall act with integrity in their relationships with colleagues, other organizations, agencies, and referral sources to achieve optimum benefits for clients.

Canon 5: Public Statements/Fees

Fees are to be established within professional standards.

Canon 6: Confidentiality

Information obtained in confidence shall be respected.

Canon 7: Assessment

The welfare of clients in the selection, application, and interpretation of assessment measures shall be promoted.

Canon 8: Research Activities

Rehabilitation counselors shall assist to expand the knowledge needed to more effectively serve persons with disabilities.

Canon 9: Competence

Professional competencies shall be established and maintained at a level at which clients may receive the highest quality of services available.

Canon 10: CRC Credential

Rehabilitation counselors holding the CRC designation shall honor the integrity and respect limitations placed upon its use.

COURT CASES INVOLVING COUNSELING PROFESSIONALS

Ethics provide guidelines for professional conduct of all counselors and serve as a basis for evaluating misconduct. When clients believe they have been unduly harmed by a professional counselor, they may ask a court of law to determine whether the counselor acted in an irresponsible manner.

The courts have acted upon issues that include: disclosure of privileged communication; failure to exercise adequate precautions for a suicidal client; sexual misconduct; invasion of privacy; and defamation (Brown, Pryzwansky, & Schulte, 1987; Barton & Barton, 1984; Fisher & Sorenson, 1985; Hopkins & Anderson, 1985; Slimak & Berkowitz, 1983). As confidentiality is perhaps the ethic most open to debate, two examples of case outcome will be described:

In *Pittsburgh Action Against Rape, 494 PA. 15, 428 A.2d 126, 1981,* the director of a rape counseling center refused to allow the files of a rape victim's statement to be scrutinized by the lawyers for the accused. A lower court found the director in contempt and ordered the release of the files. However, upon appeal, the court ruled that confidentiality was a vital and essential component of counseling services and that unless this could be guaranteed, other victims might not seek needed services.

In *Peck v. Counseling Service of Addison County, Inc. 83–062 VT. Sup. Ct., June 14, 1985,* the Supreme Court of Vermont reversed a lower court's decision and found that a mental health outpatient center had a responsibility to warn the parents of their son's alleged threat that he would burn down his parents' barn, which he proceeded to do. The court found that failure of the counseling center to warn the parents of harm to their property constituted negligence and breach of duty owed to the parents by the agency.

Even though no conclusions can be universally derived from these two court cases, as they were only heard at the state level, it was established that professional counselors are entitled to privileged communication between themselves and their clients. However, this privilege is to be deferred when there is reasonable cause to believe harm may come to either an individual or to personal property. In addition, the court has generally found that counselors and other professionals may be held to a higher standard of accountability than nonprofessionals (Hopkins & Anderson, 1985). For more detailed information on professional responsibilities and court cases, a review of the following sources may be helpful: *Ethics and the Law in Mental Health Administration* (Barton & Barton, 1984); *Psychological Consultation: Introduction to Theory and Practice* (Brown, Pryzwansky, & Schulte, 1987); *School Law for Counselors, Psychologists, and Social Workers* (Fisher & Sorenson, 1985); *The Counselor and the Law* (Hopkins & Anderson, 1985).

THE ROLE AND FUNCTION OF THE REHABILITATION COUNSELOR

The role and function of rehabilitation counselors are not easily defined because of the heterogeneity in preparation, the various settings the rehabilitation counselor works in, and the various populations served. Nevertheless, what distinguishes the rehabilitation counselor (or rehabilitationist) from other helping professionals is that rehabilitation counselors address the unique needs of handicapped individuals (Wright, 1980; Wright, 1983).

The following twenty principles by Beatrice Wright (1983, pp. xi–xvii) may serve to clarify the values by which rehabilitation counselors assist persons who have disabilities. These principles may also serve as a review for the philosophy by which the profession of rehabilitation counseling is to be guided:

1. Every individual needs respect and encouragement; the presence of a disability, no matter how severe, does not alter these fundamental rights.

2. The severity of a handicap can be increased or diminished by environmental conditions.

3. Issues of coping and adjusting to a disability cannot be validly considered without examining reality problems in the social and physical environment.

4. The assets of the person must receive considerable attention in the rehabilitation effort.

5. The significance of a disability is affected by a person's feelings about the self and his or her situation.

6. The active participation of the client in the planning and execution of the rehabilitation program is to be sought as fully as possible.

7. The client is seen not as an isolated individual but as part of a larger group that often includes the family.

8. Because each person has unique characteristics and each situation its own properties, variability is required in rehabilitation plans.

9. Predictor variables, based on group outcomes in rehabilitation, should be applied with caution to the individual case.

10. All phases of rehabilitation have psychological aspects.

11. Interdisciplinary and interagency collaboration and coordination of services are essential.

12. Self-help organizations are important allies in the rehabilitation effort.

13. In addition to the special problems of particular groups, rehabilitation clients commonly share certain problems by virtue of their disadvantaged and devalued position.

14. It is essential that society as a whole continuously and persistently strives to provide the basic means toward the fulfillment of the lives of all its inhabitants, including those with disabilities.

15. Involvement of the client with the general life of the community is a fundamental principle guiding decisions concerning living arrangements and the use of resources.

16. People with disabilities, like all citizens, are entitled to participate in and contribute to the general life of the community.

17. Provision must be made for the effective dissemination of information concerning legislation and community offerings of potential benefit to persons with disabilities.

18. Basic research can profitably be guided by the question of usefulness in ameliorating problems, a vital consideration in rehabilitation fields, including psychology.

19. Persons with disabilities should be called upon to serve as co-planners, co-evaluators, and consultants to others, including professional persons.

20. Continuing review of the contributions of psychologists and others in rehabilitation within a framework of guiding principles that are themselves subject to review is an essential part of the self-correcting effort of science and the professions.

An important point to note from the above description is the purposeful way by which individuals are described. Wright believes we need to see an individual first, then note any differences. Therefore it is more correct to say "a person who has a disability," rather than a "disabled person."

In addition, the words *disability* and *handicapping condition* must be distinguished. A *disability* is a medically diagnosed physical or mental impairment, such as diabetes, a heart condition, or the loss of a limb. By contrast, a *handicapping condition* describes the obstacles that prevent an individual from attaining some specific goal.

In the case of the person who has diabetes, he or she has a disability but may or may not have some resulting handicapping condition. Therefore, not all persons who have disabilities need the services of the rehabilitation counselor.

The concept of containment versus spread is another way to conceptualize and summarize the role of the rehabilitation counselor. The term *spread* refers to the power of a single characteristic to evoke inferences about an individual's total being (Dembo, Leviton, & Wright, 1975). The person is seen as disabled because of a specific medical condition and may be labeled inferior with respect to other physical and mental characteristics shared by all humans (Wright, 1983). For example, the person who has low vision may also be thought of as hearing impaired, or the person who is hearing impaired may also be thought of as being mentally retarded or emotionally disturbed.

The rehabilitation counselor works to help restore a handicapped person by addressing total and unique needs and consequently to minimize liabilities and to emphasize and strengthen abilities. The rehabilitation plan is thought to be based on holistic principles whereby a comprehensive rehabilitation plan should address physical, psychological, psychosocial (including the family), vocational, educational, recreational, economic and sexual areas (Rubin & Roessler, 1987; Wright, 1980).

CHRONOLOGY OF THE HISTORY OF REHABILITATION

Historically, there have been negative attitudes toward disabled persons largely due to the lack of knowledge regarding proper treatment and fear. However, this devalued status began to change during the nineteenth century when Benjamin Franklin and the Quakers established the first rehabilitation hospital in Philadelphia and Thomas Gallaudet established the first college for the deaf in Washington, D.C., in 1857.

In addition, John Itard, a French physician, took on the task of educating a child who had been abandoned by his parents and raised by a pack of wolves until he was twelve years old. Itard had some success with what was known as the "Wild Boy of Aveyron." This paved the way for others to become interested in working with individuals who display some degree of either mental retardation or aberrant behavior, or both. For example:

Samuel Gridley Howe was an earnest advocate for the blind and mentally retarded population in Massachusetts. He was instrumental in establishing one of the first schools for handicapped children in the United States. Howe found it necessary to parade the children around in public to raise needed funds to maintain the school, thereby eliciting sympathy to support his cause.

Dorothea Dix gave religious instruction to those incarcerated for a criminal offense. She found that mentally ill persons were inappropriately jailed with criminals. As a result, she became an advocate for mentally ill persons and advanced the notion that the mentally ill have special needs that were not being addressed.

Joseph Lister is credited with developing techniques for antiseptic surgery, which gave doctors the ability to correct some orthopedic disabilities. Injured Civil War veterans also aided in the acceptance of disabled persons in mainstream America.

Numerous others have followed in the footsteps of those cited above to counterattack, refute, and challenge the stigma attached to a person who has a disability. In addition, important pieces of legislation have assisted the disabled to become mainstreamed. Examples of major laws and critical events follow.

Twentieth Century

In 1913 the income tax law was passed. This opened the door to government backing of vocational rehabilitation agencies and services, based on the notion that full employment of all citizens would widen the tax base.

In 1916 the National Defense Act was passed to assist returning World War I veterans toward re-employment.

In 1917 the Smith-Hughes Vocational Act was passed by Congress, providing federal grants to states for vocational educational programs. This Act was influenced to some extent by World War I events. The act originally required states and local school districts to match federal funds. A number of skill-training programs were established in large cities. Today most high schools offer trade and industry programs as part of their curriculum, which has its origins in this Act.

In 1918 the Soldier's Rehabilitation Act, also known as the Smith-Sears Act, was passed. Recognizing that returning veterans had a need for comprehensive services, this Act provided additional monies to address career and personal counseling needs of World War I veterans.

In 1920 the Civilian Rehabilitation Act, also known as the Smith-Fess Act, was passed. This was the first piece of legislation to provide occupational, adjustment, and placement services to persons who had a disability but who were not Armed Forces veterans. Monies were provided on a 50:50 federal to state matching ratio. A person had to be sixteen years old to qualify for services.

Presidents Harding and Coolidge believed that government was best when it governed least, so neither president promoted additional federal aid to states for vocational rehabilitation. Hoover further embraced the philosophy of "rugged individualism"; as everyone was expected to be able to care for himself or herself, his administration discouraged all types of social programs, viewing them as not being in the best interest of the country. However, with the subsequent election of Franklin D. Roosevelt, services that addressed individual needs were once again supported by the government.

In 1935 the Social Security Act was established. This Act laid the foundation for permanent federal and state vocational rehabilitation programs.

In 1936 the Randolph-Shepperd Act was passed. This Act legislated that the blind have priority in operating vending stands on federal property.

In 1938 the Wagner-O'Day Act was passed. This Act made it mandatory for the federal government to purchase products from workshops for the blind.

World War II was a significant era for the growth of the rehabilitation movement. With twelve million men drafted, there was a labor shortage and a demand for industrial products to maintain war efforts. This afforded the handicapped population opportunities to demonstrate they had abilities if placed in an appropriate job.

In 1943 the Welch-Clark Act was passed. This Act is also referred to as the GI Bill of Assistance. It provided additional services, such as higher education, for returning veterans.

In 1943 the Office of Vocational Rehabilitation (OVR) was established. In some states the OVR is referred to either as the BVR (Bureau of Vocational Rehabilitation) or the DVR (Division of Vocational Rehabilitation). These agencies are the single largest employer of vocational rehabilitation counselors. Mary Switzer was appointed as the first director of the OVR and remained in that position until 1951.

Also in 1943, the Barden-LaFollette Act was passed. This bill expanded services to mentally retarded and mentally ill persons and increased services for physical and occupational restoration. Veterans were eligible for full federal funding of needs, while civilians received services supported by a 50:50 matching federal and state ratio.

In 1954 the Vocational Rehabilitation Amendments were signed by President Eisenhower, a strong supporter of rehabilitation. Federal and state contributions were changed to a 60:40 matching federal to state ratio. Services were expanded to include training monies for persons working with the handicapped population. Research grants, funds for equipment, adjustment training, evaluation of programs, and other ancillary services were funded.

In 1954 Social Security Disability Benefits (SSDB) were established. These benefits provided monies for retraining programs, as well as support monies for those persons who had a work history but were unable to work for at least one year because of a severe medical condition. Supplemental Security Income (SSI) followed. Beneficiaries of this program typically did not have a significant work history and did not earn enough money to be self-sustaining. This recipient is often the worker who is employed at a sheltered workshop. As of this writing, SSI recipients may only earn $300 per month to qualify for monies.

In 1965 the Vocational Rehabilitation Act Amendments were passed. The matching ratio for federal to state monies was changed to 75:25. Extended evaluations became available (up to eighteen months), to see whether added services would help re-employ more persons. Public offenders, alcoholics, drug abusers, as well as socially disadvantaged groups were now eligible for vocational rehabilitation funds.

Such plans as Medicare, which constitutes national health insurance for persons sixty-five years of age and older or for certain disabled individuals, and Medicaid, which provides medical assistance to needy families and dependent children of the aged, blind, and disabled, were now becoming available to Americans in need.

In 1970 the effectiveness of the Golden Era of Vocational (public) Rehabilitation was questioned. President Nixon was not a strong supporter of rehabilitation programs and vetoed an increase of monies for additional vocational rehabilitation services.

In 1971 the Javits-Wagner-O'Day Act was passed. This legislation by Senator Jacob Javits, from New York State, expanded the original Wagner-O'Day Act, whereby government agencies purchased services from workshops for the blind. Government agencies were now encouraged to purchase services from any population who had a handicapping condition.

In 1973 the Rehabilitation Act and its Amendments were passed. This Act is referred to as the billion-dollar program. The federal to state matching ratio was changed to 80:20. There was a strong emphasis to expand and prioritize services to the severely disabled population. The Rehabilitation Services Administration (RSA) was established. States were mandated to submit plans describing how they intended to serve the handicapped population. An Individualized Written Rehabilitation Plan (IWRP), which outlined short-term and long-term goals, set forth specific services to be provided, projected dates for initiation and completion of needed services, and designed a procedure to determine timeliness and effectiveness of each plan, was to be developed. The IWRP was also to be mutually developed by client and counselor, with the client verifying his or her participation in the program by signing the plan. Client Assistance Programs (CAPS) were established both as a watchdog for OVR and to provide any needed advocacy services. A compliance board for architectural and transportation barriers was to be established.

Title V of the Rehabilitation Act of 1973 is critical to know as the implications of these subsections are widely quoted:

Section 501 of Title V mandates that the federal government be nondiscriminatory in its own hiring practices and be a model agency for promoting, recruiting, hiring, and advancing workers who have disabilities.

Section 502 addresses accessibility of public buildings and of any building receiving federal funds, including most schools, colleges, and universities. Any public building built after 1976 must meet accessibility standards for bathrooms, telephones, and other needed and basic facilities.

Section 503 states that employers who receive federal contracts in excess of $2,500 must make reasonable accommodation to recruit, hire, and assist disabled persons. To reduce discrimination, hiring practices and job requirements must be related to job performance.

Section 504 has been referred to as Affirmative Action legislation, as it prohibits discrimination against the handicapped within any program, institution, or activity receiving government financial assistance. It is only a forty-five word statement, yet it has stimulated more than twenty-seven pages of regulations, with far-reaching implications. Minorities, including the handicapped, have used Section 504 to argue fair employment practices.

In 1975 the Federal Privacy Act was passed. This legislation gave all individuals the right to know what has been written about them in agency records.

In 1975 the Education Act for All Handicapped Children (PL 94-142) was passed. This special education act provides all children up to twenty-one years of age with the right to a free and appropriate public education, in the least restrictive environment. An Individualized Educational Program (IEP) must be developed for each eligible child.

In 1978, Amendments to the 1973 Rehabilitation Act were passed. This provided monies for Independent Living Services, such as housing, peer counseling, attendant care, and recreational services. Independent Living Centers were to be established and staffed on a priority basis by persons who had a handicapping condition, providing role models for those who were to take advantage of services.

During the 1980s, rehabilitation services experienced a slower growth than in earlier periods, but emphasis was placed on expanding services to many different populations. There have also been increased efforts by OVR to develop an IWRP for special education students to complement the IEP, so that upon completion of academics, vocational placement could proceed smoothly. Earlier, special education students often finished their schooling, only to wait a considerable length of time before being recognized as eligible for OVR services.

In 1980 the Mental Health Systems Act authorized additional funds to assess community services, develop national goals and priorities, and learn more about the problems, concerns, and alternative solutions for the mentally ill population.

In 1981 President Reagan proposed block grants to cut federal spending and to encourage states to take more responsibility in providing needed services.

In 1982 the Comprehensive Employment and Training Program (CETA, 1973), an employment assistance program, was replaced by the Job Training Partnership Act (JPTA). Under this Act, the importance of training was reaffirmed.

In 1986 Section 508 was added to Title V of the Rehabilitation Act of 1973. This provision ensures access to computers and other electronic office equipment in places of federal employment for persons who have a handicapping condition.

SERVICE DELIVERY

Service delivery is important to both the National Certified Counselor (NCC) and the Certified Rehabilitation Counselor (CRC). Areas of concern are the nature and needs of the population served, the agency setting, and the mission and scope of available services. Counselors need to become aware of incentives and disincentives to change, dependency needs of both the client and the counselor, recidivism, and outcome measurement strategies.

Many counselors refer their clients to other community agencies to complement available services. The extent of information to be shared and the competencies of agency personnel may be additional professional concerns.

Agencies often operate on a cost-benefit ratio model, due to limited resources of time and money. Effectiveness may be judged in terms of client outcome, making the maximizing of resources a concern. Lack of public funding may preclude service for the severely disabled population.

The NCC or CRC candidate who works in a school counseling setting, in which the client population includes minors, must be concerned with parental approval before providing services. The issue of confidentiality becomes a confounding issue as students may approach counselors with intimate problems they do not want their parents to know. Examples include issues of birth control, abortion, drug use, or peer pressure. Protocol is typically under the auspices of local administration. However, the state may also invoke and provide standards for action.

In one court case, *City of Akron v. Akron Center for Reproductive Health, Inc. (51 U.S.L.W. 4767, 1983)*, a city ordinance prohibited abortion for an unmarried minor (under fifteen years old), unless permission was granted from a parent or legal guardian. The court ruled that the ordinance was unconstitutional because of *Roe v. Wade (410, U.S.113, 153, 1973)*, which established that a woman may decide whether to terminate her pregnancy. (The reader is cautioned that this case has been identified only to illustrate the complexity of concerns when counseling minors and does not constitute a universal precedent for action.)

One area in which the counselor working with minors may circumvent parental permission is if the counselor suspects child abuse or neglect. In this case, there is an obligation to report the suspicion to appropriate authorities (Hopkins & Anderson, 1985).

Counselors who work with clients who have a different cultural base from their own have a different obligation than the counselor who works with minors. The counselor should make every effort to become familiar with multicultural norms and values. Some believe that minorities are best served by those who have similar cultural backgrounds. This philosophical argument has yet to be resolved and perhaps never will be.

Rehabilitation counselors have additional concerns regarding service delivery, such as the acknowledgment that disability is not just a client concern but also includes the concerns of family members and significant others. Feelings of inferiority, succumbing, and coping, and learning to subordinate physical attributes must also be addressed (Wright, 1983). Counselors must recognize that the extent of the various stages of adjustment experienced by those with a permanent or long-term disability may interfere with service delivery. (Wright, 1980; Wright, 1983).

Service provision for rehabilitation clients include medical restoration, work adjustment, vocational training, and living arrangements (Rubin & Roessler, 1987; Wright, 1980). Clients may either have a medical, cultural, or educational problem that affects employment or restricts lifestyle.

Concerns may also involve an appropriate place to live. Rehabilitation residences such as group homes proliferated after the Willowbrook exposé, which called attention to the mistreatment of institutionalized people. A group home living arrangement resembles a traditional home but provides professional support services. Unfortunately, there is a shortage of group homes, due to limited funds and trained staff, as well as public outcry that property values might decrease or that crime in the neighborhood will rise with the establishment of a group home.

The provision of rehabilitation services is often affiliated with a vocational outcome in which services are targeted to one of five choices: competitive placement, sheltered employment, unpaid family worker, farm worker, or self-employment.

Competitive placement is the most desired goal. This is especially true for the rehabilitation counselor who is employed in the private sector, where referrals typically involve Worker's Compensation and the emphasis is on short-term placement strategies (Rubin & Roessler, 1987). The goal of self-employment is typically not offered as a first choice by most rehabilitation counselors because of the potentially high risk of failure.

For the person who has a severe physical or mental disability, the goal of sheltered employment may be the most desirable, as support services are available on a daily basis. These workers are permitted to work at a slower pace than workers in a competitive environment.

If the goal for the client is as an unpaid family worker, services may be directed at leisure time counseling, socialization, or matters of independent living. Psychosocial clubs—modeled after Fountain House in New York City, where people socialize and help with the maintenance of the facility by cleaning, cooking, or taking care of telephone messages—may be one of the services proposed (Wright, 1980).

A QUICK QUIZ

To test your understanding of historical antecedents and the certification process, describe the following:

1. The need for certification

2. The difference between certification and licensure

3. Basic competencies for the professional counselor

4. Whether empathy is a learned skill or an innate trait

5. The differences between a self-employed counselor and one who is employed at a state or federal agency

6. The similarity and differences between the National Certified Counselor and the Certified Rehabilitation Counselor

7. Important legislation that has contributed to the rehabilitation movement

8. The impact of stereotyping

9. Coping skills as a requirement for adjusting to some loss

10. The purpose of counselor assistance and intervention.

SELECTED REFERENCES

The following references are suggested for further study:

Guide to Rehabilitation Counselor Certification (1987). Commission on Rehabilitation Counselor Certification. Arlington Heights, IL: Author.

Hopkins, B. R., and Anderson, B. S. (1985). *The Counselor and the Law.* (2nd ed.). Alexandria, VA: AACD.

National Board for Certified Counselors. (1987). *Code of Ethics.* Alexandria, VA: Author.

National Counselor Certification, Information & Application. (1989). Alexandria, VA: Author.

Rubin, S. E., and Roessler, R. T. (1987). *Foundations of the Vocational Rehabilitation Process.* Austin, TX: PRO-ED.

Wright, B. A. (1983). *Physical Disability: A Psychosocial Approach* (2nd ed.). New York: Harper & Row.

Wright, G. N. (1980). *Total Rehabilitation.* Boston: Little, Brown.

Theories to Guide the Professional Counselor

THEORIES TO GUIDE
THE PROFESSIONAL COUNSELOR

Introduction

Counseling and psychotherapy may be viewed as a process whereby a counselor (therapist) assists a client to identify, delineate, and resolve concerns that are interfering with the client's ability to experience a satisfactory lifestyle. To promote change, counselors are guided by theoretical approaches to human personality and behavior. The counselor's choice for therapeutic intervention is determined by client and counselor characteristics, the client's problems, the counseling setting, and nature of the referral. Community resources, agencies' philosophy and parameters, and other intrinsic and environmental contingencies are additional factors that may also determine treatment.

This section reviews the four main types of therapeutic interventions: psychoanalytic and neoanalytic, behavioral, cognitive, and affective. Each theory is briefly presented. For a more detailed discussion of each theory, the reader is directed to review the major reference sources cited throughout the text. A list of major reference books is also found at the end of the section.

Each chapter includes the philosophy, techniques, and strategies for each therapeutic intervention. Also addressed are the kinds of client and counseling situations in which the theory has had its greatest impact, as well as the perceived strengths and weaknesses of each theory.

Counseling Versus Psychotherapy

The terms *counseling* and *psychotherapy* have been considered by authors of recent counseling-theory textbooks as interchangeable and synonymous (Baruth & Huber, 1985; Corey, 1986; Corsini, 1984). Both terms describe a professional relationship that can provide emotional support, intellectual clarification, and an action modality to facilitate change. When professionals disagree on the meaning between these two terms, the difference rests on the depth and length of the client and counselor relationship.

The reader should be aware that a difference of opinion regarding nomenclature between these two terms exists among some professionals. For purposes of this text, *counseling* or *psychotherapy* and *counselor* or *therapist* will follow the trend established by recent counseling textbooks, in which these terms are used in a synonymous way.

CLASSICAL PSYCHOANALYSIS

SIGMUND FREUD
1856–1939

KEY CONCEPTS

Biological Theory
Closed System
Countertransference
Determinism
Dream Analysis
Early Childhood Experiences
Ego Defense Mechanisms
  Compensation
  Denial
  Displacement
  Introjection
  Projection
  Reaction Formation

Resistance
Repression
Sublimation
Eros and Thanatos
Fixation
Free Association
Id-Ego-Superego
Libidinal Instincts
Oedipal and Electra Complexes
Psychosexual Developmental Stages
Transference
Unconscious-Preconscious-Conscious Domains

P R E·V I E W   Q U E S T I O N S

---

1. What developmental period does Freud refer to as an age of innocence?

2. Which intrapsychic structure rules the "musts," "shoulds," or "oughts"?

3. What is meant by "determinism"?

4. What is the term for all psychic energy?

5. What is the ego defense mechanism whereby an individual develops positive traits to make up for limitations?

6. What happens if a psychosexual crisis is not satisfactorily resolved?

7. What level of the psyche harbors material retrievable at will?

8. What is the phenomenon whereby a client projects onto the therapist characteristics of a significant person from the client's past?

9. How do neoanalysts differ from traditional analysts?

10. What are "Freudians slips"?

Introduction

A review of major counseling theories typically begins with psychoanalytic theory, founded by Sigmund Freud (1856–1939). Numerous researchers and counseling practitioners disagree with Freud's deterministic nature of the human condition and see it as impractical for counselors. However, this theory is traditionally regarded as the historical foundation for all other counseling theories.

To review the major tenets of classical psychoanalysis, Freudian theory can be conceptualized as consisting of four separate yet interrelated ideas: (1) Freud's philosophy describing how human behavior develops; (2) the understanding of the energy conflict among the three structures of personality; (3) the critical analysis of psychosexual stage development in understanding health or pathology; and (4) ego defense mechanisms as an explanation for healthy or dysfunctional coping styles.

FREUD'S PHILOSOPHY

The underlying principle of psychoanalytic theory is that humans are in constant conflict and turmoil to resolve sexual and aggressive impulses that permeate everyday living. These impulses are biological and organic in nature, and are shared by all human beings. Unresolved concerns, often the result of early childhood experiences, help to determine adult personality.

Freud's philosophy of human behavior rests on *determinism,* the philosophical doctrine that every event, act, and decision is the inevitable consequence of antecedents. This is why Freud believed it imperative for therapists to understand the client's early childhood experiences and for therapists to undergo their own analysis. Humankind is viewed as a closed system, ruled by intrinsic demands and biological urges, similar to those of lower-order living organisms. Human beings are not believed to be masters of their own fate. Rather, free will is thought to be an illusion humankind had developed. Behavior is seemingly an uphill battle in which we must direct our energy to resolve unconscious conflicts, needs, and drives (Hall, 1954).

Freud hypothesized that the *psyche* (from the Greek, meaning "soul") is composed of three levels of consciousness: the *unconscious,* the *conscious,* and the *preconscious.* Conscious information is material readily available to a person by simple recall. Preconscious information is retrievable at will, through concentration, such as remembering an event. Unconscious material is unavailable to the person and can only be retrieved through analysis.

Psychoanalytic theorists are not as concerned with the conscious or preconscious levels as much as with material residing in the unconscious domain, due to their belief that unconscious material keeps individuals in constant anxiety as energy is directed at meeting and controlling unfulfilled needs and desires. As a result of this emphasis, classical psychoanalytic therapists postulated that the unconscious makes up the largest part of each person's personality and also predisposes people to behave with particular mannerisms (Brammer & Shostrom, 1982; Hansen, Stevic, & Warner, 1986; Wallace, 1986).

Freud believed two essential unlearned psychological drives (instincts), *Eros* and *Thanatos,* also govern our behavior. Eros, the god of love in Greek mythology, symbolizes the sum of all self-preservative, positive events in life, such as hunger, sex, art, and creativity. Eros is considered more powerful than Thanatos, as it is necessary for the survival of the species. Thanatos is symbolic of negative, aggressive, destructive behaviors, such as death or death wishes.

The *libido* describes all energy behind life instincts. It includes sexual and biological drives. Energy is directed first toward the self, then toward parents, followed by members of our own sex, and ultimately toward members of the opposite sex. Freud believed there is a tendency to use energy to seek pleasure and avoid pain. Therefore, early experiences of pleasure and pain need to be analyzed, as this information is the key to understanding adult behavior. Behavior may be further understood by recognizing the struggle among the three structures of personality: the *id*, the *ego*, and the *superego*.

Energy Conflict within the Personality

Freud defined personality as consisting of three internal dimensions: the id, the ego, and the superego. He described these intrapsychic structures to be in continuous struggle for superiority and that, although these intrapsychic structures are not compatible, there must be a sense of equilibrium or profound anxiety and abnormal behavior will result. One of the goals of Freudian therapy is to assist clients to understand, recognize, and resolve intrapsychic conflict.

The id, the ego, and the superego were thought to emerge at different developmental periods in the child's early life. Once the structure appears, it remains throughout life (Freud, 1935).

The id is thought to be present at birth. It resides in the unconscious and is not anchored to reality. It is the source of all instinctive energy, is ruled by the pleasure principle, and is not tolerant of discomfort. The id selfishly demands immediate gratification. It does not acknowledge the presence of the ego or the superego, nor does the id consider consequences, logic, or morality.

The ego is thought to emerge when the child acquires socialization skills. It apparently develops because the id alone is unable to satisfy total individual needs. The ego is controlled by the reality principle. It is referred to as the "mediator" of psychic energy (work carried out by psychological activity), or the "executive administrator" of the personality (Freud, 1960; Hall, 1954; Hall & Lindzey, 1978; Wallace, 1986). Its purpose is to balance the forces between the id and the superego. To remember the function of the ego, think of a seesaw. The ego is the central fulcrum that balances the id and the superego, found at either ends.

The superego is the last psychological structure to emerge. It develops when the child is mature enough to internalize social and cultural ethics and mores, and has developed communication skills. The superego is similar to the id in that it is predominantly an unconscious force. The superego passes judgment whether an act is "right" or "wrong." It is considered to represent the parental conscience and parental injunctions (shoulds and oughts). It has a high regard for morality and is critical of the id and the ego. The purpose of the superego is to repress the id from expressing inappropriate impulses by making the person feel guilty for his or her actions. Its goal is to strive for perfection and self-ideal (Arlow, 1984; Hall, 1954; Hall & Lindzey, 1978; Hinsie & Campbell, 1960; Wallace, 1986).

Freud believed that humans are closed, rather than open, systems; the total amount of available energy is limited and always remains constant. Therefore, the three intrapsychic dimensions are in competition for the distribution of energy. How energy is distributed is thought to be dependent on biological needs, the environment, and the current stage of development.

Psychosexual Stages of Development

Freud developed a theory of childhood sexuality after he analyzed himself when his father died (Hall, 1954). He hypothesized that during childhood development, a body area predominates as the source of pleasure and that all of our energy (libido) originates from sexual drives to satisfy this need for receiving pleasure and avoiding pain.

Psychosexual stages were believed to be biologically determined, universal, predictable, sequential, and orderly tasks that children experience. He felt that all children progress in a similar fashion from one stage to the next, and that children must resolve age-related tasks without too much or too little frustration. If a psychosexual stage was not satisfactorily experienced, the child would become fixated in one stage and as an adult would have a tendency to regress to the unfulfilled stage and manifest symptoms representative of that particular stage. This lasting preoccupation with the pleasures and issues from an earlier psychosexual stage is known as *fixation*. Severe frustration tends to produce the strongest fixations (White & Watt, 1973).

Freud referred to the first psychosexual stage as the *oral stage*. This stage begins at birth and continues until the child reaches approximately one and one-half years of age. During this stage, the child derives pleasure by sucking at the mother's breast (or bottle), thereby reducing hunger tension by oral stimulation. The baby who experiences either severe frustration or deprivation of the sucking sensation or of nutrition may not be willing to relinquish oral satisfiers as an adult, because of an unconscious feeling that oral needs will remain unfulfilled. Freud believed that the adult who has not experienced this stage successfully develops an overly dependent personality (Craig, 1980; Newman & Newman, 1984).

The *anal stage* follows the oral stage and lasts until the child is approximately three years old. During this stage, elimination of bodily waste reduces tension and discomfort. Where the oral stage demanded immediate gratification, the anal stage marks the beginning of delayed gratification and the socialization process. The ego and superego are thought to emerge during the anal stage. The child learns to delay biological urges and immediate gratification in exchange for social approval from others. The major task to be successfully experienced during this time is toilet training. If toilet training is experienced as an anxiety-producing event, the child will develop into a compulsive, cruel, stingy, and overly orderly adult who has difficulty being spontaneous or openly expressing anger. The anal-retentive adult is thought of as a person who models self-control and has passive-aggressive tendencies.

The *phallic stage* describes psychosexual tasks that must be successfully experienced when the child is between three and six years of age. The superego continues to develop during this stage. Psychic energy is directed to the genital organs, and there is an unconscious, incestuous desire for the parent of the opposite sex. The Oedipus and Electra complexes are believed to emerge during this stage.

The *Oedipus complex* is the male child's desire to remove his father from the scene so that he can have sexual possession of his mother. The *Electra complex* is the female child's desire to remove her mother from the scene so that she can secure undivided attention from her father. Freud elaborated more on the resolution of the Oedipus complex than the Electra complex, perhaps because he personally experienced this conflict. Freudian analysts believe that homosexuality may be associated with inappropriate resolution of the Oedipus or Electra complex (Baker, 1955; Hall, 1954; Stone, 1971).

The sexual conflict experienced during the phallic stage is thought to be threatening for the child. In order to reduce this threat, the child represses and buries into the unconscious all sexual feelings toward the parent of the opposite sex. The young boy fears that his father, who is stronger and more powerful than he, will punish him for his incestuous thoughts by castrating him. When the young girl realizes that she lacks the male sexual organ, she develops a sense of inferiority, called *penis envy*. She blames her mother for this lack, yet recognizes that her mother is more powerful than she, so she seeks out her mother for love and approval. To diffuse and reconcile the anxiety experienced during this stage, children of both sexes identify with the same sex parent (Hall, 1954).

In later life, Oedipal feelings may influence an adult's choice for love. Men and women who choose partners who remind them of their mother or father may be resolving this psychosexual crisis as an adult (Baker, 1955; Hall, 1954).

The *latency stage* is experienced by the child from six to twelve years of age. It is the only stage that Freud believes to be asexual. The child is still developing sexually, but there are no pervasive sexual drives, nor are any new significant conflicts expected to arise. This time is thought of as an age of innocence, a repose from the highly sexual Oedipal or Electra conflict, and a time for the body to gather energy for the coming turbulent stage of adolescence. It is a time for the child to master the environment, to further develop the superego, and to begin to develop an adult identity (Craig, 1980; Newman & Newman, 1984).

The final stage of development described by Freud is known as the *genital stage*. This stage is thought to begin at puberty and to continue through adulthood. It is a sexual stage in which the sexual impulse is typically directed toward a person of the opposite sex. During adolescence there is a reawakening of the Oedipus and Electra conflict, which may explain why many adolescents withdraw from their families and seek alliance with their peer group (Newman & Newman, 1984).

Freud's developmental stages end with the genital stage. Freud's writings indicate that adults continue to remain in the genital stage throughout life, unconsciously working to repress sexual and instinctual drives and urges (Arlow, 1984; Corey, 1986; Freud, 1935; Hall, 1954; Hansen et al., 1986; Wallace, 1986).

PSYCHOANALYTIC TECHNIQUES

The goal of Freudian psychoanalysis is to help clients bring into awareness unconscious, repressed material, to strengthen the power of the ego, and to help clients understand intrapsychic conflicts. Initially, Freud used hypnosis to help his clients. However, while working with his now famous patient, Anna O., Freud recognized the limitations of hypnosis and used a technique called *free association*, developed by Joseph Breuer, a Viennese physician. Freud was successful in relieving Anna O. of some of her hysterical symptoms and credited the technique of free association with facilitating this change (Hall & Lindzey).

During free association, the client is instructed to say anything that comes to his or her mind. Freud believed this permission would encourage the client to bring forth unresolved psychic material that had been buried and repressed, making it available for analytical interpretation. As the client free associates, the analyst takes copious notes, so that everything the client says may be retrieved and referred to for possible association with other information; this analysis is believed to assist the client in gaining and/or regaining emotional health. Dream analysis, also utilized by Freudian analysts, is applied in a similar fashion (Arlow, 1984; Hall & Lindzey, 1978; Hinsie & Campbell, 1960).

Freud believed that clients would be instinctively reluctant to bring into the consciousness material that had been previously repressed and forced into the unconscious. Therefore, the psychoanalytic therapist is constantly on guard for signs of *resistance*. Resistance is viewed as being of primary importance in the practice of psychoanalysis, since it opposes therapeutic progress. If client resistance is suspected, it is the responsibility of the therapist to confront the client and interpret the hidden meanings behind the resistance. For example, the act of arriving late for an appointment might be interpreted by the therapist as the client's unconscious demonstration of passive-aggressiveness and a technique to resist therapy. The counseling session would therefore focus on analyzing the lateness (Corey, 1986; Freud, 1935; Hall, 1954).

The concept of *transference* is another technique used by Freudian analysts. Transference occurs when highly emotional feelings, thoughts, and wishes are projected onto the therapist as the therapist takes on the characteristics of some significant person from the client's past. Typically, this projection is believed to originate from unresolved tasks imposed from an earlier psychosexual crisis. Through transference, clients understand how they use projection and other defense mechanisms as coping and/or rewarding techniques.

Countertransference is similar to transference, but it is the therapist who is projecting from his or her past onto the client. Countertransference interferes with objectivity and the ability of the therapist to be a change agent for the client. It is more damaging to the therapeutic relationship than transference. In order to minimize countertransference, psychoanalytic therapists are expected to go through their own psychoanalysis (Freud, 1935; Hall, 1954).

Freudian analysts are viewed as authoritative, nonjudgmental, passive, knowledgeable persons who clinically analyze and interpret what the client reports. Their anonymous nature permits unconscious, highly emotional conflicts, experienced in early childhood, to be transferred onto the therapist. The client is expected to lie down on a couch and to look away from the therapist, so that transference may take place. With the exception of the required free association, the sessions are unstructured. The client is expected to be committed to change through a process of critical self-examination. The client is informed that change, through understanding, may take several years. Appointments are scheduled three to five times per week. The client must be verbal and honest as everything depends upon interpretation of the material.

Classical psychoanalysis is analogous to the medical model, in which the therapist and client respectively are believed to have a superordinate-subordinate relationship. Sessions are devoid of emotional interchange. The therapist offers little self-disclosure and remains practically nonexistent.

Ego Defense Mechanisms

Ego defense mechanisms are unconscious devices that help minimize anxiety and maintain integrity. They protect the ego from becoming overwhelmed from demands made by the id and the superego. They can be either realistic and helpful ways to assist individuals to make rational decisions, or they can be used to distort reality. A description of some of the more common defense mechanisms follows (Arlow, 1984; Brammer, 1985; Corey, 1986; Hinsie & Campbell, 1960).

- **Compensation** is the development of certain traits to make up for perceived weaknesses. An adaptive example of compensation is when a person pursues a career in which strengths, rather than limitations, may be used; for example, an extroverted person may choose to work as a salesperson, while a more introverted person may choose to become an accountant. Compensation may also take on a negative form, as when a child fails to receive attention for some positive act (e.g., good grades) and so "acts up" to receive at least negative attention (Corey, 1986).

- **Denial** is a way to avoid the reality of a situation. If a situation is too traumatic or threatening, temporary denial can be a healthy coping mechanism. For example, a person who sustains a severed spinal cord as a result of a motor vehicle accident may be helped initially by denying the reality of paralysis, believing he or she will have the ability to walk again. This coping mechanism can encourage participation in rehabilitation efforts and can offer the person (and the family) some hope. However, persistent denial is considered neurotic, and not therapeutic, as the person blocks a realistic assessment and fails to cope with the situation (Kerr, 1977).

- **Displacement** is the shifting of an emotional affect from an appropriate to an inappropriate object. A boss who blames a subordinate for his or her own mistake exhibits displacement.

- **Introjection** is when an individual incorporates the values of another person (often an authority figure) into his or her own repertoire of behaving, as a way to cope with anxiety. Introjection has been thought of as a process whereby cultural and generational values are transmitted and subsequently maintained.

- **Projection** consists of an individual's denial of some characteristic disliked in himself or herself and assigning the undesired characteristic to another person. An example of this is when an individual claims another person doesn't like him or her, when in actuality, the individual is really stating that he or she does not like that particular person.

- **Reaction formation** occurs when an individual feels so uncomfortable with another person or situation that he or she acts in the exact opposite of the way that is felt. A common example is when a person is friendly toward you but behind your back speaks negatively of you.

- **Repression** is a concept used extensively in analytic psychology. This defense mechanism bans unacceptable ideas or impulses from consciousness, so that internal conflicts can be reasonably managed. Freud proposed that we all have thoughts and desires we cannot admit to ourselves, and the mechanism of repression provides an acceptable channel for these thoughts. "Freudian slips," saying something out loud and wondering why you said such a thing, is an example of repressed material. When we stumble over words, we do so because it stirs up a memory that for some reason is unacceptable, while at the same time, desirable. A main goal of psychoanalysis is to uncover the source and meaning of repressed material.

- **Sublimation** involves modifying an instinctual impulse into a socially appropriate and acceptable channel. Sublimation is thought to help the id gain external expression. For example, the workaholic may be thought to substitute work in place of sexual passion.

The Analytic Client

Certain types of clients and client problems are considered more appropriate for psychoanalytic counseling. The client must have time and money, and be committed to a long counseling process encompassing many years.

Psychoanalysis has been successfully used in cases of hysteria; phobias; psychosomatic manifestations; character disorders; and hysterical, obsessive, compulsive, and sexual disorders. Psychoanalysis is thought to be less successful for narcissistic, impulsive, sociopathic, or psychopathic disorders or when problems must be met immediately (Arlow, 1984).

S U M M A R Y

The strength of Freud's psychoanalytic approach is the emphasis on the unconscious; ironically, this is also its weakness. Freudian analysts rely upon clients to reconstruct childhood experiences. This causes the theory to be validated by subjective data and lends itself to disputation by traditional scientists as lacking a scientific base. However, whether counselors accept or refute, like or dislike, or see Freudian theory as impractical, classical psychoanalysis has been the backbone for understanding human behavior.

Psychoanalytic theory is based on abnormal personality. It has been referred to as id psychology, since Freud stressed the notion that unconscious, instinctual urges rule life and that psychosexual urges cause us to be in constant conflict.

Several of Freud's students disagreed with the emphasis placed on the id and broke away from traditional psychoanalytic thinking. These theorists are known as neoanalysts, or neo-Freudians. They include Adler, Erikson, Fromm, Horney, Jung, Rank, Sullivan, and others.

The neoanalysts base their theory on ego psychology. Their belief is that humans are reality based, have the ability to control instincts and behavior, are social beings, and are masters of their own fate. As Adler, Erikson, and Jung appear more frequently in recent counseling textbooks than other neo-Freudians, the main tenets from these three theorists are reviewed here (Corey, 1986; Corsini, 1984; Hansen et al., 1986; Wallace, 1986).

ANALYTICAL PSYCHOLOGY

CARL JUNG
1875–1961

KEY CONCEPTS

Amplification

Anima/Animus

Archetypes

CollectiveUnconscious

Dream Analysis

Eros Principle

Extraversion/Introversion

Logos Principle

Mandalas

Persona

Religion

Self

Shadow

PREVIEW QUESTIONS

---

1. How is the personal relationship between Freud and Jung described?

2. How do archetypes make themselves known?

3. What are mandalas?

4. How does religion impact on analytical beliefs regarding therapy?

5. What does the Myers-Briggs Type Indicator describe?

6. What psychic structure does the shadow reflect?

7. What archetype is considered most important?

8. What does Jung say happens at midlife?

9. What are "archetypes"?

10. How do extraverted types view their environment?

Introduction

Carl Jung is the founder of *analytical psychology*. He developed a theory of personality and psychotherapy to better understand the reason behind human existence. Therapy is preoccupied with dream analysis, fantasies, symbolism, mythology, and archetypal (historical) contents of client's thoughts. It is a therapy full of metaphors. As a result, Jungian therapy has been criticized as too elusive, abstract, esoteric, and complicated to understand clients' problems (Brammer & Shostrom, 1982; Kaufman, 1984; O'Connell & O'Connell, 1980).

Nevertheless, Jung was a brilliant psychotherapist who added another dimension to the analysis of human behavior. A review of the major tenets of this theory adds to a further understanding of the classical psychodynamic model.

BACKGROUND AND PHILOSOPHY

Jung's theory evolved partly from his own personal life experiences and partly from what he learned from his clients' self-reports. The special relationship Jung had with Freud is a good place to begin this review of analytical psychology.

Initially Jung worked closely with Freud in promoting classic psychoanalytic theory. More than three hundred pieces of correspondence passed between these two psychotherapists. Freud took a special liking to Jung and believed Jung would be his successor. The literature refers to Freud and Jung as having a father–son relationship. Freud was so impressed with Jung that he appointed him the first president of the International Psychoanalytical Association (Hall & Lindzey, 1978; Kaufman, 1984). However, their relationship was highly volatile.

Jung disagreed with Freud on some major notions regarding human behavior, including the importance Freud attached to sexuality and human life, to the exclusion of everything else, and Freud's belief that individuals are driven solely by internal instincts. Jung also differed with Freud regarding the meaning of dreams; for Freud, dreams were unresolved, infantile conflicts, and instinctual needs, while Jung interpreted dreams to represent present concerns that, when analyzed, contained future material that could warn the individual of troublesome times ahead. Also, Jung was not interested in the intrapsychic conflict of the id, ego, and superego; rather, he searched for the developmental roots of human personality. In 1913, Jung severed ties with Freud and developed his own theory of human behavior, which he called analytical psychology (Hall & Lindzey, 1978; Kaufman, 1984; Kovel, 1976; O'Connell & O'Connell, 1980).

The dissociation with Freud left Jung experiencing deeply symbolic dreams and frightening visions. As he felt himself to be on the brink of psychosis, he submitted himself to psychoanalysis. It was only after four years of psychotherapy that Jung believed his psychosis had lifted.

During Jung's four years of psychotherapy, he noticed he was drawing geometrical figures, circles, and squares. He hypothesized that by understanding these drawings, he would understand the reason for his own life and why humankind existed. He named these drawings mandalas, in which all sides of a picture are perfectly balanced around a center point. Jung believed that by analyzing both his and his clients' mandalas, additional insight into problems and solutions could be found. During therapy, Jung encouraged his clients to go further into the dream scenario by visualizing mandalas, and attaching myths, symbols, and art to the visualized pictures. This, Jung believed, would promote a more comprehensive understanding of intrapsychic conflict (Kovel, 1976).

Jung's theory of personality emphasizes the complex nature of human beings, from birth to death. Behavior results from both conscious and unconscious forces (Kaufman, 1984). All individuals strive for individuation, whereby a "God" within each of us helps us to achieve a sense of a self-fulfillment. This "God" is not affiliated with any particular religion, but rather represents a person's beliefs. Jung believed all religion has it merits and that no single religion is omnipotent.

Jung placed great emphasis on the notion that everyone is a creative being. Many of his clients were artists and other well-known people. He believed that men and women have differences in personality partly because women operate from the *Eros principle*, represented by intuition, and men operate from the *Logos principle*, making decisions based on logic and reason (Jung, 1933).

Jung saw people as either introverted or extraverted. He believed that at birth individuals have a predisposition to either one or the other of these psychological tendencies and that these innate psychological differences determine who we are and what we can become. Jung believed we each have a tendency to act in one way, to the exclusion of the other. Therefore, one side of us remains undeveloped, blocking us from becoming fully functioning persons. Jung stated that one of the reasons for his split with Freud was a difference in personality orientation. Jung described himself as an introvert, and Freud as an extravert (Jung, 1961).

Extraverted types look to the external world for meaning and value, are more interested in others, accommodate more easily to situations, and consequently are popular with other persons. Introverted types have a dispostion that is more strongly attached to internal feelings and thoughts and motivated primarily by subjective experiences. Because introverts do not seek approval from others, they are often regarded as aloof and therefore difficult to get along with and less able and willing to share emotions.

Carl Jung shared with Erik Erikson an interest in adult development and personality. Both men were concerned with issues that take place during the second half of life and both viewed mature development as a continuation of earlier life experiences.

Jung viewed an individual's personality as developing from two distinct developmental phases. Jung's first developmental period spans from birth to thirty-five years of age. The tasks to be accomplished during this period center around achieving such societal expectations as establishing a career, family, and other externally valued life successes. At about forty years of age, a person's psyche undergoes a transformation in which external goals take on less importance and one turns inward to examine the meaning of life. During the midlife transition, men take on such "feminine" traits as nurturing and artistic endeavors, and women take on more "masculine" traits of aggression and competition. Levinson's work (1978) supports Jung's theory that men experience a middle-age crisis, taking on a more caring nature in both interpersonal relationships and career goals. Sheehy (1976) also reported on midlife crises and, in her book, notes the changes in values and life emphasis that both men and women experience during this period.

THE COLLECTIVE UNCONSCIOUS

Perhaps Jung's most unique contribution in explaining human behavior is his belief in the *collective unconscious*. The collective unconscious represents inherited, repetitious experiences of past generations that are permanently embedded in the human mind. The information is transmitted from one generation to the next; thus, the information is "collected." All humans share the same collective unconscious, leading to psychic predispositions regarding perception, emotion, and behavior. Jung concluded that clients' problems or conflicts might be remnants of evolutionary material that remained unresolved (Jung, 1961).

Jung named the material found in the collective unconscious *archetypes*, a word that shares the same root as *archaic* or *archeology*, both of which mean something very old (O'Connell & O'Connell, 1980). The more common archetypes include the persona, shadow, anima and animus, and the self. They are found in mythology, art, personal dreams and fantasies, and folklore and in the deepest layer of the inner psyche. Archetypes are believed to play an important role in personality. Symbols in dreams such as birth, death, rebirth, God, devil, wise old man, and earth mother represent descriptive themes of common archetypes (Hall & Lindzey, 1978; Kovel, 1976; Kaufman, 1984; O'Connell & O'Connell, 1980).

ARCHETYPES

Anima/Animus

The anima and animus represent the notion that all individuals have both masculine and feminine traits. The concept is similar to the Chinese Taoist philosophy of Yin (masculine) and Yang (feminine), which defines masculine traits as reflecting logic, rationality, bravery, dominance, and conquest, and feminine traits as representing nurturing, reception, submission, and intuitive and artistic traits. Jung believed that socialization pressures reinforce individuals to deny and repress either the anima (in men, the woman within) or the animus (in women, the man within).

Persona

The persona is the ego's mask and is the image we present to others. It changes as we adopt different roles in everyday living circumstances, such as mother, wife and lover, and career woman. Individuals use the persona to hide true and deeper personality characteristics from others; problems result if individuals use the persona to ignore or reject their innate tendencies.

Self

The most important archetype is that of the self, our unconscious, which constantly strives for unity. The self is immersed deep within our psyche; analyzing mandalas helps individuals to better understand the self and the meaning of life. Jung believed that this search is often carried out in humankind's quest for God.

Shadow

The shadow resides behind the persona, or mask, and is similar to Freud's id. It is impulsive and uncaring of societal norms and values, yet it is not to be viewed as a negative concept. Rather, the shadow consists of beliefs or feelings we try to deny, yet desire to possess. For example, a woman may view herself as not very attractive, but in a dream she sees herself as glamourous and beautiful. In dreams, the shadow is typically the same gender as the person who is dreaming. In order to be a self-fulfilled person, we must be in touch with our shadow, otherwise we may scapegoat others for any part we reject in ourselves.

TECHNIQUES

As neurotic behavior is believed to be the result of conflict between the personal unconscious and the collective unconscious, Jungian therapists help their clients experience the unconscious as deeply as possible. The information that lies hidden is believed to have the potential to promote well-being. Exploration of the unconscious is typically carried out through the interpretation of dreams. Clients are encouraged to work on symbols during therapy and to paint and draw dream symbols in detail.

Free association, a technique used widely by Freud, was discarded by Jung, who thought of it as a reductive method. In its place, Jung used a technique called *amplification.* Dream contents were expanded and dramatized, and clients were encouraged to add myths and symbols so that a higher form of cognition could be realized (Kovel, 1976).

In contrast to Freudian analysts, who remain anonymous, Jungian analysts interact face to face with their clients. Therapy is viewed as a process of gaining self-knowledge and wisdom, in which there are no set rules for sessions; it is viewed as a healing process. The goal of therapy is the recognition and integration of the total self.

Kovel (1976) states that this therapy works well with all types of emotional disturbances but is most suited to normal individuals who are experiencing a midlife crisis or to those seeking wisdom and enlightenment about the meaning of existence. Jungian therapy is not suitable for counselors working with clients who have problems that must be resolved in a short period of time (Craig, 1980; Kaufman, 1984).

Jung has had influence on counselors in the development of personality tests. For example, the *Myers-Briggs Type Indicator* is a widely used measure of personality dispositions and preferences based on Jung's theory of types. It has been found suitable for upper elementary school children to adults. It provides four bipolar scales that can be reduced to a four-letter code or "type" of Extraversion or Introversion, Sensing or Intuition, Thinking or Feeling, and Judgment or Perception. Eysenck's Introversion-Extraversion Scale, Rotter's Incomplete Sentences Blank, and various other word-association tests employ Jungian personality typology as the foundation from which the tests were constructed (Anastasi, 1982).

SUMMARY

Jung was a prolific writer who hypothesized about the nature and orgin of the human race. He provided therapists with numerous clinical techniques so that human suffering could be minimized. The chief and most salient feature of analytical psychology is the belief in the collective unconscious and in archetypes. The most important archetype is the self, which represents our unconscious and is striving for oneness, unity, wholeness, and meaning to life.

Jung has been criticized as being too mystical and too preoccupied with archetypal representation of earlier human experiences. His theory is based on much abstract thinking, which may be too esoteric or difficult for many clients to grasp (Brammer & Shostrom, 1982; Kovel, 1976).

PSYCHOSOCIAL DEVELOPMENT

ERIK ERIKSON
1902–

KEY CONCEPTS

Bipolar Conflicts
Ego Diffusion
Ego Psychology
Epigenetic Principle

Psychosocial Crises
Psychosocial Stage Developmental Theory
Self-Determinism

PREVIEW QUESTIONS

---

1. How does id psychology differ from ego psychology?

2. How do psychosocial crises differ from psychosexual crises?

3. During what stage does the child learn stereotypic and prejudicial behaviors?

4. During which psychosocial stage is creativity fostered?

5. When does the question "Who am I" emerge?

6. What is the last psychosocial task?

7. If an individual lacks a clear sense of life, what psychosocial stage has not been successfully met?

8. What is meant by epigenesis?

9. At what stage is peer pressure encountered most?

10. How do cultural and social demands affect development?

Introduction

Erik Erikson was a disciple of Freud. He adhered to classical psychoanalytic principles but expanded on Freud's teachings by developing a theory of human develoment based on ego psychology. Proponents of ego psychology believe that humans are self-determined beings who have the ability to govern themselves through reasoning. This is in contrast to classical Freudian belief, which places instincts as the power and source of behavior (Brammer & Shostrom, 1986; Hall & Lindzey, 1978).

Erikson is most noted for a psychosocial theory of human development. He was the only psychoanalytic theorist to develop a series of developmental stages that cover the entire life span. His stage theory differs from Freud's in that he did not believe that a particular body zone dominates each developmental period, nor that each crisis originates from a psychosexual basis. Rather, he postulated psychosocial development results from an interaction between biological, maturational, and environmental needs and demands. A critical psychosocial crisis accompanies each stage of development and must be resolved for healthy maturation.

ERIKSON'S EPIGENETIC PRINCIPLE

An *epigenetic principle* is a biological plan for growth that has an orderly and systematic sequence from inception to death. Erikson borrowed this term from the pure sciences to describe a natural process of human psychosocial development. Individuals are believed to experience a naturally blossoming or unfolding of maturity. Environmental and intrinsic conditions are believed to have an influence on growth and an impact on individual mannerisms and chosen lifestyle. In essence, Erikson's principles describe a process that credits both nature and nurture as contributing factors for human growth and behavior (Erikson, 1950; Newman & Newman, 1987).

Erikson's epigenetic principle presumes that each individual will pass through a predictable and set order of stages. These stages are the product of social, biological, and environmental demands imposed on the person. Each stage varies in age to accommodate inherited and cultural factors that impact on maturation. The individual must adjust to demands both psychologically (internally) and behaviorally (externally) to relieve tension and enter the next stage in a healthy way.

Critical developmental tasks accompany each stage. The individual must master a set of particular skills and competencies and continue to build on this knowledge in later stages. If earlier stages are met with satisfactory resolution, one has a greater chance to experience a more fulfilled adult life than if developmental crises failed to be satisfactorily resolved. Both the stages and the tasks are believed to be universally experienced (Erikson, 1968).

Erikson's model is similar to Freud's model in that both share a critical stage developmental philosophy toward growth and healthy or dysfunctional maturation. Erikson is more optimistic than Freud, who believed that a person was doomed to have difficulties in later life if an earlier developmental crisis was left unsatisfied. In Erikson's view, a person can, with extra attention, make up for an unfulfilled crisis at some later developmental period.

Erikson believed the way an individual initially resolves each psychosocial crisis plays an important part in how subsequent crises will be resolved. This pattern of response is also a contributing factor in the formation of the personality (Erikson, 1950). In a subtle way, the notions of self-fulfilling prophecies and reinforcement theory permeate Erikson's writings.

In contrast to Freud, Erikson believes the ego is not dependent upon the id, but rather the id and the ego are separate and unique entities. The id controls the person with its impulsive nature. The ego represents rational cognitive thought based on conscious behavior. Erikson believes the ego is the intrapsychic structure that rules human behavior and that the ego becomes strengthened with successful resolution of each psychosocial stage.

Erikson believed it is within each individual's power to choose a lifestyle representative and consistent with his or her own values and goals. He stressed, however, the value of a loving and supportive environment in attaining life satisfaction. Social conditions are thought to have mediating powers that can either enhance or deter success at each stage (Erikson, 1968).

Erikson added another dimension to psychoanalytic theory. He acknowledged that social connectedness is critically related to healthy maturity. He was one of the first psychotherapists to address the powerful influence that others have on an individual's personality formation and the choice of lifestyle. Freud paid little attention to this aspect of individual development, but Adler and other neo-Freudians typically included the impact of significant others as an important influence in human development (Erikson, 1968; Kitchener, 1978).

THE NINE PSYCHOSOCIAL STAGES

Erikson originally identified lifespan development as consisting of eight stages. Later, other developmental theorists documented the vast differences between the young and the mature teenager. Hence the adolescent stage has been considered by contemporary researchers as two distinct critical periods, and the notion that there are nine developmental stages has been widely accepted. The first four stages parallel Freud's psychosexual stages and are descriptive of tasks related to infancy and childhood. The fifth and sixth stages concern adolescent crises. The last three stages occur during adulthood and old age and are related to individual accomplishment tasks (Erikson, 1982; Newman & Newman, 1984).

Each stage consists of descriptors that have bipolar tendencies. Erikson hypothesized that both positive and negative experiences contribute to a person's ability to resolve developmental tension and conflict. The critical nature of each stage and task is influenced by cultural expectations, and its importance is placed on a continuum and is rated according to some personal standard. To move from one stage to the next, the individual must disengage from one set of criteria, replacing old ideals and values with new ones. If the person fails to shift priorities, he or she becomes confused. Erikson called this *ego diffusion* (Erikson, 1964).

Stage One: Trust versus Mistrust

The first stage takes place from birth to one and a half years of age. Infants must rely on others for primary needs of food, water, and shelter. This stage parallels Freud's oral stage.

When babies are cold, wet, or hungry, they must count on their caretaker to remove their discomfort. The infant who perceives the caretaker to be dependable develops a sense of trust in others. Erikson has identified trust versus mistrust as the first critical task or psychosocial crisis experienced by the individual. Mutuality with the caregivers is needed for healthy maturation.

A sense of confidence develops from successful resolution of the first psychosocial crisis. This feeling and cognition are generalized by the baby to other people in the environment. The infant senses that he or she will not be deserted and that needs will be met. The trust engendered further enables an infant to learn to delay gratification and minimize anxiety with onset of discomfort.

The child who learns to trust his or her world will become a trustworthy adult. The child who fails at this activity may become an adult who is overly cautious and suspicious of others; the development of intimate relationships with others may also become blocked. Erikson believed the proper mix of trust versus mistrust is instrumental in promoting an attitude of hopefulness, the enduring belief that it is possible to fulfill wishes. Unsuccessful resolution of this stage causes an individual to withdraw from others and to portray an affect of social and emotional detachment (Erikson, 1964, 1982).

Stage Two: Autonomy versus Shame and Doubt

Autonomy versus shame and doubt distinguishes Erikson's second psychosocial crisis. The child is from one and a half to three years of age. The task to be learned successfully is physical bodily self-control. Children learn this skill as they master toilet training. Freud referred to this period as the anal stage.

Erikson believed that the crisis experienced during this stage goes beyond the child experiencing success in toilet training and includes the control of other impulses. The child learns to recognize that internal powers of self-control enable him or her to develop a sound sense of autonomy. It also permits the child to recognize the limits of control over others. If the child is overprotected or not encouraged to master self-control or is punished and labeled "messy," "bad," and so forth, a sense of shame and doubt develops. The child questions his or her own ability to deal effectively with the external environment.

As the child gains a sense of autonomy, boundaries are tested. This helps to explain why this stage is often referred to as the "terrible twos." The child begins to experience a sense of right versus wrong. This lays the foundation for the emergence of guilt.

Parents or caretakers who permit the child to experience decision-making help the child see that there may be a broad interpretation to resolving a problem. Tolerance of others becomes a learned phenomenon. The child learns there is no single or absolute answer to life circumstances. If autonomy is denied, the child is more likely to reject and stereotype others who are different. The adult who is compulsive is thought to have had difficulties that blocked successful coping during this critical second period.

Stage Three: Initiative versus Guilt

The third stage describes the three- to six-year-old child. It is comparable to Freud's phallic stage. Erikson considered it critical for the child to acquire initiative during this time. Failure would result in feelings of guilt.

To be successful, the child must be provided the opportunity to explore the world and seek answers to questions and goals. It is believed that children who are permitted to learn by experiencing their environment gain self-confidence. As a result, they are more likely to take appropriate risks in later developmental periods. If not, they become fearful and lack assertiveness.

Children use play to learn to imitate and identify with others. They gain a sense of the purpose of things, how they fit into the world, and their relationship to others. They begin to deal with abstract issues and to use creativity in investigating the environment and in problem-solving.

Adults who failed to meet this psychosocial crisis are thought to lack a clear sense of their own personality. They feel prohibited from pursuing valued goals. As a result, they may be more outer- (other) directed than inner-directed. The outer- or other-directed person is more apt to live by rules imposed by others. This may result in frustration and a sense of futility to life.

Stage Four: Industry versus Inferiority

Industry versus inferiority describes Erikson's fourth developmental stage, ranging from ages six to eleven. This stage parallels Freud's latency stage.

In contrast to Freud, who believed this age span to be less dynamic than other ages, Erikson viewed this developmental period as the most decisive stage for ego growth and identity formation (Erikson, 1950). The child now goes to school and must learn to get along with peers, teachers, and other authority figures. Success during this stage leads to a belief in self. Feelings of self-value and importance are necessary to compete with others. The importance of socialization and group membership is recognized by the child as a critical element.

The notion of feeling competent, in relation to self and others, is a reflection of having a sense of being industrious and not inferior. Situations in which the child can realize success are beneficial. Success with educational demands is one way the child learns he or she has mastered this psychosocial crisis. The child should be encouraged to apply energy to focused, realistic, and attainable activities. If the child is unsuccessful during this critical period, feelings of inferiority may persist in subsequent stages.

Stage Five: Group Identity versus Alienation

This stage represents tasks for the thirteen- to seventeen-year-old. Group membership is critical. Erikson believed that if the early adolescent fails to acquire a group identity, alienation and role confusion will be experienced. This stage is comparable to Freud's genital stage, his final stage of development.

The primary task during this stage is for adolescents to develop a sense of who they are in relation to their world and to others. Adolescents recognize that they have a repertoire of roles: son or daughter, brother or sister, student, peer, and friend. They view the various roles as distinct and separate entities.

The young teenager is experiencing many physical changes during this time. Girls typically begin menstruating, and their breasts begin to develop; boys develop body hair and their voices deepen. It is a period that signals childhood has ended. Attraction to others permeates thoughts, resulting in an inordinate amount of self-consciousness as they question whether others are experiencing similar physical and psychological changes.

The notions of loyalty and fidelity emerge as psychosocial issues to be resolved. Confusion between parental versus peer morality may be experienced. Values clarification exercises may be especially helpful during this developmental period.

Stage Six: Individual Identity versus Indentity Confusion

The critical tasks for older adolescents eighteen to twenty years of age include gaining autonomy from parents, experimenting with life roles, choosing a career, and forming a male or female identity. If the adolescent fails to gain a sense of individual identity, role diffusion results.

A heightened sense of personal values emerges with successful resolution of this stage, paving the way for enhanced commitment and acceptance of the self. Older adolescents now fully recognize the ownership of various roles (e.g., son or daughter, student, worker, lover) and various responsibilities. They recognize self-morality guides decisions and they begin to experience the strong impact of family life. They may acknowledge they are more "like" than "unlike" their parents.

During this stage, adolescents are faced with making a career choice. They recognize that their decision has implications for living a particular lifestyle. They acknowledge there must be some accommodation and integration of various roles and values to maintain a consistent identity.

Stage Seven: Intimacy versus Isolation

During the early adulthood stage, the individual is twenty-three to thirty-four years old. The notion of "love" emerges as a dominant theme during this developmental period. It is critical for persons to achieve intimacy. If they fail, isolation is experienced; confidence in self is a prerequisite for success in this stage.

Erikson's notion of intimacy is the ability of a person to share his or her life with another person of either sex without being fearful that one's own identity will be lost. Before a person can be truly intimate with others, the individual must have ego strength. There must be a sense of trust, autonomy, and self-identity. If the individual has not met previous crises with success, self-preoccupation, to the exclusion of others, will result in feelings of loneliness and isolation. The success of both career and marriage indicates that the person has resolved this stage successfully.

Stage Eight: Generativity versus Stagnation

Middle adulthood describes this stage, in which the individual is between thirty-five and sixty years old. The critical element at this time concerns generativity versus stagnation. Both the management of a career and a family emerge as central activities. There is increased interest in caring for the next generation, either through work or raising children, or both. Self-fulfillment is realized by sharing knowledge and experiences with others. "Caring" best describes the critical tasks to be accomplished during this psychosocial period. Restlessness results if the person fails at either career or family tasks.

The midlife crisis is experienced during this developmental period. There is a realization that the body has changed physically and that one is not as adept as in earlier years. Introspection accompanies this crisis and adults search for ways to cope with aging. Divorce, career change, and extramarital affairs are problems that may emerge during this stage.

Stage Nine: Integrity versus Despair

This later adulthood stage is experienced when the person has lived more than sixty years. Erikson refers to this time in terms of ego integrity versus despair. Social support is critical.

During this stage, the individual must cope with physical changes that accompany aging. Older people must believe they have led a meaningful, productive, and worthwhile life that has provided them with some intrinsic satisfaction and has benefited society in some way. This attitude enhances ego integrity and permits the person to accept the realization of human mortality. Those whose life was not felt to be satisfactory despair and may experience maladjustment during this final stage of growth.

SUMMARY

Erikson's theory views healthy development as an epigenetic process during which life proceeds in an orderly and universal fashion. Each stage of growth is met with a psychosocial crisis that must be resolved. These critical demands are the product of internal and societal expectations and are culturally based. Maladaptive coping skills are believed to be linked to unsuccessful resolution of an earlier psychosocial developmental period.

Crises are identified as having bipolar tendencies. Success or failure of crises can help explain adult personality. The way individuals resolve a crisis may also help describe why they have a particular orientation to life events and decision-making patterns.

Erikson founded his stages of life-span psychosocial development using ego psychology principles. Ego counselors believe that humans are self-directed cognitive beings who base their decisions on a rational thought process.

INDIVIDUAL PSYCHOLOGY

ALFRED ADLER
1870–1937

KEY CONCEPTS

Cognitive Approach
Compensation for (Organ) Inferiority
Early Recollections
Family Constellation
Faulty Assumptions or Basic Mistakes
Growth Model
I-Thou
Lifestyle

Misbehavior
Paradoxical Directives
Private Logic
Pushbutton Techniques
Self-Fulfilling Prophecy
Social Interest/Social Connectedness
Socio-Teleological-Holistic Approach
Superiority

PREVIEW QUESTIONS

---

1. Why are early childhood experiences viewed by Adlerian therapists as critical events?

2. Why is it necessary for all individuals to recognize that they have both superior and inferior qualities?

3. How does the Adlerian therapist explain pathology?

4. Why is it important for individuals to relate to one another?

5. What does the term "private logic" describe?

6. How is lifestyle constructed?

7. What would Adler say of a person born with a handicap?

8. How would an Adlerian therapist use dreams?

9. What influence does birth order have on personality formation?

10. What are the four goals to misbehavior?

Introduction

Alfred Adler was the founder of *individual psychology*. He viewed human behavior as being within the conscious control of the individual. Particular courses of action are deliberately chosen by individuals for the purpose of demonstrating both to self and to others each person's uniqueness as a human being. Adler acknowledged that certain modifying factors, such as genetics, early childhood experiences, and environmental factors, heavily influence personality and actions, but he stressed that an individual's conscious thoughts, beliefs, and logic govern behavior.

Adler emphasized that if a person's logic is faulty, behavior will be dysfunctional and will result in an unsatisfactory lifestyle. Therapeutic efforts are directed at assisting clients to discover inconsistencies or "fictions" in their logic through a re-educational process.

Individual psychology has a cerebral emphasis and is classified as a cognitive therapy. Other writers have viewed Adlerian therapy as sharing tenets with behavioral principles, while some interpret Adler as an existentialist. For purposes of this book's organization, Adler will be considered under the general classification of therapists who ascribe to a neo-analytical philosophy.

BACKGROUND AND PHILOSOPHY

Adler began his career as a classical psychoanalyst. He was trained by Sigmund Freud. He broke away from Freud in the early years of the Freudian movement as he, like other neo-analysts, rejected Freud's sexual etiology of neurosis.

Adler believed that therapy should be concerned with current events rather than with historical reasons for pathology. This attitude placed the responsibility for resolution of problems on the client, rather than on the environment. Therapeutic sessions had a here-and-now focus. He viewed the role of the therapist as that of an empathic listener, clarifier, and educator (Adler, 1963; Corey, 1986; Dreikurs, 1961; Dinkmeyer, Pew & Dinkmeyer, 1979; Hansen, Stevic & Warner, 1986; Wallace, 1986).

Adler's theory has been referred to as a *socio-teleological-holistic approach* (Corey, 1986). Individuals are motivated by social forces (socio); all behavior is goal-directed and has an ultimate purpose (teleology); and people cannot be divided into parts, nor can any part of a person be studied in isolation (holism). The term *individual psychology* is descriptive of Adler's belief in the uniqueness of each human being.

Adler believed that, early in life, each individual chooses a life goal or life script to fulfill individuality and compensate for inferiority. Efforts are consistently expended by the individual to live up to his or her life goal, which results in habitual ways of responding to situations. The chosen goal acts as a self-fulfilling prophecy, and the individual acts consistently according to self-imposed expectations. The choice of a life goal is a result of both genetics and environmental experiences. Motivation to achieve a life goal is driven by an inherent need by every individual to master and influence his or her environment and to believe that he or she is valuable and is contributing to the welfare of others (Adler, 1964).

The choice of a lifestyle is the most distinctive theme by which Adlerian therapists understand human behavior (Hall & Lindzey, 1978). Lifestyle choice is propelled by four major criteria: (1) early childhood experiences, (2) place and perceived function in the family constellation, (3) need for social connectedness, and (4) drive for superiority.

Lifestyle

An individual's lifestyle is made up of individual characteristics, perceptions, long- and short-range goals, and private logic. Our lifestyle choice verifies our thoughts and actions and governs decisions in life. For example, the careers we choose, the choice of mate, and how we dress, all represent efforts that maintain our self-talk. The pattern of acting and reacting becomes habitual, due to expectations and reinforcements from self and others. By the time we reach early adulthood, habits are integrated as part of our personality. Essentially, a young child's behavior is thought by Adlerian therapists to be fundamentally the same throughout life (Dreikurs, 1961).

The young child develops a notion of self through trial and error and feedback from others. Ways to master the environment are learned, as are ways to secure approval and receive attention from others. Techniques that are successful and satisfy needs are those perceived by the individual as being reinforced by others. These reinforced behaviors become lifelong habits that influence and maintain a person's current and future actions and perceptions. Each individual subsequently continues to select goals that fulfill and reinforce individual identity and gain social approval.

Lifestyle can be conceptualized as a circular, self-perpetuating, predictable type of reaction and as a mechanism that supports and exemplifies the power of a self-fulfilling prophecy. As the construction of lifestyle is a product of inner perceptions and environmental response, believed to be willfully chosen by each individual, a dissatisfactory lifestyle can be changed by developing insight into dysfunctional behavior, and by challenging and clarifying beliefs through a cognitive restructuring process.

Family Constellation

An individual's birth order or place in the family constellation is also believed by Adlerian therapists to be a strong and important factor in the choice of a lifestyle. The ordinal position, as well as the psychosocial circumstances surrounding the birth of the child, is thought to govern and strongly influence a person's way of being. As no two children are born under exactly the same circumstances, this belief ensures that each person will hold a unique place in the world.

Adlerian therapists have reached some conclusions regarding lifestyle choice and family constellation. The first child is more likely to become a leader who has conservative attitudes. The second child tends to become a rebel and is more competitive. If the second child is born soon after the first child and is the same gender, there is a greater likelihood that the second child will be predisposed to having an extraverted personality, seeking approval and attention from others outside the nuclear family. The lifestyle choice that the older child finds successful in assuring his or her place in the world is likely to be completely opposite from the second child's choice. For example, if the older child excels at academics, the second child may excel in athletics, music, or art. Adler believed that the interaction between siblings has a profound influence in the choice of a lifestyle. It may be even greater than the interaction between child and parent (Dreikurs, 1961; Hall & Lindzey, 1978).

Social Connectedness

The theme of social connectedness is related to choice of lifestyle. Its importance in the formation of the personality is repeatedly addressed by Adlerian therapists (Dreikurs, 1961). Adler believed that people are primarily social beings who have a strong inclination to belong and be recognized as valuable to society. Moreover, life would be without meaning if people were unable to do things for others.

Adlerians believe that social connectedness is essential for the survival of the human species. If individuals did not believe that they need others, they would have no reason to cooperate, and the human race would decline (Hansen et al., 1986; Mosak, 1984).

Superiority

The drive for superiority is a goal shared by all human beings. Adlerians believe all individuals are compelled to master their environment, as this establishes their uniqueness as a person and validates their existence. In order to achieve a sense of superiority, each individual must recognize and accept the notion that inferiority is a natural part of being human. Healthy persons work to rid themselves of inferiority. A person who rejects the notion of universal inferiority will be unsuccessful at mastering the environment. Ability will become exaggerated, resulting in pathology, dysfunctional behavior, and dissatisfaction with life.

The person who retreats through fantasy or projection, or who denies reality is inappropriately striving to overcome inferiority. Adler perceived neurosis to be the result of faulty beliefs and fictional, unrealistic goals. Individuals are self-determined beings who willfully and consciously choose whether or not to be productive (Ansbacher & Ansbacher, 1956). Adler shifted the etiology of neurosis from the medical model Freud espoused to a cognitive-behavioral, antideterministic, more hopeful model (Dreikurs, 1961; Mosak, 1984).

Compensation for inferiority is an ongoing task for all humans. Individuals strive to strengthen an inferior part of the body through either extensive training or some other way to minimize organ inferiority (Adler, 1963). Dreikurs (1961) considered what a person is born with less important than what he or she does with it.

In the drive for superiority, it is critical that there also be concern for, or social interest in, the welfare of others. Without this dimension, the strive for superiority will become pathological. In addition, there must be congruence between individuals' views of themselves and how others view them (Ansbacher & Ansbacher, 1956).

Adlerians believe individuals may use misbehavior in striving for superiority and that misbehavior always has some self-fulfilling purpose. Dreikurs and Dinkmeyer, well-known Adlerian therapists who initiated much interest in Adler's teachings in the United States, developed explanations to understand a child's misbehavior. They view misbehavior as being intentional and as having a payoff whereby either attention is gained, power is sought, revenge is taken, and/or deficiency or defeat is declared. By applying this explanation, parents and teachers have found they are able to parent and teach more effectively (Dinkmeyer, Pew & Dinkmeyer, 1979; Patterson, 1980).

TECHNIQUES

Adlerians are noted for using any technique that attracts attention and arouses the client. The underlying belief of individual psychology is that insight paves the way to change basic mistakes, private logic, and fictional goals (Dreikurs, 1961). Any technique that challenges the client to unravel faulty logic is encouraged.

Adler was one of the first therapists to use the technique of *paradoxical directives*, which involves the exaggeration of a behavior to increase awareness of it. Marital and family therapists often use this technique to promote change in the family system (Corey, 1986; Dreikurs, 1961; Hall & Lindzey, 1978; Hansen et al., 1986; Mosak, 1984; Wallace, 1986).

Adlerian therapists hold a humanistic attitude toward clients. The therapist must be genuine, treat clients with respect and acceptance, and be an empathic listener, clarifier, and educator. Adler believes therapists must be responsive and spontaneous. Adler encouraged the client-counselor relationship to be in I-Thou terms where the atmosphere is relaxed and both parties face one another. Goals must be identified and mutually agreed upon by client and counselor (Buber, 1957; Dreikurs, 1961; Mosak, 1984).

A thorough understanding of the client's perceived lifestyle, goals, and early memories is typically gathered during the initial sessions. With this focus on the client's perceptions, Adlerian techniques have been included as part of phenomenological therapy. In addition to being thought of as an early humanist, Adler is also considered an early phenomenologist.

Asking clients to recall their earliest memories and to describe their impression of the family constellation is thought to reveal inner logic and assists the counselor to more fully understand the client's style of life. These questions are posed to clients during the early stages of therapy. The Adlerian counselor would subsequently provide cognitive interpretations of the client's responses and check with the client to verify hunches (Adler, 1963). Therapy has a here-and-now focus; past dreams are not analyzed for unconscious motives but rather are seen as a way to solve problems. Dreams are viewed as a possible rehearsal for future action (Mosak, 1984).

The role of the counselor is to explain the client's mistakes in a way that is acceptable to the client. As the main source of maladjustment is considered to originate from a sense of inferiority resulting in low levels of self-confidence and self-esteem, the therapist relabels inferior attitudes as *acts of discouragement* and facilitates change by providing support and encouragement to the client. Social participation is also encouraged to decrease feelings of isolation and aloneness, and to enhance feelings of belonging and value.

Most people who come to counseling know they are dissatisfied with life but lack an understanding of why they act as they do. The Adlerian counselor's job is to help clients gain insight into basic mistakes and recognize the purpose a behavior serves or the gains derived from it. Adler referred to successful therapy as an "aha" experience (Adler, 1963; Mosak, 1984).

Clients learn to understand their lifestyle, as well as the complex and unique reason for their choice. It is explained to clients that once a lifestyle is chosen, it remains throughout life and unknowingly dictates all actions. However, as we cognitively create a life script, a change in life script is possible through education. (Adler, 1963; Corey, 1986; Dreikurs, 1961; Hansen et al., 1986; Mosak, 1984; Wallace, 1986).

SUMMARY

Adler's theory of psychotherapy and psychopathology rests on the belief that humans have an intellect to make decisions based on creativity and self-directed thinking. Adler viewed action, thoughts, and feelings to be in accordance with an individual's subjective experiences. There are no victims; rather, individuals are masters of their own fate (Corey, 1986; Hansen et al., 1986).

Individual psychology has a number of applications to persons or situations. In the United States, Dreikurs and Dinkmeyer are known as Adler's disciples. Their research has demonstrated that Adlerian tenets assist children, adults, couples, and families who have a variety of complaints. Child guidance clinics and schools have adopted many Adlerian techniques. Parent and teacher training workshops have been widely based on Adlerian philosophy (Dinkmeyer et al., 1979).

Individual psychology views pathology as a function of an inferiority complex; a person who feels discouraged has not mastered his or her environment. The purpose of counseling is to assist the client in cognitively discovering and unraveling faulty logic, fictions, and reasons for a dissatisfactory lifestyle. Clients are also encouraged to develop relationships with others. Clients must accept self-responsibility if therapy is to be successful.

As a result of Adler's emphasis on social connectedness and self-responsibility through education, individual psychology has been recognized as a major contribution for a number of current contemporary counseling theories. Adler's ideas have been used by humanists, existentialists, cognitive therapists, and behaviorists, in group, family, and individual counseling (Corey, 1986; Dreikurs, 1961; Hall & Lindzey, 1978; Hansen et al., 1986; Mosak, 1984; Patterson, 1980).

BEHAVIOR THERAPY

B. F. SKINNER
1904–

KEY CONCEPTS

BASIC ID
Chaining
Classical Conditioning
Cognitive Restructuring
Contracts
Discrimination
Emotional Flooding
Extinction
Generalization
Learning Principles
Multimodal Approach

Operant Conditioning
Punishment
Reductionistic Model
Schedules of Reinforcement
Scientific Method
Shaping
Social Learning Theory
Stimulus
Systematic Desensitization
"Tabula Rasa"
Vicarious Learning

PREVIEW QUESTIONS

---

1. What type of reinforcement schedule is best for developing new behaviors?

2. What is the difference between classical conditioning and the operant model?

3. Why is Skinner's model considered to be an individually limiting or deterministic theory?

4. What does the Lockean notion of "tabula rasa" describe?

5. How can behaviors be extinguished?

6. How does negative reinforcement differ from punishment?

7. How does primary reinforcement differ from rewards?

8. What behavioral technique was made renowned by Joseph Wolpe?

9. Why is it that reinforcers differ from person to person?

10. Why is it important for the client and counselor to mutually develop a behavioral contract?

Introduction

At about the same time Freud was proclaiming the virtues of psychoanalysis in Europe, John B. Watson was advancing the merits of behavioral counseling methods in the United States (Haas, 1979; Wilson, 1984). In contrast to Freud's probing of the unconscious to resolve emotional and physical distress, Watson's belief was that if psychology was to be considered a science, only observable behavioral change that could be scientifically isolated was worthy of study and reporting. Upon this belief and the principle of "tabula rasa," set forth by John Locke, the foundation of behavioral counseling was laid.

Watson based his theory on Ivan Pavlov's classical conditioning studies, in which a conditioned stimulus (bell) was paired with an unconditioned stimulus (food) to produce a conditioned response (a dog salivating). In this now famous and classic experiment, Pavlov was able to demonstrate that when two events are simultaneously presented, the second event will take on the quality of the original event. In his experiment, Pavlov presented food to a hungry dog that salivated in response to the food. Pavlov then paired giving the food to the dog with ringing a bell in order to elicit salivation. Subsequently, Pavlov rang the bell without the simultaneous presentation of the food and found that, through conditioning, the dog salivated. He repeated this experiment numerous times and concluded that learning is a function of manipulating the environment. He called this type of learning, in which an antecedent stimulus produces a conditioned response, *classical conditioning* (Pavlov, 1927).

Watson applied Pavlov's principles to the psychology of learning in human beings. He took an 11-month-old boy named Albert and found that, by pairing a loud noise (UCS) with a harmless white rat (CS), he could elicit a fearful response (CR) in Albert. Watson continued his studies and found that Albert remained fearful upon presentation of the rat, even when the unpleasant loud noise was absent. Through this experiment, and others, Watson successfully documented that humans learn by association.

Watson's views were not favorably accepted by contemporary researchers, who were also in the process of developing hypotheses to explain human development and behavior. It was not until B. F. Skinner published his studies on the Skinnerian black box, in which rats learned how to manipulate a maze and secure food, that behavioral principles were accepted as a means of understanding human actions (Hall & Lindzey, 1978).

As a result, B. F. Skinner is considered the father of *behavioral counseling*, as it is known today. His research was heavily influenced by E. L. Thorndike, who demonstrated the power of consequences in learning, maintaining, and extinguishing behaviors (Patterson, 1980).

Skinner's model of learning is referred to as *operant paradigm, operant conditioning,* or *instrumental learning.* Whereas Pavlov's model was based on physiological, biological, and reflexive actions and primary reinforcers such as food, water, shelter, and antecedent behavior, Skinner's model emphasized voluntary willed actions, consequential behavior, and second-order conditioned responses, such as praise, love, self-esteem, and self-actualization (Maslow, 1968).

The concept—that reinforcers act to control behavior and determine the degree of certainty or probability that the behavior will occur again—describes the major philosophy behind behavioral counseling. Other well-known behavioral researchers who share Skinner's beliefs include J. Krumboltz, C. Thoreson, and R. Hosford (Corey, 1986).

PRINCIPLES OF THE OPERANT MODEL

Behavioral theories rest on the assumption that people are not innately good or bad; rather, each of us has a neutral personality that is formed by learned environmental experiences and controlled by external events. The ability to change some undesired behavior can be accomplished through a selective and conscious process in which correct reinforcers that maintain dysfunctional behavior can be scientifically identified.

The most difficult part of a behavioral program is to gather accurate information that isolates and describes the role of specific reinforcers. Once correct reinforcers are identified, ways to shape desired behavior can be developed (Patterson, 1980).

Shaping mechanisms consist of laws of reinforcement, extinction, generalization, and discrimination. They must be operationalized into specific and clear terms so that a desired behavioral plan is clearly understood.

Skinner rejected notions of drives, motives, feelings, and other internal states as reasons for behavior. He defined individuals as reacting to a repertoire of behavior appropriate to a given set of contingencies. The body itself is thought of as a machine in the sense that it is a complex system regulated by actions that are shaped by evolutionary patterns of survival and adaptation (Skinner, 1938, 1953, 1974).

Behavior therapy has been called a reductionistic and mechanistic model, as human potential is seen as outside the power of the individual and limited by environmental forces. Individuals are seen as reactive, passive organisms influenced by manipulation and who must wait to receive information from their environment. Skinner rejected the notion that humans are free and in control of their destinies. These beliefs define both behaviorism and psychoanalysis as deterministic theories (Brammer, 1985).

PRINCIPLES OF REINFORCEMENT

Behavioral counseling is considered action therapy in which reinforcers explain behavioral responses. The concept of reinforcement maintains that a stimulus which follows a behavior can either increase or decrease the likelihood that the behavior will occur again.

There are two classes of reinforcers: positive and negative. A positive reinforcer is usually pleasurable; it is a stimulus that when applied following an operant response strengthens the probability that the response will occur again (e.g., watching TV after completing homework). A positive reinforcer is not necessarily a reward, as rewards are given on a conditional basis for completion of a task. The person who receives the reward may or may not value it. If the reward is not valued, it will not act as a reinforcer. Numerous studies have documented a link between positive reinforcement and desired behavior change (Groden & Cautela, 1981).

A negative reinforcer involves the use of an aversive stimulus that, when removed or withdrawn following an operant response, strengthens the probability of that response. A negative reinforcer is not synonymous with punishment. Punishment refers to the decrease of a response with the presentation of an aversive or unpleasant stimulus (e.g., getting a parking ticket for an expired meter). Skinner (1953) found punishing rats only resulted in temporary suppression of some behavior. He concluded punishment is not a powerful or permanent method of extinguishing certain behaviors and should only be used when positive alternatives are not found satisfactory.

In deciding whether a stimulus acts as a reinforcer or punisher, ask what effect presentation or withdrawal of a stimulus has on behavior. If the stimulus increases the probability that some behavior will recur, it is a reinforcer. If the stimulus decreases the likelihood that some behavior will recur, it is a punisher (Groden & Cautela, 1981).

To understand how reinforcers operate, a baseline of desired behavior is developed. This permits the translation of general goals into concrete measurable ones. A design is schematically developed, a reinforcer is introduced, and behavior is observed; a reinforcer is withheld and behavior is observed; and the reinforcer is reintroduced and behavior is observed. The researcher or clinician notes any and all changes in behavior as a result of this manipulation.

Sometimes an inadvertent stimulus, which appears to act in a stimulus-response pattern, is accidently viewed as a reinforcer of behavior. For example, superstition, as in the wearing of a lucky shirt to win a game or pass an examination, could be viewed as an accidental reinforcer. The inadvertent stimulus-response mechanism would not hold up to the rigors of scientific testing and would eventually be determined as a coincidental factor that produced a particular outcome.

SCHEDULES OF REINFORCEMENT

Schedules of reinforcement and punishment refer to the regularity with which patterns of stimulus follow operants and the effect they have. There are two general classes of reinforcement schedules: *continuous* and *intermittent*.

A continuous schedule is the simplest version, involving reinforcement after each occurrence of a behavior. This approach is most effective for developing new behaviors but is least effective for maintaining behaviors. Once a particular response is conditioned, it is not economical to maintain behavior this way, and an occasional or intermittent schedule should be developed.

Skinner (1938, 1953) proposed two main classes of intermittent reinforcement schedules: *fixed* and *variable*. A fixed reinforcement schedule describes reinforcers that are provided after a person exhibits some desired behavior a certain number of times. A variable schedule describes a situation in which a certain number of responses are consistently required for reinforcement. Typically the variable rate is calculated according to some mean or average time the desired behavior is expected. Fixed or variable reinforcers are also provided based on the number of responses. This is called a *ratio rate*. Reinforcers may also be provided at some fixed interval during which a certain amount of time must elapse between actions.

Behavioral therapists have found the more recent association a particular stimulus has on some outcome, the greater the likelihood it will prevail as the stimulus-response bond. Through a process of *chaining*—stringing together several associations or responses to change—and shaping, discrete behaviors become connected, forming an elaborate reinforcing system. Generalization through chaining and shaping of behavioral responses becomes complex to track, but a series of stimulus-response-reinforcer can be developed after careful observation (Bijou, 1976; Munn, 1974).

Extinction principles explain how to decrease a behavior by either ignoring it or withholding reinforcers. For example, parents who ignore the temper tantrum of their two-year-old are employing principles of extinction. The difference between negative reinforcers, punishment, and extinction is that in the latter case no consequence follows behavior, while in negative reinforcers and punishment something is taken away.

TECHNIQUES

Behavioral techniques can be generally viewed as a process involving the selection and documentation of appropriate reinforcers to construct precise operational definitions for some desired goal. Throughout the process, observations of change are noted and recorded. If the desired behavior is not realized, a new plan is developed. This type of plan modification and redevelopment is done as many times as needed.

The role of behavioral therapists is viewed as a learning process; through continual evaluation, the counselor helps the client discriminate and define the problem. The therapist works as an "applied behavioral scientist," using systematic observation, quantification of data, and hypothetical-deductive reasoning to develop a meaningful procedure (Corey, 1986; Thoresen, 1966).

Clarity of responsibilities is a strong theme employed by behavioral counselors. Explicit contracts are developed between the client and counselor, which spell out roles, responsibilities, expectations for each person, what is to be accomplished by whom, and when some agenda is due. This is believed necessary for a clear and concrete understanding of desired goals.

Although the process appears to be mechanistic, the counselor takes the time to establish rapport and to be nonjudgmental and accepting toward the client. Behavioral therapists had been previously charged as being too reductionistic and applying band-aid solutions to complicated, multifaceted client problems. Behavioral therapists recognize there may be a problem with oversimplification of the client-counselor relationship and, like other therapists, work to maintain an open attitude toward treatment (Brammer, 1985; Groden & Cautela, 1981).

Problem-solving, decision-making techniques, and behavioral rehearsals are often part of the therapeutic process. The counselor typically assigns homework to provide the client with direct experiences that contribute to some behavior change (Groden & Cautela, 1981; Patterson, 1980; Wilson, 1984).

Behavioral therapists vary as to how the environment shapes and influences the individual. A wide range of approaches have been used to help clients to change undesirable behaviors. Three different approaches are reviewed below: systematic desensitization principles, developed by Joseph Wolpe; the multimodal approach, developed by Arnold Lazarus; and social learning theory, developed by Albert Bandura.

Joseph Wolpe (1958, 1973) documented success in working with phobic and anxious clients by developing a behavioral intervention technique known as *systematic desensitization,* based on the theory of reciprocal inhibition. Wolpe used imagery techniques to teach clients to manage anxiety through a process of counterconditioning. He paired bipolar situations perceived by the client as threatening or unpleasant with pleasurable stimuli and relaxation techniques.

Wolpe's system was to instruct clients, during therapy, to develop a hierarchy of least anxious to greatest discomfort situations and to inform the therapist each time anxiety or fear was felt. With this transmission of information, the therapist would instruct the client to stop imagining the scene and relax. Wolpe's system of rehearsing various levels of anxiety in a safe environment desensitized the client by diffusing and distracting the memory that perpetuated the anxiety. His techniques have been widely replicated by other researchers, in a variety of situational problems (Brammer, 1985). For example, Masters and Johnson (1966) reported the use of Wolpe's basic approach to treat sexual anxiety and dysfunction.

Arnold Lazarus worked with Wolpe, and together they used a number of creative behavioral techniques to help clients attain some desired behavior (Krumboltz & Thoresen, 1976). Lazarus subsequently devised the multimodal approach, a cognitive-behavioral map that incorporated the three human experiental modalities of cognition, action (behavior), and emotions (affect). He helped clients thoroughly assess their behavior by paying attention and tracking the importance or "firing order" of components. Lazarus named these components the BASIC ID, an acronym for behavior, affective responses, sensations, imagery, cognitions, interpersonal relations, and drugs (or a biological modality).

Through his *multimodal approach*, Lazarus believed he could help people understand the multifaceted and complex nature of behavior and actions. He employed the use of a variety of mental and physical techniques to assist clients and believed clinical effectiveness to be a function of the counselor's ability to employ technical eclecticism and flexibility in working with clients. Known for his personalistic and individualistic approach as a therapist, he rested much of his theoretical base on social learning theory (Lazarus, 1971, 1976).

Albert Bandura is the founder of *social learning theory*. He believed humans learn from direct and obvious reinforcement, as well as through imitation and role modeling (Bandura, 1977). He emphasized the importance of *vicarious experiences* and the selection of social role models in personality formation. Bandura and Walters (1963) hypothesized that an individual plays an active role in determining the classes and intensity of behavior to be imitated through some internal mediation process and that the choice of a role model is heavily influenced by individuals viewing other individuals as similar to themselves (Bandura, 1977, 1979).

Shaffer (1979) summarized both the cognitive and behavioral processes believed to be present for the acquisition of behavior through observational and social learning as follows:

1. An individual must be capable of attending to and must pay attention to a particular event.

2. An individual must be able to retain or remember critical features of an event so that events can be recalled.

3. An individual must have available motoric reproduction skills and needs to be able to physically perform the particular behavior.

4. An individual must have motivation to acquire a particular behavior.

Social learning theorists believe individuals have the ability to reinforce themselves and that immediate reinforcers are not necessary every time a behavior is desired. This method teaches individuals to be self-reliant by selecting appropriate role models. It also addresses the importance of cultural expectations in the acquisition of behaviors and helps to explain the transmission of behavior across generations. For example, research has identified perpetual familial patterns of alcoholism, obesity, and child abuse (Mischel, 1973).

Behavioral therapists use a number of other techniques to help clients change dissatisfactory behaviors. *Emotional flooding* is a process whereby the client is instructed to think deliberately of a situation that causes anxiety and to hold onto the anxiety until the point of energy depletion or exhaustion. This is a form of paradoxical intervention, an exaggeration of the problem. A technique known as *implosive therapy* is similar to flooding but is psychodynamic in nature (Watson & Marks, 1971).

Other behavioral techniques include imagery to change behavior or behavior modification, in which a token economy acts as a reinforcement mechanism. In aversive therapy, a noxious unconditioned stimulus, such as shock, is paired with an undesirable behavior to produce some consequence. Thought stopping and other cognitive restructuring activities are additional techniques used by the behavioral therapist (Corey, 1986; Wilson, 1984).

Effectiveness in changing behavior is judged by how differently the client acts as a result of counseling intervention techniques. Specific, rather than general or global, goals are addressed. Selected goals must be measurable and attainable, and there must be some mechanism for feedback. Therapy is centered around client interests and counselor competency and is guided by professional counselor ethics. (Patterson, 1980; Wilson, 1984).

Behavioral techniques are most successful when targeted to specific, culturally accepted ways of behaving. The client must be active in the counseling process and willing to assume responsibility for initiating and maintaining change. Individuals who have sociopathic tendencies or who do not have the discipline to change their behavior are inappropriate candidates for behavioral counseling interventions.

SUMMARY

Behaviorism began as an effort to understand human behavior through the application of the principles of learning, using the method of scientific inquiry. Behavior theories originated with Pavlov's and Watson's classical conditioning, antecedent stimuli, or respondent learning theories. Skinner's theory of the operant model—that behavior is a function of consequences—describes the philosophy of contemporary behaviorists, who believe that environment shapes individual responses, leading to an increase, decrease, or no change in particular behaviors. Both theories demonstrated that a neutral stimulus can become a conditioned stimulus that creates a predictive response when paired with an original unconditioned stimulus.

Behaviorists are convinced of the importance of an objective way to measure change through empirical investigation. They believe that a specific behavior—and not the origin of some action—is the critical point for counseling intervention.

The emphasis of behavioral therapy is on assessment, evaluation, and accountability. Strategies for change start with helping the client formulate specific goals; this is followed by identification of stimulus-reinforcer mechanisms that maintain particular behaviors. New stimulus-response links to produce some desired change are subsequently identified; this eventually leads to a process of acceptable generalizations for similar situations. A written contract is developed by the client and counselor in order to decrease ambiguous goals and outline both client and counselor responsibilities (Corey, 1986; Skinner, 1953; Wilson, 1984).

REALITY THERAPY

WILLIAM GLASSER
1925–

KEY CONCEPTS

Attitude toward Mental Illness
BCP
Eight Steps for Therapeutic Intervention
Failure Identity
Irresponsibility

Positive Addictions
Responsible Hedonism
Responsibility
Success Identity
The 3 R's of Therapy

PREVIEW QUESTIONS

---

1. How does Glasser view maladjustment or pathology?

2. What is Glasser's view of mental illness?

3. Why is perception so important?

4. How is responsible behavior defined?

5. How important a part do genes play in personality development?

6. How does Glasser view anti-anxiety medications?

7. How important are early childhood experiences in personality formation?

8. What is the role of transference in reality therapy?

9. Do reality therapists need to be concerned with cultural norms?

10. What is the relationship of exercise to mental health?

Introduction

William Glasser, the founder of *reality therapy*, was trained as a psychiatrist and classical psychoanalyst. He became frustrated with the lack of progress being made when using Freudian techniques for the institutionalized delinquents who were his patients. He hypothesized that traditional analytic techniques with their emphasis on dysfunctional, dissatisfactory, and abnormal behaviors perpetuated, rather than helped change, inappropriate emotional and behavioral problems. He discontinued the use of psychoanalytic techniques, much to the dismay of his colleagues. In its place, Glasser insisted that his clients take responsibility for their own actions by concentrating on the present, rather than the past. In 1965 Glasser published *Reality Therapy: A New Approach to Psychiatry*.

Glasser believes therapy must have a here-and-now focus. There is little concern with the etiology of a problem or critical tasks to be accomplished during a particular developmental period. What happened in the past is history and cannot be changed.

Glasser describes his type of therapy as behavioral, with actions promoting positive change (Glasser, 1984). Other researchers describe Glasser's theory as a cognitive-behavioral approach in which logic and the development of rational, concrete thinking are used to overcome emotional difficulties (Hansen, Stevic, & Warner, 1986; Pietrofesa, Hoffman, & Splete, 1984). Although the categories overlap and are arbitrary, both modalities stress the role of the therapist as a teacher who helps clients learn more satisfactory ways to control their environment.

PHILOSOPHY

Glasser formulated reality theory based on the belief that behavior is under the control of perception (BCP). The brain is believed to work as a control system that decodes internal messages and develops a plan of action to resolve the need. Thoughts, feelings, and actions are all under the control of the same cognitive system. Personality, successful adjustment, and/or maladjustment rely on the perceptual interpretation of needs—the only reality for the person.

Individuals learn to have either a *success identity* or a *failure identity* by consciously choosing particular behaviors that are thought to satisfy needs. If perception is accurate, the person engages in responsible behavior that satisfies personal needs and does not prevent others from satisfying theirs. The responsible person is viewed as having a *success identity* (Glasser, 1965, 1984).

A *failure identity* results from faulty perception; it is fostered by irresponsible acts that spread to the person's total personality, resulting in a pervasive personality deficit. The person who "acts up" views this response as an effective mechanism to satisfy needs and repeats this behavior. The medical model, with its "sick" label, reinforces irresponsible behaviors by removing responsibility from the individual. Descriptors that portray the client-counselor relationship in doctor-patient terms are considered antitherapeutic by Glasser (Glasser, 1984).

Feeling loved and valued is necessary for acting responsibly. A proper growth environment begins with the parent-child relationship, in which the child knowingly experiences love, self-worth, and value. A loveless life promotes feelings of anxiety, self-blame, depression, and withdrawal from society. To challenge and help change this, the therapist uses early counseling sessions to develop rapport and reinforce the notion of worthiness for every human being (Glasser, 1965; Glasser & Zunin, 1973).

Although Glasser classified his therapy as a behavioral theory, he rejected Skinner's reinforcement theory of organizing stimulus-response conditions for desired actions. Glasser believes that behavior emanates from internal, rather than environmental demands, and that individuals have a choice in responding to some need (Glasser, 1984).

TECHNIQUES

Glasser describes the counseling relationship as a one of teacher-pupil. The counselor is a teacher who instructs clients to control their own world through the use of logic and reason. The therapist is active, directive, and confrontive in "pinning down" clients to understand exactly what it is they want from life, and then challenges clients to take more effective control over their life. Both client and counselor sit face to face and attempt to engage in a meaningful, productive, honest dialogue (Glasser, 1984).

The teaching of responsibility is viewed as a developmental process. The first lesson is the "do it" stage. This refers to the desire of the client to take the initiative to improve. The second stage stresses a "positive symptom person" outlook. The client is taught to act constructively by expressing self-needs, while concurrently considering the effect of expressing those needs on others.

Worthiness of self and others is stressed throughout the counseling process. Clients are taught to be good to themselves and to create positive addictions. Focus on healthy activities such as a proper diet and regular exercise is encouraged; these helpful activities promote and lead to feelings of competence and value. Glasser refers to individuals partaking of "responsible hedonism," seeking pleasure while weighing the circumstances and consequences of behavior (Glasser, 1984; Wubbolding, 1981).

The "3 R's" of reality therapy—"right," "responsibility," and "reality"— are viewed as essential elements that clients must accept as part of a successful therapeutic process. *Right* refers to the belief that healthy people evaluate their own behavior and modify it to fit within some accepted cultural norm. *Responsibility* refers to the ability of the client to satisfy personal needs without preventing others from realizing their needs. *Reality* refers to the recognition that individuals have limitations for fulfilling self-needs and that this is a universal reality experienced by everyone.

Therapy has a here-and-now focus. Dwelling on the past and those behaviors that failed to contribute to a successful identity is not viewed as a therapeutic technique. However, past successful behaviors are discussed in therapy as a way of helping clients recognize that they have had the ability in the past to use proper ways to resolve concerns. Humor is introduced as a therapeutic mechanism that dissipates tension brought about by the recognition of faulty behaviors. Humor also teaches clients that it is okay to laugh at their own mistakes.

A contract between client and counselor is developed that states a clear and specific plan of action. The client must agree to participate fully. Clients are reassured that change is difficult but that persistence will pay off. Clients are encouraged to be creative, spontaneous, and curious. Because a success identity is produced by positive addictions, meditation or any other activity that can be done alone is encouraged. Activities that are noncompetitive and able to be performed without becoming self-critical are therapeutic (Corey, 1986).

Glasser identified eight steps that describe the practice of reality therapy (Glasser, 1984):

1. The counselor must develop rapport and help clients understand what it is they *really* want from life. The counselor must be genuine and demonstrate acceptance toward the client.

2. The counselor asks the client what he or she is doing to satisfy perceived needs. A focus on current behaviors encourages clients to take responsibility for themselves.

3. The counselor evaluates the behavior the client is using to meet needs. The counselor helps the client establish a linkage between perception and actions.

4. A plan for desired behavior is developed.

5. The client must be committed to follow the plan. The counselor teaches a step-by-step plan of action.

6. The counselor must accept no excuses as to why the plan is not producing success. If the plan is incorrect, a new plan must be developed.

7. The counselor must be careful not to punish the client for failing to follow the agreed plan. Punishment may actually be a manipulation on the part of the client to sustain dysfunctional need gratification.

8. The client and the counselor must refuse to give up. All problems can be solved, given the right plan of action. An attitude of persistence will result in success.

Reality therapy prides itself on being a jargon-free, nonmystical, and down to earth type of therapy. Its popularity rose during the 1950s and 1960s, and it has been used since that time for people of all age groups and in a variety of mental health settings (Ivey & Simek-Downing, 1980).

In 1969 Glasser wrote *Schools Without Failure*; this book emphasizes that learning without failure, as well as discipline without punishment, teaches responsible actions, which have the potential to satisfy needs. Glasser's therapy has since been used widely by educators.

SUMMARY

The major theme of Glasser's reality therapy is responsibility through awareness that is both logical and grounded in reality. The ability of the individual to be responsible leads to a success identity, while irresponsibility leads to a failure identity.

The role of the therapist is as a teacher. The counseling process is viewed as a dialogue between client and counselor. Failure to reach desired goals is viewed as the client's unwillingness to make needed changes.

Therapists are unconcerned with symptomatology, diagnosis, or prognosis. All behavior is thought to be under the control of perception (BCP), in the here and now (phenomenology). Reality therapy uses an action-oriented or behavioral modality to promote change. Glasser believes it is easier to order oneself to take some action than to convince oneself to feel better (Corey, 1986).

RATIONAL EMOTIVE THERAPY

ALBERT ELLIS
1913–

KEY CONCEPTS

ABCDE Model
Awfulizations
Cognitive Model
Cognitive Restructuring
Confrontation

Homework
Musturbations
Rational and Irrational Beliefs
Self-Talk

PREVIEW QUESTIONS

---

1. What is the role of parental influence in adult personality?

2. What must individuals do to lead a satisfactory life?

3. What is the single most important role of the therapist?

4. How would RET treat the id, ego, and superego?

5. What follows disputation in the RET model?

6. What is bibliotherapy?

7. How long does a rational emotive therapist work with a client?

8. Should individuals be overly concerned with how they are viewed by others?

9. What can the individual do to stop negative self-talk?

10. How is RET similar to reality therapy?

Introduction

Albert Ellis, the founder of rational emotive therapy, commonly known as RET, was trained as a classical psychoanalyst. Like many other therapists, Ellis became dissatisfied with Freudian techniques and the lack of progress made by his clients. He believed therapy was too long and tedious a process, and he questioned the therapeutic outcome of psychoanalysis.

Ellis turned to the principles of learning theories for a better understanding of the interactions among human actions, behavior, health, and pathology. From these studies, he developed a model of short-term practical therapy that could be easily applied to a variety of emotional and behavioral disorders (Ellis, 1962, 1967, 1984; Frey & Raming, 1979).

The basic premise of RET is the belief that cognitions produce self-talk that leads to either a satisfied, healthy, happy person, or a dissatisfied, maladjusted, unhappy person. People are thought to think, emote, and behave according to how the intellect processes information. Words provide the mechanism for the interpretation of information and cause emotional and behavioral consequences. Misperceived or misguided verbalizations produce cognitive errors, which Ellis refers to as "irrational beliefs." Over time, irrational beliefs become habitual patterns of behavior, and the person is viewed by himself or herself as either successful or unsuccessful.

The role and function of the rational emotive therapist is as a teacher. The therapist actively challenges clients' irrational beliefs and demonstrates the ABCDE method for refuting faulty beliefs. The therapist assumes a direct, confrontive approach and is not as concerned with developing a close relationship with the client as much as helping the client develop a satisfactory lifestyle within a reasonably short period of time (Baruth & Huber, 1985; Walen, DiGiuseppe, & Wesler, 1980; Ellis, 1984).

Rational emotive therapy has been popular since the 1950s. Because it holds up to the scientific rigors of hypothetical-deductive reasoning, it has been widely researched. The results of numerous studies have indicated RET to be a successful philosophy and technique for clients who have diverse cognitive concerns (Baruth & Huber, 1986; Ellis, 1984; Patterson, 1980).

PHILOSOPHY

Rational emotive therapy centers around the principle that humans have higher order intelligence with the ability to construct cognitive structures from both a rational and irrational basis. Ellis believed that a cerebral process known as *cognition* governs intellect; it is the most important determinant of human emotion and behavior, as people think, emote, and behave in accordance with how information is processed. When people interpret activities from a rational basis, the result is healthy, adaptive functioning. When people interpret activities from an irrational basis, emotional problems such as anxiety, anger, depression, guilt, and hopelessness result.

Words or verbalizations, referred to as "self-talk," describe the individual's internal thought process that governs the way an event is interpreted and acted upon. Each individual is a free, self-determining being who has the inherent power and control to live a happy life. Each individual also has the inherent power to lead a dissatisfactory or miserable life (Wallace, 1986).

Ellis believes early childhood experiences and a biological predisposition contribute to how events are interpreted. Children are viewed as gullible and suggestible because of a basic need for love and attention. The way in which significant others (e.g., parents, family, friends, and teachers) treat the child becomes a pattern that contributes to a habitual way of responding to the environment as an adult and to an individual's personality (Ellis, 1967).

Rational emotive therapy places responsibility for actions and behavior on the individual. Only the self can make a person act. Blaming others is neither rational nor logical. We innately and consciously choose either to be governed by ourselves in a satisfactory way or to permit ourselves and others to govern us with the use of irrational, illogical ideas. Therefore, satisfaction, or the lack of it, is under the control of each individual and is considered an internal event (Baruth & Huber, 1985; Ellis, 1967, 1984).

Rational emotive therapists believe that maladjustment or dissatisfaction with life is either a product of faulty messages from the self and others, or of too much time and energy spent listening to negative self-talk. Cognitive errors are those that contain unproven assumptions and carry a message implying there is a single or "right" way to carry out a particular activity. Ellis uses the term "musturbations" to describe messages that contain absolutes. These absolute messages serve to promote emotional or behavioral dysfunction.

Words such as "should," "must," "ought to," and "have to" are descriptive examples of "musturbations." The term "awfulizations" conveys a similar message and includes such words as "hopeless," "awful," "horrible," "terrible," or "unbearable." Overgeneralizations, oversimplifications, and exaggerations are other examples of absolutistic messages that contribute to unhealthy thoughts and actions (Ellis, 1967, 1984; Walen, DiGiuseppe, & Wessler, 1980; Wallace, 1986).

Ellis describes behavior as a bipolar dimension. Satisfactory behavior results from interpreting verbalizations from a logical, rational perspective. Dissatisfactory behavior results from illogical, irrational interpretations or from "musturbating" or "awfulizing"—convincing oneself something is final, rather than inconvenient or disadvantageous. When circumstances are viewed as worse than they really are, one does not see oneself in control or as having a way out of the situation (Ellis, 1973).

Ellis believes that people who are unhappy or who portray themselves as maladjusted and dysfunctional and who become emotionally disturbed are really telling themselves a chain of false sentences. Ellis identifies eleven common "irrational beliefs" that lead to dysfunctional emotions and behavior (Ellis, 1967, p. 61):

1. It is absolutely essential for an individual to be loved or approved of by every significant person in his or her environment.

2. It is necessary that each individual be completely competent, adequate, and achieving in all areas, if the individual is to be worthwhile.

3. Some people are bad, wicked, or villainous, and these people should be blamed and punished.

4. It is terrible and catastrophic when things are not the way an individual wants them to be.

5. Unhappiness is a function of events outside the control of the individual.

6. If something could be dangerous or harmful, an individual should constantly be concerned and think about it.

7. It is easier to run away from difficulties and self-responsibility than it is to face them.

8. Individuals need to be dependent on others and have someone stronger than themselves to lean on.

9. Past events in an individual's life determine present behavior and cannot be changed.

10. An individual should be very concerned and upset by other people's problems.

11. There is always a correct and precise answer to every problem, and it is catastrophic if it is not found.

To counteract common faulty perceptions, Ellis uses a cognitive and behavioral model to teach self-directed behaviors and minimize distortions of reality. Cognitive models emphasize the notion that awareness and perceptions govern behavior and that communication is needed to interpret what is thought and perceived. Behavioral models stress the importance of understanding the components and effects of stimuli and reinforcers in producing some action.

TECHNIQUES

The rational emotive therapist uses various *cognitive restructuring* techniques to challenge clients to refute absolute and unrealistic demands that lead to maladaptive thoughts and behaviors. *Cognitive restructuring* is a general term that describes how the therapist uncovers and teaches clients to refute illogical thinking, understand internal values and statements, and restructure faulty beliefs to become rational and logical ones (Ellis, 1973; Stone, 1980).

The first step in RET is for the client and therapist to agree on what specific goals will be addressed and the specific actions needed to reach these goals. The client is instructed to describe undesirable self-defeating emotions and ineffectual behavior in terms of self-imposed statements. The therapist helps the client self-explore these statements and conclude whether they emanate from a rational, logical, scientific base or from an illogical or irrational base.

In the second stage of therapy, the therapist teaches and forcibly challenges the client to recognize self-sabotaging statements and how he or she is responsible for maintaining dysfunctional consequences. Ellis believes the single most important element of therapy is for the counselor to vigorously confront the client to act on irrational behaviors. Therapy is considered hard work. Confrontation and active participation by the therapist are needed to attack and wear down the client's resistance to change. As a result of this attitude, Ellis has been referred to as a harsh counselor who belittles people to force change (Patterson, 1980).

Ellis does address the necessity of a client-counselor rapport for change to occur. However, he views the relationship between client and counselor to be of little importance as an ingredient for successful therapy. Rapport is seen only as an advantageous mechanism that facilitates a teaching-learning environment (Baruth & Huber, 1985; Ellis, 1984; Walen, DiGiuseppe & Wessler, 1980).

Ellis developed a simple schema known as the *ABCDE* method to illustrate how cognitions play a role in developing and maintaining emotional and behavioral disturbance. The process begins with an *activating* event (A), whereby some stimulus or circumstance forces some response. At first, it is believed (A) causes some *consequence* (C). However on closer inspection, (C) is actually found to be the result of internal self-talk which is mediated by a person's thoughts and *beliefs* (B). If thinking is confused or illogical, irrational beliefs will result in self defeating behaviors (Ellis, 1973).

The rational emotive therapist expands the ABC model to ABCDE; clients are taught to *dispute* (D), challenge, and debate faulty beliefs and then to note the *effect* (E) of the disputation, replacing irrational statements for rational ones. Disputations must be vigorously attacked, in the belief that people have a tendency to revert to habitual ways (Baruth & Huber, 1985).

Clients are assigned specific homework assignments to practice the ABCDE method. The client is typically asked to keep a record of how many times and under what circumstances the homework assignment was actually carried out, as well as what descriptors were used to recognize the ABCDE pattern. This process to dispute irrational beliefs continues until topics that produce disturbed consequences disappear (Ellis, 1984; Shertzer & Stone, 1974).

Homework also includes teaching the client to throw away "absolute" words and the "musturbations" or "awfulizations," which imply the situation is hopeless. Overgeneralizations, oversimplifications, and exaggerations are also brought to the attention of the client, who is taught to disavow these expressions. In place of absolutes, the client is taught to interpret messages cognitively by using the logical-empirical method of science, in which beliefs can be tested and verified (Ellis, 1967, 1984).

Bibliotherapy is the assigning of topical reading materials for the client; it is another technique often recommended by the rational emotive therapist. Other techniques to increase cognition include role-playing, thought-stopping, assertion training, desensitization, and other methods to rehearse functional behaviors. Ellis agrees any technique that helps people think about why they are acting in the manner that they do has merit. He has even referred to RET as an eclectic model with eclectic techniques (Ellis, 1973).

Sessions are structured. Assessment and readiness to change are continually challenged. RET is designed as an efficient short-term therapy in which the therapist and client meet weekly for five to fifty sessions (Ellis, 1984).

The goal of RET is to teach the client to take responsibility for emotions and behavior by analyzing self-talk, substituting logic and reason for illogical and irrational beliefs, and stopping negative self-statements. This approach is expected to refute self-defeating behaviors and promote a sense of satisfaction with the self and with life. Clients are told repeatedly that they alone have the internal power to create their own happiness or unhappiness. They are taught to accept the world as it is, and not as they believe it should be, for they have no power to control others or their environment.

Clients who have well-developed language and cognitive abilities respond best to RET, as it depends on words to challenge irrational beliefs. RET is not recommended for children under ten years old or for those who have low mental or limited problem-solving abilities. RET may also be contraindicated for individuals who are out of contact with reality, or who are highly manic, schizophrenic, autistic, or brain injured (Ellis, 1984; Patterson, 1980).

RET has been criticized as underestimating the importance of affective or emotional reactions. Overuse and overconfidence with the use of the scientific method may result in misguided therapeutic plans, as total human behavior cannot always be reduced to a single event. Also, the highly directive therapist may impose the therapists's belief system upon the client and intimidate the client by using too much authority, which may result in the client withdrawing from therapy or may minimize client responsibility (Corey, 1986; Patterson, 1980).

S U M M A R Y

Rational emotive therapy is considered one of the major cognitive models, in which clients are provided with direct guidance and taught how to live a more satisfactory life through the application of logical, rational thinking. It is hypothesized that unpleasant emotional and behavioral consequences cause people to seek counseling.

Rational emotive therapy is a re-educative model in which accountability and evaluation are emphasized. The approach for promoting change is structured and systematic. Behavioral assignments serve as reinforcers to integrate newly learned emotions and actions.

The prime determinant of anxiety is believed to stem from internalized negative sentences, referred to as "self-talk." Emotional disturbance results from indoctrinating oneself with "musturbations" or "awfulizations."

The goal of RET is to challenge the client's belief system, point out irrational beliefs, and show how to correct mistakes in reasoning, thereby eliminating undesirable emotions. Irrational, illogical thoughts are believed to distort reality and serve a self-defeating purpose. Unfounded nonscientific beliefs are attacked as lacking merit. Clients are taught to think rationally and logically through cognitive restructuring exercises. Improvement, rather than a "cure," is expected (Ellis, 1967).

There is some similarity between RET and both Alfred Adlers's individual psychology and William Glasser's reality therapy. Ellis, Adler, and Glasser share the view that the power to live life either as a satisfied or dissatisfied person lies within the individual.

The greatest difference among Adler, Glasser, and Ellis is the emphasis of each theorist. Adler's emphasis is on social interest, Glasser's emphasis is on responsibility, and Ellis's emphasis is on cognitions and the consequences of irrational self-talk.

Other cognitive theorists include Aaron Beck, a leading authority on depression, who developed the Beck Depression Inventory, and Donald Meichenbaum, who emphasized cognitive restructuring and rehearsal of a new internal dialogue. Eric Berne, the developer of transactional analysis, has also been classified as a cognitive theorist.

TRANSACTIONAL ANALYSIS

ERIC BERNE
(1910–1970)

KEY CONCEPTS

Adapted Child
Archaeopsyche
Contamination of Ego States
Critical Parent
Ego Psychology
Ego States
Exteropsyche
Free Child
Games
Karpman Triangle

Life Position
Life Script
Neoanalytic Approach
Neopsyche
Nurturing Parent
Racket
Strokes
The Adult
Transactions

P R E V I E W   Q U E S T I O N S

---

1. What two major writers developed TA principles?

2. What is the role of parenting styles in the development of the adult personality?

3. What are the three ego states?

4. What ego state is comparable to Freud's superego?

5. What does it mean when an ego state is contaminated?

6. What does the *I'm OK, You're OK* transactional style imply?

7. What does an egogram represent?

8. What is a third-degree game?

9. What is a racket?

10. What three abnormal games are found on the Karpman Triangle?

Introduction

Eric Berne is the founder of a cognitive approach known as *transactional analysis* (TA). Berne was trained as a psychiatrist and Freudian psychoanalyst and based the tenets for TA on neoanalytical principles. As a therapist, Berne was interested in developing a therapeutic technique of a shorter duration than the approximate five years needed for classical psychoanalysis. He was also interested in developing a technique for small group therapy. Transactional analysis fulfills both goals.

Berne popularized TA as a major system of counseling with *Games People Play* (1964) and *What Do You Say After You Say Hello?* (1972). Thomas Harris further contributed to the development of TA with his book *I'm OK—You're OK* (1967).

Berne and Harris developed therapy as a practical intervention that has a here-and-now approach. They integrated into the methodology of transactional analysis various concepts of ego psychology that stress individuals have the ability to think, express their feelings, and make decisions that result in self-fulfillment. Methods are concrete, easily practiced, and taught to clients by using commonly understood, jargon-free language. The emphasis is on interaction and transactions between persons. The approach has been found to be easily adaptable to a variety of situations and problems and has proved especially helpful for group counseling (Berne, 1964; Dusay & Dusay, 1984; Harris, 1972; James & Jongeward, 1971).

PHILOSOPHY

Transactional analysts view personality and healthy or dysfunctional behaviors to be greatly influenced by both overt and covert messages received by the infant and toddler. The child learns a way of transacting with others; and a plan, known as a *life script*, develops. This causes an individual to respond to others in the environment in a familiar and habitual way. The goal of transactions is to receive recognition, known in TA terms as *strokes*, from others. Each person is believed to be compelled to seek strokes continuously. This pattern contributes in part to personality formation, described as a product of learning and reinforcement.

There are three intrapsychic structures: the *parent*, the *adult*, and the *child*. These structures are known as ego states and serve as conductors to receive recognition. The habitual pattern of interacting with others and preferring one ego state over another also contributes to each individual's personality and how he or she views the world (Berne, 1964).

Individuals are viewed as rational cognitive beings who consciously and deliberately interpret and organize their environment to receive strokes, which can be positive, negative, conditional, or unconditional. The "payoff" that results establishes and reinforces a belief system for continuation of intrapersonal transactional patterns with significant others. This, Berne believes (1964), helps to explain the existence and availability of both functional and dysfunctional behaviors.

The therapist's job is to teach and explain how adult actions, cognitions, and feelings, known as *rackets*, contribute to repetitive behaviors with corresponding emotions. The client is taught to challenge and change early script messages and to learn to recognize healthy and functional transactions.

Ego States

Ego states are defined as "coherent systems of thought and feelings manifested by corresponding patterns of behavior" (Berne, 1972, p. 11). They explain intrapersonal functioning based on the three intrapsychic structures of the personality: the parent, the adult, and the child. All individuals contain these three states within their personality. The ability to activate any state is a conscious and deliberate choice and a function of the individual's interpretation of the situation. Only one state is able to be dominant at any given time. Each state inherently contains its own observable gestures, mannerisms, words, thoughts, emotions, and body postures.

The parent ego contains attitudes and behaviors learned from parents and other authority figures. Within the parent state are two substates. The *critical parent* is where rules are found. Values, judgment, and actions, which are based on parental injunctions, direct the person toward behaviors based on moral inferences; these contain the "shoulds," "oughts," and "musts." The *nurturing parent* is that part of the parent ego that offers support and encouragement and tends to soften or balance the fault-finding nature of the parent. This ego state is also known as the *exteropsyche* and is analogous to Freud's superego (Berne, 1972).

The adult ego, or *neopsyche*, houses the center of thinking. It is the rational, unemotional part of the individual. Reality testing and accountability are found in this element of the personality, which is concerned more with facts than with feelings. Decisions are based on the intellect and on principles of logic. The adult has been compared with Freud's ego (Berne, 1972).

The child ego, or *archaeopsyche*, is comparable to Freud's id. It contains impulses that are intuitive, spontaneous, and playful. This ego state is considered to be the most valuable part of our personality and an important clue to personality, as the foundation of our self-concept is believed to originate here (Corey, 1986). Feelings of sexuality reside in this element of the personality.

Two substates reside in the child ego state. The *natural child* is playful and uninhibited and experiences total freedom. The *adapted child* is influenced by parental injunctions and "right" versus "wrong" beliefs. It is where feelings like guilt, anger, or frustration emerge and where self-reprimand lies. The *little professor* is found in the child ego state. This describes a child who uses adult-like reasoning to receive strokes (Corey, 1986). The child ego is filled with emotions. The individual is described as "childlike," meaning natural, innocent, carefree, and dependent on others for strength and protection (James & Jongeward, 1971).

Transactional analysts believe all three ego states reside within each person. Only one ego state can predominate at any given time. The use and selection of one ego state over another for a particular transaction is circumstantially prescribed and dependent upon interpretation of how a similar situation was met in the past.

TECHNIQUES

Transactional analysts view the therapist's role as a teacher and resource person whose job is to explain transactional analysis from both a structural and transactional perspective. The counselor is active and confrontive and is willing to share his or her own beliefs about the nature of human behavior (Berne, 1972).

The process begins by examining all transactions and determining whether the level of interaction is complementary or crossed, as well as the "game" that is being played and the "racket" and "payoff" that are perpetuated out of habit and transformed into a "life script." Ego states are schematically depicted by circles, triangles, arrows, and bar graphs to aid in teaching clients to understand, identify, and apply transactional principles.

Transactions are described as a unit of response between two individuals' ego states. In complementary transactions, the vectors are parallel. One ego state "speaks" to another person's similar ego state. For example, the adult speaks to the adult of another person. This leads to smooth communication, which is open and straightforward. "Games" are avoided, permitting the communication to proceed indefinitely.

In crossed transactions, the ego state of one person communicates with another's ego state that is not parallel to the first. A common state is when the adult speaks to the parent or the child speaks to the parent. The result of a crossed transaction is that communication is broken off. There is misunderstanding, hurt, or anger. Ulterior motives and "hidden" or "implied" messages are found in crossed transactions. A "game" is played that results in one-upmanship, a loser and a winner, and where one person receives a "payoff" at the expense of the other person (Berne, 1964).

Healthy functioning is viewed as a balance among the three ego states and by selecting an ego state that is appropriate for the particular situation. Transactions between individuals should be smooth and not crossed (Berne, 1972).

Life Positions

Harris (1967) identifies four life positions or transactional patterns in which persons learn to receive "strokes." The search for strokes is believed to be an innate need each individual seeks and, while positive strokes are desired, negative strokes are preferable to none.

I'm OK, You're OK is the mentally healthy way to receive strokes. It views the self and others as having a positive identity. It is the goal of therapy as it results in a success identity.

I'm OK, You're not OK is when others are blamed for miseries. The antisocial person, the revolutionary person, or the criminal is believed to have this life script, which is thought to be the product of a lack of stroking, or of stroking that is conditional. Early in life, this person learns not to rely on or trust others and therefore has difficulty trusting himself or herself.

I'm not OK, You're OK is when the individual feels powerless. This transaction describes the pleaser or martyr. The person is basically unhappy, lacks positive self-regard, and is constantly searching for strokes. Depressed persons or those contemplating suicide may have this life script.

I'm not OK, You're not OK is when daily hopelessness is felt. There is rejection of both self and others, and schizoid behavior may result. The individual fears making decisions, as the anxiety for severe punishment is omnipresent. This life position is thought to originate when a person never receives strokes as a child.

Life positions are developmental and associated with growth stages; they arise from the unconscious. In the *I'm not OK* script, the infant feels inferior, inadequate, and subordinate to others. As we gain competency and become less dependent on others, we discover other transactional patterns that serve to meet our needs (Harris, 1967).

Games

The transactional analyst helps clients understand the life positions and life script through an analogy by asking: "What game is being played so that a certain 'payoff' can result?" Games operate at both an overt and covert level and are referred to as first-degree, second-degree, and third-degree games. They may be played to avoid or elicit intimacy (Berne, 1964).

Overt games describe communication where the payoff is known. For example, in "Would you help me do the dishes?"; the message is clear and direct, and the person receiving the communication is able to respond in a candid fashion.

By contrast, when communication is implied, rather than stated, there is an ulterior motive within the message, and the payoff is not directly known. For example, if the person desires help doing the dishes and instead of directly asking for help says, "I have a headache, but the dishes need to be done . . ."; one is left to guess the hidden message and confusion results. Covert communication tends to contain messages that imply, "Now I've got you, you SOB." The therapist's job is to help clients learn to state their needs and avoid "games" (Berne, 1964).

Berne (1964) referred to first-degree games as those in which the payoff is innocuous and no one gets seriously hurt. Second-degree games are more hurtful. Third-degree games are characterized as deadly serious, played for keeps, and ones that represent dysfunctional roles in life. Karpman (1968) depicts abnormal or dysfunctional life roles and the victim, the persecutor, or the rescuer, illustrated as a drama triangle.

People play games to receive strokes, to fulfill a life script, and to maintain their racket. Life scripts lead to strong beliefs regarding relationships with others and the importance of environmental circumstances. An *egogram* describes a technique that provides clues to a life script.

Egogram

The egogram is a symbolic representation of how much time and energy is spent in any single ego state. An emotionally healthy person has a bell-shaped egogram in which the adult ego state is found in the center, surrounded on each side by the child and the parent. The three ego states are depicted as separate and distinct entities, uncontaminated by any other ego state. This implies that the person is healthy and well balanced, as he or she makes use of all three ego states proportionately and appropriately.

If the egogram is skewed, one ego state is exaggerated at the expense of the others, implying abnormality or an unhealthy lifestyle (Corey, 1986).

S U M M A R Y

Transactional analysis is considered a short-term, pragmatic method for helping people attain a satisfactory lifestyle. Transactional analysts are committed to demystifying the therapeutic process by teaching clients consciously to observe and analyze their interactive behavior in various circumstances and with various persons (Corey, 1986).

Transactional analysts believe that each of us has the ability to be self-acutalized and to change a life script learned in childhood. Normal personality is represented by an *I'm OK* life position, in which each of the three ego states is used appropriately and proportionately, and where games to receive recognition or strokes are avoided. More than one hundred studies have supported the use of TA as a clinical method for therapeutic change (Corey, 1986).

EXISTENTIAL THERAPY

VIKTOR FRANKL, ROLLO MAY, & IRVIN YALOM
1905–   1909–1989   1931–

K E Y   C O N C E P T S

Anxiety

Courage to Be

Eigenwelt

Existential Aloneness

I-Thou

Logotherapy

Meaninglessness

Mitwelt

Ontology

Phenomenology

Responsibility and Self-Awareness

Search for Meaning

Self-Actualization

Self-Transcendence

Umwelt

PREVIEW QUESTIONS

---

1. What person is credited for existential psychotherapy in Europe?

2. Who are two persons credited for existential psychotherapy in the United States?

3. Is existentialism a self-determined or deterministic form of therapy?

4. What is "existential aloneness"?

5. What does "logotherapy" mean?

6. What does *umwelt* mean?

7. How does an individual become self-actualized?

8. What is the role of formal assessment to the existential therapist?

9. What is an I-Thou relationship?

10. What type of client or situation may be contraindicated for existential therapy?

Introduction

Existentialism is more an attitude or philosophy toward life and the human experience than a clearly defined system of psychotherapy. Its roots can be traced to philosophers such as Dostoevski, Kierkegaard, Nietzsche, Heidegger, Sartre, Buber, and others who believed the potential for self-actualization was realized through individual freedom and self-responsibility.

Existential psychotherapy emerged during the 1940s and 1950s from a small group of psychoanalysts who were unhappy with Freudian concepts of determinism and the mechanistic approach of the behavioral psychologies. They shared a concern for *ontology*, the science of being and existing, and *phenomenology*, the use of the current experience as the source for data, and they incorporated these beliefs in their work with clients (Corey, 1986; May & Yalom, 1984; Patterson, 1980).

Existential therapy was not founded by any single psychotherapist. Viktor Frankl developed *logotherapy* using existential principles and philosophy in Europe. In the United States, Rollo May and Irvin Yalom are major writers who represent the existential attitude toward health and pathology.

Existential therapy is described as providing clients with the power of actively choosing sometimes painful, but fulfilling alternatives. The final decision for a lifestyle is up to the individual, who must accept the consequences for his or her actions. Failure to live up to individual potential can result in guilt, meaninglessness, isolation, and the feeling that we are victims of others and our environment (Patterson, 1980).

PHILOSOPHY

Existentialism is grounded on the assumption that individuals are free, rational beings. Existence is said to precede essence. This means that what people do with their lives is more important than genetic makeup or environmental circumstances. Human nature is believed to be good and destiny self-determined. Self-responsibility must prevail if individuals are to be happy and self-actualized. There is no blaming others for our unhappiness. Rather, each of us alone must give a sense to the meaning of our life, and we alone must decide how we will live.

In order to be responsible, we must have self-awareness. This promotes freedom and a commitment to discover and value one's identity. Without self-awareness, meaningful relationships with others cannot be established. It takes courage to recognize that a successful or unsuccessful life is a product of self-direction.

The knowledge that actions are individually chosen creates internal anxiety, which existentialists consider an essential ingredient for being and a condition of life that is universally experienced. Normal anxiety is believed to be necessary for growth and change.

Awareness of our own mortality and of death reinforces anxiety, as this reminds us that the time to become self-actualized is not infinite. It results in *existential guilt*, which is the wasting of time and the failure to accept responsibility for thoughts, actions, and behavior. Guilt permits the individual to rationalize that he or she is a victim and that life and happiness are outside the power of individual control. Guilt can also serve as a positive force, as it can promote the utilization of one's potentialities.

One of the aims of therapy is to help the client confront anxiety as fully as possible. The therapist does this by transforming anxiety to fear. Fear is a concept that can be operationalized by objective criteria. It can then be reduced to more finite and precise meanings, until the fear becomes so dissipated that it is no longer experienced (May & Yalom, 1984).

The concept of *existential aloneness* implies that each of us is ultimately alone, as no one else can fully experience another person's exact feelings. This aloneness can be either a freeing or enslaving experience. The decision as to how to interpret aloneness resides within each individual.

Existential therapists teach clients to draw from their inner strengths and accept themselves as unique individuals. Happiness is referred to as an internalized concept. The notion that others cannot make us happy is stressed repeatedly. Clients are reinforced to accept themselves and accept the responsibility for their own actions. This reliance on the self permits individuals to become more resourceful and ultimately more satisfied with life (Frankl, 1959).

Each individual must define his or her own search for the meaning of life. The counselor's job is to help the client recognize the philosophy that living and choosing are synomyous, as well as to learn to live with the realization that a life plan is under the will of the individual.

As a living system, humans are always in the process of becoming and working toward self-actualization. We live in three worlds simultaneously: *Umwelt* refers to the biological or physical world around us. It includes internal needs, drives, and instincts. *Mitwelt* refers to the world of relationships with others. *Eigenwelt* is the world of self-identity and self-awareness, where the meaning of events is personally experienced (May & Yalom, 1984).

The central theme to the existential movement is the notion that self-awareness promotes freedom, responsibility, and a commitment to discover one's identity, permitting the establishment of meaningful relationships with others. This lesson, although universally known, is sometimes denied. The role of the existential therapist is to highlight and reinforce this attitude.

VIKTOR FRANKL AND LOGOTHERAPY

Viktor Frankl was trained as a psychiatrist. He studied classical psychoanalysis under the direction of Freud but rejected the deterministic nature of Freud's teachings, as he viewed life as self-determining, purposeful, dynamic and experiential. He saw self-actualization as a process of becoming fully human through subjective and ongoing experiences.

Logotherapy is based on Frankl's personal experiences as a prisoner in a Nazi concentration camp. He believed that although he could not control conditions around him, he had the inherent power to control his internalized responses to the austere environmental conditions he experienced. He believed human suffering could be redirected into human achievement. He developed an existential approach to explore the meaning of life and named his therapy *logotherapy*, which means "healing through meaning" (Frankl, 1959, 1979).

Frankl's main tenet rests on the belief that as humans each of us has the power to direct our own life. No matter how repressive the environment, we alone are responsible for promoting either our own happiness or unhappiness.

Each of us must have a reason for life and must believe that we are free to make choices. The belief that we are free compels us to be responsible and fosters creativeness in achieving tasks. Life is viewed as an interconnection between the freedom of will, will to meaning, and meaning to life (Frankl, 1959).

Freedom is both an external and internal phenomenon. Although external freedom may not always be possible, internal or spiritual freedom can never be taken away. Frankl believed that people who think they have control over their destiny choose life; and that people who think they are robbed of personal control choose death. Logotherapists believe death gives life meaning. Those who fear death, fear life; and consequently the will to live loses its meaning (Frankl, 1959).

Frankl considers the drive for pleasure (Freud) or the drive for power (Adler) as oversimplifications of the meaning of life. He considers the will to have meaning in life the motivating force for living, loving, and working toward self-actualization. The aim of therapy is therefore to expand self-awareness and increase self-responsibility.

ROLLO MAY

Rollo May introduced existential psychotherapy to the United States during the 1950s. May studied with Alfred Adler, a neoanalyst, and with Paul Tillich, an existential philosopher. May was trained as a clinical psychologist and was interested in exploring the meaning of anxiety. He concluded that anxiety is an essential component to life, as it enhances intelligence, creativity, and positive change. One of the aims of May's psychotherapy was to reduce anxiety to fear, as fear can be clinically and objectively dealt with (Corey, 1986; May & Yalom, 1984; Wallace, 1987).

May is not a pure phenomenologist or existentialist in the sense that perceptions alone are believed to be the sole determinant of behavior. May believed we exist in a world of reciprocal totality, dependent on both ourselves and others for our existence, and that through self-interpretations, we are co-creatures of our own phenomenology. Our intellect and consciousness permit human freedom to be creative. Human creativity enables the individual to become self-actualized and minimizes inherited tendencies or predispositions (Wallace, 1986).

TECHNIQUES

The existential therapist avoids systematic techniques, a formal diagnosis, or formal assessment. The therapist must enter the world of the client's subjective experiences without preconceived notions. The event itself is not what counts, but rather the perception and interpretation of the event. History-taking or a review of past psychological reports may distort the counselor's understanding of the client's problem and be disruptive to the existential process of healing.

The counselor's attitude is reflective of an open, human, responsive person who views therapy as a spontaneous and experiential encounter or shared journey with no predetermined route. Empathy is viewed as the key to the therapeutic process. The focus is on the here and now. The atmosphere is nonthreatening and judgment free. The client may be confronted but in a supportive way (Frankl, 1959, 1979).

The counselor must put all his or her own needs aside and concentrate on being with the client. The communication of unconditional positive regard and genuineness is an essential ingredient to the existential therapeutic experience. Self-transcendence, the rising above one's needs to reach out to the other, is required by the counselor (Corey, 1986; Patterson, 1980).

The client-counselor relationship is defined in I-Thou terms that imply equality between persons or a horizontal relationship (Buber, 1957). The counselor is not seen as an expert or technician who has the answers for a successful life. The counselor is there to support, nourish, and help the client enhance self-awareness. Existentialists believe that to do this, the therapist must enter the client's world and suspend any predetermined agenda; feedback is immediate and ongoing.

To help the client get in touch with the self, any technique the therapist believes will help the client is tried. For example, the therapist may bring a mirror into the counseling session and ask the client to speak to his or her mirrored reflection.

To develop awareness of the reality of both life and death, the therapist may ask the client how and where he or she would like to be in the future. Therapists may direct the client to write his or her epitaph. Both Frankl and May used paradoxical directives, the exaggeration of a symptom, to help obsessive, compulsive, and phobic clients change (Corey, 1986; May & Yalom, 1984).

THE EXISTENTIAL CLIENT

There are some criticisms and limitations to existential therapy. It may not be appropriate for clients who are in a crisis situation, as the process is subjective and esoteric. The process may also be difficult for a low-functioning person to understand and implement. Also, existential concepts are difficult to operationalize, and the unavailability of a rigid methodology makes it difficult for researchers to judge its therapeutic effectiveness.

S U M M A R Y

Existential therapy is a philosophy in which the counselor operates on the principle that to be human is to be free, and to be free is to be responsible. Techniques vary and are flexible.

Existentialist therapists help clients become aware of choices, thereby becoming fully human. They encourage individuals to become involved in a process of self-exploration; there is a spiritual dimension to existential counseling, something not stressed in other counseling therapies.

The ultimate goal of therapy is to help the client reduce the anxiety of nonbeing and to reclaim lost power. Throughout therapy, it is stressed that others cannot be expected to fully understand an internal event that one individual is experiencing. Each of us is alone in this world. Aloneness promotes creativity, which facilitates self-responsibility.

It is difficult to teach or learn existentialism as a therapy. It is more an attitude toward life, than a model to be followed. It is considered a client-centered type of therapy in which the emphasis is upon helping the client recognize potential and growth, rather than on specific problem-solving.

PERSON-CENTERED THERAPY

CARL ROGERS
1902–1987

KEY CONCEPTS

Affective Model
Authenticity
Closed-Ended Questions
Congruence
Counselor Attractiveness
Empathy
Genuineness

Humanism
Immediacy
Incongruence
I-Thou
Positive Regard
Self-Actualization
Unconditional Positive Regard

PREVIEW QUESTIONS

---

1. How does Rogers define maladjustment?

2. What is the difference between congruence and incongruence?

3. What is the role of the counselor in person-centered therapy?

4. What is empathic listening?

5. What is the result of acting as others wish us to act?

6. In an effort to be genuine, should counselors "blurt out" whatever they are experiencing?

7. What do humanists believe regarding self-actualization?

8. What is "emotional knowing"?

9. What does Rogers say about the nature of the human condition?

10. Would Rogerian therapy be a difficult modality for the person who has schizophrenic tendencies?

Introduction

Carl Rogers founded an affective type of counseling approach known as person-centered therapy. The basic assumption of affective models is the belief that emotions are attempts to communicate and express both positive and negative experiences. If attempts to communicate are blocked, the individual will experience an elevated state of frustration. This leads to acting, feeling, and behaving in an incongruent or inconsistent way. Over time, incongruency results in maladjustment. Health is restored by the release of negative and unproductive self-communication (Meador & Rogers, 1984; Rogers, 1962).

Person-centered therapy is a holistic humanistic theory with a here-and-now focus. Rogers viewed persons as indivisible with regard to thoughts, emotions, and actions. He rejected both environmental determinism and Freudian determinism. He believed human nature is good and forward moving. There is a strong identification with existentialism in that the perceptual experience is given much importance and the process of self-actualization is viewed as a continuous phenomenon. Rogers also identified with humanistic or "third force" psychology, in which there is optimism regarding the potential of the human condition and therapy is directed at the release of inner potential (Corey, 1986; Maslow, 1968; Meador & Rogers, 1984; Patterson, 1980).

Rogers originally called his therapy nondirective or client-centered therapy. In 1974 Rogers and his cohorts renamed his theory person-centered therapy to reflect more adequately the emphasis that counseling is a process that believes in the power of the self (Meador & Rogers, 1984).

The counseling process centers around the notion that unconditional positive regard from the counselor frees the person to get in touch with his or her own feelings. This permits self-acceptance and self-responsibility and leads to persons having a sense that they are in control of their life and moving forward toward self-actualization. The counselor acts as a facilitator who is genuine and authentic. There are no specific techniques or rigid rules, but the client is encouraged to trust the counselor. Rogers believes this can only be achieved if the counselor is willing to be an empathic and active listener. It is believed positive regard from others permits constructive personality growth and change, emotional security, and optimal use of abilities (Rogers, 1957).

PHILOSOPHY

Rogers developed his theory with the belief that humans possess the capacity to be rational, social, realistic, and self-directed. He believed we behave in terms of how we internally perceive things, not how things appear to others. This is known as the *phenomenal field*. When the counselor enters, accepts, and tries to understand the client's inner world, there is a better sense of the reality that disposes individuals to choose one decision over another. Therefore, part of the counseling process involves encouraging clients to open up themselves to others and test the reality of inner world perceptions (Rogers, 1961b).

Rogers views humankind as basically good, rational, socialized, and constructive. He rejects the Freudian concept that individuals are basically self-destructive with little or no control of their own destiny. Individuals have enormous potential and strive to find the special meaning that reflects the uniqueness of each person's life (Rogers, 1961a, 1977).

The therapeutic process is described as epigenetic; there is progressive discovery of deeper and deeper levels of self-awareness. To explore the self, the client is offered a supportive environment. This allows the client to eventually gain a more accurate perception of the self. The counselor is there to act only as a catalyst or facilitator. No interpretations or directions are provided, as it is believed that within each of us resides the power to choose actions that promote self-worth and self-actualization (Meador & Rogers, 1984; Patterson, 1980; Rogers, 1957).

Self-actualization is a universal need. It is interpreted as an evolving process whereby the individual feels a sense of achievement or self-fulfillment. It comes about by being honest with our emotions, and by not suppressing or constraining them. When others have positive regard for us, self-actualization and feelings of self-worth are expedited. Persons who feel good about themselves are free to demonstrate positive regard to others. Put another way, as a person satisfies another's need for positive regard, the person fulfills this same need in himself or herself.

In 1970 Rogers published a book on the *encounter group model*. He saw group members as having the potential to help others develop positive self-regard and hypothesized that acceptance by others may be the missing link in maladjusted persons. This supports and reinforces his belief that respect from others is critical in the development of a healthy personality.

If feelings of maladjustment are to be changed, it is essential that the client be provided with a warm and caring relationship. This will permit the client to change, grow, and understand the basis for dissatisfactions in life. The counselor must present himself or herself as genuine to encourage the client to freely explore his or her own feelings and develop deeper self-understanding.

TECHNIQUES

Like existential therapy, person-centered therapy constitutes more an attitude than techniques to be taught. Three factors influence therapeutic change: the client, the counselor, and the relationship. In addition, there are three conditions that facilitate the client's commitment to the counseling process: unconditional positive regard, congruence or genuineness, and empathy (Meador & Rogers, 1984; Rogers, 1957).

The client and counselor must engage in psychological contact—the client in a state of incongruence, vulnerable and anxious, and the counselor congruent and genuinely invested in the relationship. The counselor must communicate empathy and unconditional positive regard to the client, and the client must perceive, internalize, and accept this. The relationship must demonstrate authenticity of feelings and the avoidance of intellectualism. There is a focus on immediacy, saying what you feel at the present moment, and on concreteness, which is the concentration on the specific content and context of what is being said (Rogers, 1967; Truax & Carkhuff, 1967).

Rogers believed strongly that the client-counselor relationship is the most important condition for therapy. The counselor must care for the client in a nonpossessive, unconditional way in which reservations or evaluations are suspended. This nonjudgmental, nonevaluative atmosphere with its here-and-now focus is believed to have the potential to release the self and foster growth.

The client must be given unconditional acceptance as a unique individual. Rogers termed this *unconditional positive regard* (UPR); that is, the counselor communicates to the client a deep and genuine caring and the recognition of human value. Unconditional positive regard involves a willingness to share equally in the client's happy or sad feelings, successes or failures. Acceptance and unconditional positive regard helps engage the client in the process of therapy and leads to constructive personality change (Rogers, 1961a).

Counselor genuineness, known also as *congruence*, is also a critical factor for a positive therapeutic experience. Congruence is the matching of physiological experiencing with awareness and communication. It is like dropping a facade and being in touch with who you are and how you act. Congruence is thought to reduce barriers between the client and counselor (Patterson, 1980).

The counselor models a congruent way of being, and the client learns to appreciate and model this same behavior. Trustworthiness and attractiveness, in terms of like and respect, follow. The result of congruence is that it becomes an instrument that promotes the client to become more self-reliant. This promotes feelings of self-acceptance and reduces barriers between the two persons involved in the counseling process. The lack of congruence results in defensive and ambiguous behavior, with maladaptive behaviors continuing to be experienced.

The counselor must be aware of the feelings he or she is experiencing and be able to communicate them to the client whenever appropriate. This does not mean the counselor should impulsively say anything that comes to mind. It does mean the counselor has a responsibility to share an honesty that has the potential to promote growth, development, maturity, improved functioning, and improved coping (Rogers, 1961b).

Empathic understanding is another condition for therapeutic change. It is described as the counselor sensing what the client is experiencing at the moment. It is a form of "emotional knowing" of the client's feelings and problems. It is similar to a sense of being in the client's shoes and experiencing the client's inner world. Although a person can never fully understand what another person is experiencing, the inclination to go through what the client is feeling can in itself be of value. Empathy encourages the client to continue to emote and permits the client to become more fully involved in his or her own circumstances (Corey, 1986).

The counselor communicates empathic understanding by reflecting or paraphrasing the client's expressed feelings. If there are inconsistencies in what is being said, and what is implied through nonverbal behaviors, the counselor may point out unaware, hidden feelings or attitudes suggested by the client. The counselor may demonstrate to the client a sharing of personal experiences with the client to indicate that he or she is not alone with regard to certain feelings. Active listening skills have been developed by a number of other researchers (e.g., Egan, 1982; Ivey & Authier, 1978; and Truax & Carkhuff, 1967).

Rogers did not see therapy as a diagnostic or cure process. He avoided the doctor-patient terminology and preferred the use of "counselor" over "therapist" to reduce the possibility that the counselor may hide behind a professional role, reducing genuineness. Rather, he believed that counseling is a vehicle through which strengths and abilities can become recognized. He employed an I-Thou attitude with his clients and established a comfortable atmosphere so that parts of the self previously denied might emerge (Meador & Rogers, 1984).

The philosophy of counseling is to create the self as a resource that paves the way for self-actualization. Otherwise, individuals will begin to impose evaluations from others on themselves and behave as others expect. By hiding individual identity to please others, behavior is thought to become unpredictable and irrational, resulting in incongruence and abnormal development.

The process of counseling is to help the client gain insight into personal experiences and to challenge a dysfunctional style of living, permitting individual potential to be expressed. This responsibility implies the counselor must have organizational and focusing skills to keep the client's talk from wandering aimlessly from topic to topic (Rogers, 1957).

Closed-ended questions that result in yes or no responses are avoided. Instead, open-ended questions that encourage clients to elaborate are chosen. There is summarization at the end of each counseling session to remind the client of the positive exchange of the session.

Numerous researchers have investigated the causal difference in behaviors when working with clients using the Rogerian modality. The results of these studies have supported person-centered therapy as an effective change agent (Meador & Rogers, 1984; Rogers, 1961b).

SUMMARY

Roger's person-centered therapy is based on the notion that we are rational, self-directed beings who determine our own fate. He believed in the principles of genuineness, congruence, and empathy as therapeutic techniques that lead to self-actualization. He viewed problems as inconsistencies or incongruencies between internal and external messages.

The capacity to discard unsuccessful ways is further enhanced when the counselor demonstrates unconditional positive regard to the client. The client learns to be free to express thoughts and feelings and to become aware of inconsistencies. This results in an attitude of inner freedom and fosters self-responsibility, permitting self-value and self-actualization to be experienced.

GESTALT THERAPY

FREDERICK (FRITZ) PERLS
1893–1970

KEY CONCEPTS

Confluence

Dialogue

Figure-Ground Experiences

Here and Now, What and How

I-Thou

Layers of Neurosis

Projection

Retroflection

Self-Awareness

Systems Theory

Unfinished Business

Wholeness

PREVIEW QUESTIONS

---

1. What is meant by an event having a figure-ground experience?

2. How important is confrontation to the Gestalt therapist?

3. What is generally meant when someone says they are guided by existential principles?

4. What does Perls say about early childhood experiences having an influence on adult behavior?

5. What unique techniques do Gestalt therapists use to help clients work through some impasse?

6. What does Perls say about the nature of human potential?

7. What is the major reason why defense mechanisms are used?

8. What is the meaning of gestalt?

9. How do incomplete gestalts become complete?

10. How does systems theory define pathology?

Introduction

Frederick (Fritz) Perls is the principal founder of *Gestalt therapy*. Perls trained as a Freudian analyst but rejected Freud's deterministic beliefs regarding the human condition and the dualistic nature of thoughts, feelings, and actions. Perls also rejected Freud's notion that unconscious motives provide the impetus to satisfy unmet needs or that talk therapy is the exclusive mechanism for resolving concerns. Rather, Perls viewed psychological health to be a product of self-responsibility for moment-to-moment actions, promoted and facilitated by self-awareness, and by actively experiencing the environment.

Gestalt therapy is an affective and experiential type of therapy that concentrates on existential principles, which have a here-and-now focus. This form of therapy stresses actions as a means of promoting awareness. Cognitions are downplayed as they interfere with spontaneity and authenticity.

Gestalt refers to a form of holism in which the individual's total experiences are greater than the sum of their parts. Holistic principles are guided by *systems theory*, which states that an individual's actions are influenced by the actions of others and with the critical events in the environment. Perls used systems theory to organize the principles for Gestalt therapy.

The concept of *unfinished business* plays a central part in Gestalt therapy. Many of the principles and techniques are directed at assisting clients to become aware of unfinished business, so that they may be restored to wholeness.

The Gestalt therapist employs numerous techniques to facilitate client awareness and promote self-congruency. Any technique believed to heighten client self-awareness may be tried. The ultimate goal of therapy is for the client to achieve authenticity through self-regulation. An I-Thou relationship is maintained throughout therapy to elicit positive regard and permit the client to experience fully any unresolved issues.

PHILOSOPHY

The philosophy on which Fritz Perls founded Gestalt therapy came from his interest in integrating existentialism, phenomenology, and psychoanalytic techniques with psychodrama techniques developed by J. L. Moreno. Systems theory is a field theory perspective, according to which an ecological interdependence exists between the person and his environment. This theory also helped Perls develop hypotheses regarding the nature of human behavior, healthy functioning, and maladjustment (Perls, 1973; Patterson, 1980).

Perls viewed humans as living organisms who move toward the construction of meaningful wholes, or gestalts, to promote balance with their immediate environment. Thoughts, feelings, and actions are all one and part of the lawfulness of nature. Actions are self-determined and selected by an individual as a way to control his or her own fate.

Anxiety or neurosis is viewed as the organism struggling against unification, unaware there is a lack of synchrony among parts. Perls referred to this as an unnatural splitting of gestalts. The holistic nature of the human experience is violated, and stress becomes more pronounced as the person is out of balance (Perls, 1969a).

Perls did not view anxiety as a totally negative experience. In systems theory anxiety is a natural event caused from a constantly changing state of affairs. It is necessary for growth and engagement in the process of self-actualization. Persons who are healthy have successfully learned how to properly adjust to change and the accompanying internal chaos and disequilibrium. They grow from experiences by adapting and assimilating new information into their way of being, forming a new equilibrium. The process is dynamic and ongoing and is only as successful as a person desires it to be.

Individuals who are frustrated and unable to successfully handle anxiety lack awareness to cope with change. They feel helpless and victimized by circumstances. They have reached an impasse, in which they block new information and do not permit resolution of new events. There is much unfinished business, causing anxiety to become exaggerated. Life is viewed as having an infinite number of unfinished business or incomplete gestalts (Perls, 1969a).

Maladjusted people permit opinions of others to govern their life. They are in a state of confluence where no boundary exists between themselves and others. Their identity is fuzzy and enmeshed with others. They live through introjections and injunctions imposed by others, such as, the "oughts," "musts," or "have to's."

To perpetuate and maintain a dysfunctional lifestyle, individuals may employ ego defense mechanisms. One example Perls referred to is withdrawal from healthy life through the process of projection. Projection, the reverse of an introjection, is when parts of the personality that are inconsistent with our self-image are denied and placed on others. Dysfunctional persons may also engage in a process known as *retroflection*, as a means of keeping impulses under control. Retroflection is the turning back to oneself what one would like to do to others; it can be positive or negative. (Corey, 1986).

The healthy person views life as a changing, dynamic, self-imposed experience; he or she recognizes experiences as unique and separate from others. Psychological growth is a conscious process that occurs through awareness of needs, motivation to resolve frustrations, and the willingness to take self-responsibility. This is a risky attitude as success or failure depends on each individual. The person must have a clear sense of needs, be in touch with reality, and feel good about himself or herself. There is a sense of reliance on the ego for making decisions and for keeping the demands from the id and the super-ego in proper perspective (Perls, 1970).

Perls described anxiety as a gap between the now and the later (1969a). When too much energy is spent in planning for the future, we are distracted from living fully for the current moment. As nothing exists except the "now," worrying about past or future events is nonsensical. The past is only helpful to see how it has significant bearing in current actions. One aim of Gestalt therapy is to help clients to get in touch with immediate needs, permit growth, and finish business.

The concept of unfinished business is a central theme in Gestalt therapy. Unfinished business refers to unexpressed and repressed emotions, such as pain, guilt, anger, and grief. When change is imminent, equilibrium is disrupted, causing resentment. Resentment is the number one reason why people do not let go of unresolved concerns. A person is more likely to have a need for closure on issues that are closer in proximity and similar to perceived values than on issues that are not as personally related.

By not fully experiencing and having closure of emotions, the individual demonstrates inconsistent, self-defeating behaviors. To be rid of this negativism, the individual must return to old unfinished business and work toward some acceptable resolution. If life is a series of incomplete gestalts, feelings become fragmented and life has little meaning. A lack of closure ultimately causes maladjustment and dissatisfaction with life (Perls, 1969a).

Perls believed all thoughts are governed by an awareness process referred to as *figure-ground* relationships. During the perception process, a figure emerges in the foreground. This is material a person is paying attention to, which commands the greatest attention. This information or perception stands out in relief against a background that takes on a lesser important property.

Any event has the potential to have a figure-ground configuration. It depends on the need at that moment and the level of awareness directed toward the experience. Perception is constantly reorganizing, and figure and ground objects may shift in emphasis, forming a new gestalt. Two people may interpret the same situation differently and may place different parts as figure or ground characters. If there is no closure to the experience, new gestalts cannot be formed, and business will be left unfinished. The person remains at an impasse.

Perls identified five layers of neurosis and modes of defense that individuals must strip off to reach psychological maturity. Perls likened this process to the peeling of an onion (Perls, 1970).

The first layer a person must remove is the *phony layer*. On this level, games of inauthenticity are played to maintain stereotypes. People live according to rules imposed by others and become frustrated and resentful if others continue to deny their own uniqueness.

The second layer to shed is the *phobic layer*. The person is fearful others will recognize and reject his or her uniqueness. To avoid rejection, he or she maintains an image of what others think he or she ought to be. This leads to incongruent and inconsistent behaviors causing the individual to act suspicious and without self-regard.

An *impasse layer* follows. The person is stuck and fearful of maturing without environmental support. He or she continues to permit others to direct him or her to avoid what is perceived as catastrophic consequences. Risks are avoided. Without risk, there is the tendency to imagine ourselves as victims of circumstance. An impasse persists with this attitude. Therapy and self-awareness are necessary to confront and experience honest feelings and help us work through impasses in life.

The *implosive level* is when the individual becomes willing to expose his or her true self and permit others to see his or her uniqueness. It is a vulnerable time but if the individual endures, he or she will move forward and learn to appreciate himself or herself as genuine and special.

The *explosive layer* is the letting-go of phony roles and expectations of others. The person releases energy that has been built up from the previous four layers. He or she experiences a sense of relief that he or she had the strength and willingness to become authentic.

Perls believed each individual is responsible for determining his or her own fate. Every human being is thought to have unlimited potential. Therapy is believed to be a mechanism whereby clients can release their own potential. The client-counselor relationship is established in I-Thou terms, with the counselor sharing feelings and perceptions, using modeling techniques to help clients make contact with moment-to-moment experiences (Perls, 1969b).

TECHNIQUES

Gestalt therapy uses a collection of techniques designed to assist clients in working through impasses. The therapist asks clients to focus on "what" and "how" questions. "Why" questions are avoided, as they take away from the immediacy of experiences or may allow clients to hide behind rationalizations or blame others for their misery. The ultimate goal of therapy is to emphasize to the client that he or she must take responsibility and become aware of here-and-now experiences.

Any technique that the therapist believes will promote client self-awareness is tried. For example, client questions are changed to "I" statements; "can't" statements are changed to "won't" statements. Other examples include: "I've got a secret," and then having the client imagine how others would feel if they were to learn this secret; "exaggerating or prescribing the symptom," where the client is asked to act out a magnified version of the problem; and "staying with the feeling" by fully confronting and immersing the self in this experience (Levitsky & Perls, 1970).

Perhaps the best known of all Gestalt techniques involves a two-chair dialogue of unexpressed, often conflicting, parts of the self. These techniques are a form of role reversal and include *topdog/underdog, empty chair*, and *hot seat* methods.

The topdog (or overdog)/underdog technique permits the part of the person that represents an overbearing conscience—the topdog (Freud's super-ego)—to get in touch with that part of the person that defies the conscious, but who may also be submissive or a whiner—the underdog (Freud's id). In the empty chair technique, two chairs are facing each other, and the client talks from one chair to an imagined person in the other chair, who may have an opposite or different view of the situation. The hot seat is often used in group counseling, where one client has the exclusive attention of the therapist for a given period of time, and group members give feedback on how they were affected and how they could draw an analogy to their particular problem (Levitsky & Perls, 1970).

Gestaltists teach clients that change and growth occur by becoming more aware of all five senses and not relying on any one sense exclusively. Most other therapists rely exclusively on verbal communication for therapeutic gains. Perls viewed real communication as being beyond words alone. He felt that an overconcern with cognitions is representative of a kind of neurosis that permits fragmentation, rather than integration, of the person (Perls, 1969a).

Gestalt is an action and experiential therapy. Perls believed that sitting still in the therapeutic session perpetuates a neurotic split between the body and the mind. The client is urged to play out all feelings during therapy, including figures from the past, dreams, or ways the client is feeling toward the counselor (Koval, 1976).

To complete unfinished gestalts, the therapist makes no interpretations as these are seen as antitherapeutic. Rather, attention is paid to obvious experienced material (Perls, 1969a, 1973).

Confrontation is a key element in the Gestalt approach. The client is a person in need and who is experiencing something incongruent or inconsistent in their total being. Therapy must direct attention to the inconsistencies to correct and stop dysfunctional behaviors.

THE GESTALT CLIENT

Gestalt therapy is often conducted in groups or in a workshop setting. It does not focus on the group process, per se, but rather on immediate happenings and observable behaviors that get in touch with split parts of the self. It is considered short-term therapy and is an intense experience. Concentrated effort to change is expected to be seen in a three-month period (Koval, 1976).

Clients who bottle their feelings and need permission to release their emotions may find Gestalt therapy especially helpful. Gestalt therapy is not as well suited for those seeking supportive counseling (Levitsky & Perls, 1970).

The goal of Gestalt therapy is to help clients become aware of what they are doing, here and now, what and how. There is a focus on the process of what is happening, rather than the content. When there is awareness of completing a gestalt, the client has a sense of experiencing "aha."

SUMMARY

Gestalt therapy shares some beliefs with existential humanism. The counselor's job is to be a catalyst who promotes awareness of the body and mind. The client is urged to play out all feelings to facilitate the completion of unfinished gestalts. The verbal content of therapy is downplayed, as it permits clients to rationalize or blame others for their plight.

Perls's theoretical beliefs revolve around the notion that mind, body, and actions form a whole, or gestalt. If one part of the person is not congruent with the others, needs will not be met and gestalts will remain unfinished, resulting in anxiety and maladjustment.

The goal of Gestalt therapy is to promote self-responsibility and to unify the organism, thereby completing gestalts. The client learns to assume ownership of feelings and uniqueness as a human being. This is risky, because it may initially result in self-rejection and create anxiety. However, without anxiety, there is no growth. Therefore, therapy is viewed as a no pain, no gain phenomenon.

MISCELLANEOUS

K E Y   C O N C E P T S

Accommodation

Assimilation

Attending

Clarifying

Closed System

Concrete Operational Thought

Confronting

Conventional Morality

Cybernetics

Eclecticism

Empathizing

Evaluating

Expertness

Feedback

Focusing

Formal Operational Thought

Group Dynamics

Homeostasis

Immediacy

Interpreting

Modeling

Open System

Pacing

Paraphrasing

Preconventional Morality

Preoperational Thought

Postconventional Morality

Probing

Reflecting

Self-Disclosure

Sensorimotor Intelligence

Silence

Summarizing

Supporting and Reassuring

Systems Theory

Trustworthiness

PREVIEW QUESTIONS

---

1. How many participants constitute an ideal group?

2. What is the difference between concrete and formal operational thought?

3. What is the weakness of an eclectic model?

4. What is the locus of pathology in dysfunctional families?

5. How does confronting differ from interpreting?

6. What does it mean to be the identified patient?

7. What is a general goal to counseling?

8. What is the preferred counseling model?

9. How could empathy be related to postconventional morality?

10. What communication skill describes the ability to sense another person's situation from that person's point of view?

Introduction

In addition to the traditional counseling theories, there are additional theories and techniques that guide counselors in the understanding of human behavior. Examples include electic models, marital and family therapy, group counseling and dynamics, cognitive development, moral development and communication skills. A brief review of these may be found in this section.

ECLECTIC MODELS

Eclectic counselors hold that no single theory of counseling can meet the diverse needs of all clients. These counselors choose concepts that appear to be the best from diverse sources or styles. A personalized counseling approach combines directive and nondirective theories and techniques. An early proponent of the eclectic view is Frederick C. Thorne (Thorne, 1961).

Eclectic counselors are typically well-read and skilled clinicians who have thoroughly studied counseling theories and deliberately selected a preferred counseling style representative of their own belief system. They must have the skills to devise an appropriate therapeutic plan from beginning to end, using the techniques that work best for them. As with all theories, the effectiveness of the plan must be continuously evaluated, and the counselor must be amenable to modifying or changing the approach as circumstances warrant.

An eclectic model does not imply that techniques are used at random or that techniques work for some unknown reason. Rather, eclecticism has a systematic and intentional integration of parts of major counseling theories that have been scientifically validated by researchers as therapeutic mechanisms. One example of an eclectic approach is Arnold Lazarus's multimodal model, known as the *BASIC ID* (Brammer, 1969; Corey, 1986).

The strength of the eclectic approach is that it has greater potential to deal with a wider and more diverse range of problems than can be achieved with any single method. A major weakness or criticism is that the counselor may err in selecting the most appropriate method to help the client and that consistent results are also hard to document scientifically (Shertzer & Stone, 1974).

A 1982 study by Smith asked psychologists what theory best described their counseling practice. He found the eclectic approach the most popular (41.2 percent), followed by the psychoanalytical approach (10.8 percent). This finding implies a contemporary trend toward eclecticism in which therapists individualize their approach when helping clients resolve issues and concerns.

MARITAL AND FAMILY THERAPY

Marital and family therapy is a specialized branch of counseling that is attracting a growing number of counseling professionals. Because it has its own certification process, which is sponsored by the American Association of Marriage and Family Therapy (AAMFT), only a brief discussion of this therapy is presented here. For a thorough discussion of theoretical positions, the reader is directed to books by Brown and Christensen (1986), Goldenberg and Goldenberg (1985), and Nichols (1984).

The major difference between marital and family therapists and individual therapists is in the choice of a theoretical foundation to guide the practice of counseling. *General Systems Theory* by von Bertalanffy (1968) guides the marital and family practitioner. Family rules, roles, boundaries, subsystems, triangles, and communication styles are analyzed to discover dysfunctional patterns. Individual therapists pay little attention to concepts implied by systems theory.

The family is seen as an open system that interfaces with and receives information from the environment. As this is an ongoing and dynamic process, new or added information mandates the system to accommodate to change. This upsets the equilibrium of the system, forcing the restructuring of a new homeostasis.

As people grow accustomed to habitual ways of living, a new homeostasis is not always wholeheartedly accepted. It is sometimes easier to resist change, in the hope that the change will disappear if it is not addressed. Resistance by individual family members and the system as a whole to reorganize and adapt to a new way of doing things causes problems. If the resistance continues, it becomes the source of disruption that destroys the coherence of the existing system.

When the system is not operating smoothly, an identified patient or victim emerges. The role of this person, often the weakest or most vulnerable family member, is to become symptomatic so that help may circumvent the destruction of the system. The therapist who works in a one-on-one relationship with a client is typically first sought out to help the symptom bearer resolve what is initially viewed as pathology within the individual. If this approach does not work, referral to a family therapist may be recommended (Goldenberg & Goldenberg, 1985).

The family system therapist views the locus of pathology as residing within the system itself. Although one person carries the symptom, the problem is thought to be owned by all family members; thus, much attention is paid to relationships, interaction patterns, and their consequences.

The process and techniques a family therapist chooses to help the family are guided by the therapist's particular style and theoretical orientation regarding the etiology and resolution of the problem. Many family therapists share a belief system conceptually similar to that of therapists who work with individual clients. An extra dimension most family therapists subscribe to is the emphasis on communication and metacommunication (unspoken) patterns between and among family members.

A major goal of family counseling is to help family members view the family as a system made up of different members who are both connected with, yet differentiated from each other. A person is viewed as differentiated if ego strength is intact, and the person feels appreciated and valued as a unique human being.

The job of the therapist is to unite the family so that stress can be more adequately handled. A goal the family therapist must also be prepared to deal with is to provide guidance, in the event the family chooses not to stay a united entity.

There are some similarities and differences between family and group therapy. No attempt will be made to list all the similarities and differences between these two types of therapeutic interventions. However, a simple analogy portrays family therapy as having as its emphasis the enhancement of communication skills for personal relationships, which will continue long after counseling is completed. In group therapy, although group members typically do not have a history or a future once therapy stops, the emphasis is also to help individuals (strangers) develop successful transactional patterns with others. In both approaches, people are viewed as the product of social context, the environment, and other people.

GROUP DYNAMICS

Counselors who work in a variety of settings and with various populations use a group approach as a counseling modality to help their clients. Because the counselor typically has limited time and large case loads, the group approach is an efficient means of providing services to more than one client during a given time period. In addition, the group technique aids in member socialization. This is helpful, as many clients report feelings of isolation and are without significant others to whom they are able to relate. The group may also aid in reality testing and may provide the impetus, motivation, or commitment for the client to implement desired changes.

To be a group leader, the professional counselor must be familiar with group dynamics:

An optimum size for a group ranges from five to eight people. Suitability to join a group should be determined by a screening process in which each potential member is interviewed personally by the counselor. Group members should be made up of individuals who appear to be compatible and who share some identity or common base.

Groups generally have a specific focus. The group may be organized as a problem-solving group or as a growth-oriented group.

The logistics and structure of the group must be established either before the group assembles for the first time or during the first meeting. The time, place, length of the sessions, and how often the group will meet must be agreed on by all. Groups typically meet for one to one and one-half hours. If the group members are young students or a special population in which the members have a shorter attention span than one hour, the time may be adjusted accordingly.

Groups generally sit in a circle arrangement, to promote interaction by all members. The placing of a coffee table in the center of the circle may reduce initial anxiety by protecting both the physical and psychological personal space of individual members.

It must be decided whether the group is to be open or closed. In an open group, new members may enter the group at either a designated time or at any time. In a closed group, all members start and finish counseling together.

The group leader's counseling style is critical to the progress of the group and to the formation of cohesion between members. The counselor must be open and must have the ability and willingness to note both verbal and non-verbal transactions to group members. Some groups are co-led, with two counselors sharing the leadership role. In this arrangement, the counselors must have some compatibility. The group may also be leaderless, run without a formal leader. When this is part of the group dynamics, group members usually take turns as the facilitator, or a single person may assume the responsibility of leadership. Any appointment must be a group decision. An alternate group is typically led by a counselor but is leaderless for a particular session. The response to this strategy can provide valuable feedback to the role played by group members when the usual leader is unavailable.

Group members may take on specific roles in a group. For example, the *gatekeeper* acts as an expediter, making sure all group members actively participate in the group process. This person may also establish norms that he or she may find comfortable. The use of this role may keep the focus directed at others, thereby avoiding working on the gatekeeper's own personal problems. The *harmonizer* or *conciliator* keeps emotions from polarizing, while the *follower* will swing in any direction the group members choose. The *scapegoat* is the person to whom group members may project hostility, while the *energizer* may promote needed enthusiasm for the group (Corey, 1985; Forsyth, 1983; Napier & Gershenfeld, 1985; Yalom, 1985).

The ethics of using a group modality cannot be as well controlled as in individual counseling, because confidentiality cannot be guaranteed to group members. However, during the first meeting, the group leader should address this topic and ask members not to discuss the contents of the counseling sessions outside the group.

In the early sessions of the group, there will be anxiety, apprehension, and uneasiness among group members. This is typical, as individual members may fear nonacceptance, exposure of personal weaknesses, or intimacy with other group members. The professional counselor will recognize anxiety as a natural phenomenon and use it as a constructive and bonding force.

As with individual counseling, group counseling proceeds in stages. The first stage typically involves forming a working relationship. The counselor may begin the group session by suggesting a catalytic activity or structured exercise to loosen up group members, facilitate a working relationship, and build trust among group members. The middle stages comprise working on problems, resolutions, and alternatives. The final stage is the termination stage; this may be an especially unsettling time for clients, because feelings of abandonment or loneliness may occur. The counselor may want to schedule six-week and three-month follow-up meetings to minimize the stress of group disengagement.

COGNITIVE DEVELOPMENT

Human behavior may also be studied from a cognitive and developmental perspective. One of the most well-known researchers in this field was Jean Piaget, who developed a cognitive model in which development was believed to occur in a series of qualitatively distinct, predictable, approximate age-related stages (Piaget, 1926, 1972). Stages are characterized by increased complexity and are a product of four factors: biological, experience, cultural values, and equilibration (the balancing force of interactions) (Newman & Newman, 1987).

Piaget hypothesized that humans adapt to the environment through schemas or schemes. This is a mental structure, a blueprint or construct, in which new experiences are interpreted in terms of existing schemes (known as *assimilation*), or where familiar schemes are modified to incorporate new information (known as *accommodation*). Piaget used the case study method to test and verify his hypotheses.

Piaget identified four major stages, and some substages, which describe a normal pattern of cognitive development. Stages cannot be skipped or omitted from sequence, as successive stages are based on earlier experiences.

Stage I: Sensorimotor Intelligence   0-2

From birth to two years, the child adapts, anticipates, and experiments with the environment through sensorimotor means. By the end of the second year, the child is able to pretend, have some success with easy puzzles, and recall some memories.

Stage II: Preoperational Thought 2—7

From two to seven years, the child is able to use symbols and words to describe actions and events. Thoughts are unsystematic and illogical. The child thinks only from his or her own perspective (egocentric) and is unable to incorporate others' rules.

Stage III: Concrete Operational Thought 7—11

From seven to eleven years, the child is able to use some logic, to create hierarchies of different classes, and to categorize certain relationships. The concept of *reversibility,* the ability to undo an action and return it to its original state (as in clay), plus the concept of *conservation,* whereby physical changes do not alter the mass, weight, number, or volume of a substance can now be recognized.

Stage IV: Formal Operational Thought 12↑

From 12 years on, the child has the ability to possess formal operational thought. The child is able to use logic, to anticipate consequences, to use abstract thought, and to see alternative solutions to decisions. As Piaget's last cognitive stage, this stage is expected to stay with individuals through life. However, not everyone achieves this stage to the same degree.

MORAL DEVELOPMENT

Lawrence Kohlberg has written extensively on the Piaget developmental approach to morality. Kohlberg posits five stages and further subdivides these stages into three levels (Kohlberg, 1969, 1984). They are as follows:

Level 1: Preconventional Morality

In this level, consequences to the self guide moral behavior. Two stages comprise this level. In Stage 1, *Punishment-and-Obedience Orientation*, the child fears getting caught and being punished. The seriousness of a violation is judged in terms of the amount or severity of the punishment received. In Stage 2, *Naive Hedonism (instrumental orientation)*, human relations are governed by concrete reciprocity and one is only obligated to those who help him or her. Rules are conformed to gain rewards or satisfy personal needs. Violations are viewed as relative to the intent of the action.

Level 2: Conventional Morality

This level is characterized by a concern for meeting social expectations. There is a desire to conform and a belief that each of us has a duty to live up to socially defined roles. Two stages comprise this level. In Stage 3, there is a *Good Boy or Good Girl Orientation*, in which moral behavior is a function of pleasing others so that recognition or approval results. In Stage 4, *Authority and Social-Order-Maintaining Morality*, there is a belief that authority and rules exist for the benefit of all and we must be obedient so that social order may be maintained.

Level 3: Postconventional Morality, or the Morality of Self-Accepted Moral Principles

This level is characterized by an internal commitment to moral principles imposed by the self, but governed also by principles shared by others. Two stages comprise this level. In Stage 5, *Morality of Contract, Individual Rights, and Democratically Accepted Law*, morality is arrived at through democratic reconciliation of differing viewpoints, which are flexibile but residing within the will of the majority. In Stage 6, *Morality of Individual Principles of Conscience*, Kohlberg views moral development as cognitive, and the product of maturation, stimulation, and active thinking. Stage 6 is the "highest" stage of moral reasoning in which persons define right and wrong on the basis of self-chosen ethical principles. There is much individual variation, and empathy for other viewpoints may be more tolerated than at earlier stages. Some people never reach this last stage.

As with Piaget's stages, Kohlberg's stages have a defined sequence that is developmental, moving from a lower to a higher stage, and universal for all. Moral thinking at a higher stage always includes lower stage morality, similar to the idea that Piaget used when developing his cognitive model (Shaffer, 1988).

COMMUNICATION SKILLS

Several researchers have identified communication skills as essential for all types of counseling; the counselor's verbal and nonverbal responses are key elements for helping clients explore and work on personal concerns (Egan, 1986; Ivey, 1971; Truax & Carkhuff, 1965). Some of these elements include:

- **Attending** is a form of active listening where the counselor makes some gestures to imply he or she is listening carefully to the client. There can be minimal verbal responses to which the counselor responds in a single word such as "yes," "uh-huh," or "continue." The use of this skill encourages the client to explore personal issues without fear of judgmental attitudes.

- **Clarifying** allows the counselor to help clients say what they really wish to say. Vague material is simplified and brought into sharper focus. Concreteness is the clarification of material by being specific.

- **Confronting** challenges clients to address discrepancies between what they say, what they feel, and how they act. Festinger (1957) addresses this with his *cognitive dissonance theory* when he says clients act, say, or feel in contradictory ways to avoid discomfort and thereby maintain equilibrium. Confrontation may be needed to develop awareness and encourage progress. For confrontation to work, it must be supportive and timely.

- **Empathizing** is the counselor's ability to vicariously experience the feelings, thoughts, or attitudes of the client. It reassures clients that their point of view is understood and accepted.

- **Evaluating** allows the counselor to appraise the counseling process and the dynamics of the client-counselor relationship. It is used to understand the movement and direction of the counseling sessions.

- **Expertness** conveys to clients that they may have confidence in the counselor as he or she possesses the necessary skills to help them. Typically this is demonstrated by such evidence as a diploma, visible in the office.

- **Feedback** is made by the counselor and lets the client know that what has been conveyed has been heard correctly. It offers an external evaluation of how the client appears to others and helps to increase the client's self-awareness.

- **Focusing** pinpoints one topic by helping the client concentrate on a single idea or feeling, rather than wander aimlessly or ramble on about some irrelevant topic.

- **Genuineness** allows the counselor's true self to interact with the client in a sincere and honest manner. The counselor removes any facade or front portrayed to the client. This action and mannerism tends to facilitate and open up the counseling process.

- **Immediacy** refers to the counselor's ability to deal with a situation at a particular moment. This complex skill attempts to demonstrate how each party is being affected by the other. The use of immediacy permits hunches to be shared and discrepancies pointed out.

- **Interpreting** is the presentation of information by the counselor in a way that is deeper than the way the client described a situation. Timing is a critical element as information needs to be conveyed in such a manner that the client will listen to a suggested interpretation.

- **Modeling** allows the counselor to demonstrate desired and appropriate actions. The use of modeling provides clients with examples of socially acceptable behaviors.

- **Pacing** describes a situation in which counselors only encourage clients to proceed at a pace that may be comfortable for them.

- **Paraphrasing** is a brief restatement of the client's basic message. It is used by the counselor to check the understanding of the message, so that a deeper meaning may result.

- **Probing** allows the counselor to ask open-ended questions to probe a particular concern. Open-ended questions ask how, what, when, where, and why, and encourage the client to proceed. Closed-ended questions have only a simple yes or no answer; these questions inhibit responsiveness and should be avoided.

- **Reflecting** is paraphrasing an emotional message with the counselor mirroring the affect. This approach permits clients to become more aware of their feelings and at the same time reassures clients that they are understood.

- **Self-Disclosure** is used by the counselor to let the client know that he or she is not the only person who has had a particular experience. The counselor must use self-disclosure in a discrete manner and must be aware of his or her own emotions and thoughts, which, if unresolved, may interfere with the counseling process.

- **Silence** is the refraining from verbal and nonverbal communication, which may be difficult for both the counselor and the client. The use of silence emphasizes that the client has responsibility for input and direction. Silence also gives the client time to reflect on his or her own feelings.

- **Summarizing** allows the counselor to bring together ideas and feelings that the client has stated either during a counseling session or over a period of counseling sessions. It is often done before termination. Clients should be given a chance to summarize the counseling sessions, confirming that they have understood progress and resolutions.

- **Supporting and Reassuring** reassures clients that they possess the wherewithal to move forward; its use promotes an atmosphere whereby the client is encouraged to face difficult decisions.

- **Trustworthiness** are qualities and mannerisms that demonstrate the counselor's sincerity, openness, and consideration.

CONCLUSION

Despite preferred differences for the deliverance of therapeutic assistance, the general goal of all therapies is to help clients attain positive mental health, feel a sense of self-confidence, and have positive relationships with others. This is brought by helping people develop an attitude of self-responsibility, and tolerance for others, in which individual uniqueness is recognized, and differences are appreciated.

In essence, the job of professional counselors is to make their services obsolete. Therapy helps clients become integrated, independent, self-aware, and self-reliant persons who become able to cope with future problems without counselor assistance or intervention.

To test your understanding of the various theories, name the researcher or counseling theory that best describes the following statements:

1. You came into the world tabula rasa.

2. Your life script prescribes your personality.

3. You have not resolved a crisis during your first five years of life.

4. The best way for a counselor to understand a client is by understanding the client's inner world.

5. You are "sick" and need to be cured.

6. It is not essential to have structure in counseling sessions.

7. You have developed a feeling of inferiority.

8. You need to accept responsibility for your actions.

9. Experience your conflict!

10. Your position in the family structure is important.

11. Therapy can be described as an "aha" experience.

12. Clear specific goals must be stated in therapy.

13. Behavior is a result of reinforcers.

14. The main function of a therapist is as a teacher.

15. There is no formal diagnosis or history taking.

16. Injunctions of others have bogged you down.

17. Refuse to accept any excuses for not succeeding in life.

18. Your perception of the problem is critical.

19. There is no such thing as mental illness.

20. No single theory of counseling works best.

21. The main goal of therapy is to:
   Help clients develop social interest.
   Help clients know they have free will.
   Explore unconscious material.
   Finish unfinished business.
   Accept and show genuininess to the client.
   Teach specific skills.
   See different forms of communication patterns.
   Teach responsibility.
   Demonstrate how emotions contribute to problems.

22. What therapies use the following therapeutic techniques?
   Thought stopping
   Paradoxical intentions
   Anything that works
   Paraphrasing and reflection
   Dream analysis
   Family constellation
   Analysis of resistance
   No techniques
   Identifying rackets
   Transference and countertransference
   Imagery
   Systematic desensitization
   Homework

The following references are suggested for further study:

Baruth, L. G., & Huber, C. H. (1986). *Counseling and Psychotherapy: Theoretical Analysis and Skills Applications.* Columbus, OH: Charles E. Merrill.

Brammer, L. M., & Shostrom, E. L. (1986). *Therapeutic Psychology: Fundamentals of Counseling and Psychotherapy.* (4th ed.). Englewood Cliffs, NJ: Prentice-Hall.

Corey, G. (1985). *Theory and Practice of Group Counseling.* Monterey, CA: Brooks/Cole.

Corey, G. (1986). *Theory and Practice of Counseling and Psychotherapy.* (3rd ed.). Monterey, CA: Brooks/Cole.

Corsini, R. J. (Ed.), (1984). *Current Psychotherapies.* Itasca, IL: F. E. Peacock.

Craig, W. C. (1980). *Theories of Development: Concepts and Applications.* Englewood Cliffs, NJ: Prentice-Hall.

Egan, G. (1986). *The Skilled Helper: A Systematic Approach to Effective Helping.* Monterey, CA: Brooks/Cole.

Erikson, E. H. (1982). *The Life Cycle Completed.* New York: Norton.

Hall, C. S., & Lindzey, G. (1978). *Theories of Personality* (3rd ed.). New York: Wiley.

Hansen, J. C., Stevic, R. R., & Warner, R. W., Jr. (1986). *Counseling: Theory Process* (4th ed.). Boston: Allyn & Bacon.

Ivey, A. E., & Simek-Downing, L. (1980). *Counseling and Psychotherapy: Skills, Theories, and Practices.* Englewood Cliffs, NJ: Prentice-Hall.

Napier, R. W., & Gershenfeld, M. K. (1985). *Groups, Theory and Experience.* (3rd ed.). Boston: Houghton Mifflin.

Wallace, W. A. (1986). *Theories of Counseling and Psychotherapy: A Basic Issues Approach.* Boston: Allyn & Bacon.

Yalom, I. D. (1985). *The Theory and Practice of Group Psychotherapy* (3rd ed.). New York: Basic Books.

Career Counseling Theories, Occupational Resources and Tests, and Ability to Interpret Test Results

Section III

Career Counseling Theories, Occupational Resources and Tests, and Ability to Interpret Test Results

---

KEY CONCEPTS

Ability to Interpret Test Results
Achievement Tests
Analysis of Variance and Covariance
Aptitude Tests
Career Maturity
Chi Square
Client-Centered Placement
Coefficient of Correlation
Compromise versus Optimize
Correspondence
Crystallized and Fluid Intelligence
Dictionary of Occupational Titles
DPT Code
F Ratio
Guide for Occupational Exploration
Halo Effect
Holland's Six Personality Types
Intelligence Quotient
Interest Inventory Tests
Job-Finding Club
Likert Scale
Maslow's Hierarchy of Needs
Mean, Median, and Mode
Multiple Regression
Nominal, Ordinal, Interval, and Ratio Scales
Normal Distribution
Norms
Occupational Outlook Handbook
Parametric and Nonparametric Tests
Percentile Rank
Personality and Intelligence Tests
Raw Scores

Reliability-Split Half
Sedentary-Light-Medium-Heavy-Very Heavy Work
Selective Placement
Situational Assessment
Stable-Unstable-Multiple Trial Patterns
Standard Deviation
Standard Error
Standard Industrial Classification Manual
Standard Occupational Classification Manual
Standardized Tests
Stanines
Trait-Factor Approaches
Trends in the Work Force
Type I and Type II Errors
T-Scores
t-Test
Underemployment
Validity-Content, Criterion, Construct, Face, Internal, External
Work Samples
Work Satisfaction and Satisfactoriness
z Score

PREVIEW QUESTIONS

1. What is one occupation that is expected to shrink over the next decade, and one that is expected to flourish?

2. Is it practical to apply the Trait-Factor Approach to career counseling for clients who are looking for a midlife career change?

3. What ego defense mechanism did Brill believe was used when selecting a particular career?

4. What type of job would be suitable for persons who had as their prominent personality type a realistic orientation?

5. Why is it necessary for career counselors to become familiar with the working conditions of various jobs?

6. What would a DPT code of . . . 412 imply?

7. What test battery is administered at state employment offices?

8. Under what circumstances would a work sample be helpful?

9. What are three measures of central tendency and what is the purpose of each?

10. How does reliability differ from validity?

CAREER COUNSELING THEORIES

Introduction

A career choice has implications far beyond the work itself. It includes how and what a person may spend time and money on, where the person may live, as well as political attitudes; it even has implications for the choice of friends or a spouse (Neff, 1985).

In addition, when people are provided with an opportunity to do stimulating work—which is preferred and appreciated—the economy at large gains, as productivity may be enhanced. For example, the *Hawthorne effect* is a term coined after an intensive study of productivity in the Hawthorne Plant of the Western Electric Company. The researchers found that paying attention to workers suggested that the presence of an observer may cause employees to be more productive (Roethlisberger & Dickson, 1939).

Indeed, there are a myriad of counseling concerns that the counselor may address through career counseling. These may range from career and/or personal satisfaction or dissatisfaction with life, unclear or contradictory goals, unfulfilled expectations, or feelings of isolation, due to lack of privacy and self-control (Neff, 1985; Osipow, 1968). Fredrickson (1982) summarizes the important role career counseling plays for professional counselors by saying there may be no other area a professional counselor may have more influence than by assisting clients with career choice.

The process of career counseling includes helping clients integrate and apply an understanding of themselves and environmental demands. This knowledge can be helpful in bringing about a career decision that may result in personal fulfillment, throughout the life span, and across the many dimensions of a person's life (Fredrickson, 1982; Holland, 1959; Issacson, 1985; Quey, 1968).

146

Trends in the Work Force

To assist clients, career counselors need to become familiar with projected trends in the work force, as this data is related to career guidance. This information may be found in the *Occupational Outlook Handbook* (1988–1989). It is based on projected statistics in the size and composition of the population. Some of the expected trends include:

- In the next fourteen years, the population of the United States will grow more slowly than during the previous fourteen years. By the year 2000, three out of every four workers will be between the ages of 25 and 54. Colleges, the armed forces, and retail establishments that service the youth are expected to shrink.

- More women and minorities are expected to be employed. Whereas in 1972 only 39 percent of the labor force were women, by the year 2000, this number is expected to increase to 47 percent. More jobs may be available in the western states than in the Northeast because of migration patterns.

- The United States is expected to shift from a goods-producing economy to a service-production economy. There will be increased opportunities in such fields as banking, insurance, health care, education, data processing, and management consulting. As these jobs require formal education or training, there will be an expanded need for college graduates. Jobs for high school dropouts will be limited. However, more young people are expected to go on to college. This may result in a surplus of college graduates working below their skill level. This phenomenon is known as *underemployment*. Minorities such as women and the disabled have experienced underemployment to a greater degree in the past than white males, despite legislation of affirmative action guidelines to prevent discrimination (Neff, 1985).

Theories that guide the career or vocational counselor can be divided into trait and factor theories, in which the worker and the work environment are matched (Parsons, 1909; Williamson, 1939); personality theories, in which occupational choice is dependent upon individual biological, genetic, and personality factors, critical incidents during growth and development, and other childhood experiences (Roe, 1956; Hoppock, 1957; Brill, 1949; Holland, 1959); structural and developmental approaches, in which career development is seen as a lifelong process, rather than an isolated event (Ginzberg, Ginsburg, Axelrad, & Herma, 1951; Super, 1957; Tiedeman & O'Hara, 1963); and behavioral and social learning experiences, in which consequences and reinforcers play a major role in career selection (Mitchell, Jones, & Krumboltz, 1979).

Trait-Factor Approaches

Parsons (1909) and Williamson (1939) are credited as major researchers in trait-factor career counseling. According to this pragmatic model, individual differences and job tasks are identified and joined together. Basically, this approach recognizes that people have different traits, that each occupation requires a unique set of characteristics, and that the function of career counselors is to match people with jobs. To do this, the counselor provides tests that identify and measure individual differences and then matches the results against various occupational requirements. The process is considered to be rational and cognitive, with career choice seen as a single event. There is one right job for each person and one type of person for each job. World War II recruits were assigned jobs in the military based on this approach, which also laid the foundation for interest inventories and aptitude tests. This paradigm has been discarded for the most part by contemporary career counselors as too simplistic (Issacson, 1985).

Personality Approaches

Anne Roe (1956) viewed career choice to be a result of genetics, early parent-child interactions, personality traits, and psychoanalytic principles whereby both conscious and unconscious needs govern behavior. Roe believed that the child who grows up in a warm accepting climate would be more likely to select a career that is person or service centered, while the child who grows up in a cold rejecting environment would be more likely to choose a job that has few interpersonal demands. Roe also believed a person's vocational potential and resulting choice to be directly related to family circumstances, including cultural background, parental attitudes, and socioeconomic status. She sought to superimpose a career model that would explain career levels according to Abraham Maslow's *hierarchy of needs* (1954), in which lower order physiological needs take precedence over higher order self-esteem and self-actualization needs. Roe was the first researcher to define a taxonomy of occupational groups, further subdividing occupations into skilled, semiskilled, and unskilled work.

Some of Roe's tenets were supported by applying the Rorschach Ink Blot Test and the Thematic Apperception Test. A major criticism of Roe's theory is the difficulty in testing it empirically, as early recollections and individual case studies must be relied upon to either support or refute hypotheses (Carkhuff, Alexik, & Anderson, 1967; Osipow, 1983).

Hoppock (1957) expanded on the needs approach to career development by applying Henry Murray's (1938) needs-press theory; that is, individuals are thought to be motivated by the need to reduce tension. Vocational development and career aspirations could be explained by the selection of an occupation that meets a person's current needs (lower order); a new job is sought when needs change or when different needs emerge (e.g., higher order needs) (Osipow, 1983).

Brill (1949) used psychoanalytic theory to explain career selection, with the choice of an occupation serving to express unconscious psychic forces. He focused on the theme that ego defense mechanisms (i.e., sublimation) are connected to vocational choice. He viewed work as an outlet for expressing typically unsociable desires. The classic example is the surgeon, butcher, or prizefighter, who chooses such a career in order to act out socially unacceptable sadistic impulses.

John Holland (1959, 1973) based his theory of career counseling on psychological needs theory. A preferred hierarchy or pattern of responses is developed in order to deal with the demands of life. Holland believed that the work environment could be similarly classified according to the demands and needs of the job. Connecting these two beliefs, he hypothesized that a combination of a career and work environment is sought that will gratify individual needs.

Holland developed a hierarchy of six occupational environments that represent major life styles and patterns of relationships between the individual and the work environment. People are characterized in terms of one of six types, with one type most prominent, and a second or third type reflecting a particular coping style. The six types are *realistic, investigative, artistic, social, enterprising,* and *conventional.* These patterns are placed in a hexagon in which the closest ones to each other are most alike, opposite corners are least alike, and intermediate corners have an intermediate relationship. For example, an RIA profile demonstrates the expression of consistent interests, and an RSE pattern indicates inconsistency in reported interests.

A *realistic* orientation is characterized by a preference to deal more with concrete things, such as machines, data, or tools, than with interpersonal skills or abstract situations. The realistic type is interested in activities that require motor coordination and physical strength, typically associated with masculine traits. Engineers, accountants, and people in the agricultural and technical fields are included in this group.

An *investigative* orientation characterizes those who are thinkers and solve problems by the use of intelligence. They avoid close interpersonal contact and do not have a need to dominate or persuade others. These people enjoy abstract scholarly pastimes, hold less than conventional attitudes, and possess a high degree of originality, verbal, and math skills. The scientist or mathematician is found in this group.

An *artistic* orientation describes those who have an esthetic orientation and a strong need to express themselves. They rely more on feeling and imagination than on concrete cognitive tasks. They dislike structure and like tasks that permit expression of emotions. The artistic person is considered more feminine than masculine, more nonconforming than conforming. Artistic types may be found in occupations related to music, literature, the dramatic arts, and other creative fields.

A *social* type seeks attention and close interpersonal relationships. The social person tends to be uninterested in problem solving or in activities requiring manual dexterity or physical skills. This type of person may be found in teaching or counseling situations.

An *enterprising* person likes to use persuasion to manipulate or dominate others. This type is adventurous, is concerned with power, and tends to use status for satisfaction. The politician, salesperson, and self-employed entrepreneur represent enterprising persons.

A *conventional* or conforming person has a great concern for rules and regulations. This type likes structured and practical jobs. They tend to subordinate personal needs. A clerical occupation is an example of a conventional typology.

Holland believes that stereotypes of particular jobs exist in the minds of most people and influence the choice of a career. When considering a career, we project ourselves in terms of these stereotypes and make a statement about ourselves by projecting perceived and desired identity into occupational titles. For Holland, career choice is a function of occupational knowledge, and insight and understanding of both ourselves and the world of work (Holland, 1959, 1973). His theory may be the one chosen as most popular by contemporary counselors. The Strong Vocational Interest Inventory, one of the most widely used interest inventory tests, is based on his theory.

STRUCTURAL AND DEVELOPMENTAL THEORIES

Ginzberg, Ginsburg, Axelrad and Herma (1951) view vocational choice as developmental, covering a span of ten to fifteen years. The process takes place over three periods: Fantasy, Tentative, and Realistic. Each stage has a unique description. The Tentative and Realistic periods have several substages.

At first, the person fantasizes about various careers. Reality factors are not addressed. The person moves on to a tentative-choice period, in which some reality is introduced. Eventually, a final choice is made on the basis of reality of needs, abilities, and environmental demands.

The process was first thought irreversible. Ginzberg et al. (1951) first believed it was almost impossible for persons to change their career, as an earlier choice prevented movement into other fields. However, the theory was reformulated as it was recognized that many people go on to formal training beyond their original intentions and interruptions such as military service can lead to career change (Ginzberg, 1972).

Ginzberg et al. (1951) also originally viewed vocational choice to be a compromise of interests, capacities, and values. Later revisions changed *compromise* to *optimize*, with individuals seeking an occupational fit of career preparation, realities of the world of work, and intra-individual determinants (abilities, interests, and aptitudes). Ginzberg et al. also restated the decision-making process of vocational choice as one that parallels an individual's working life span, rather than as one that restricts the process to a developmental period (Ginzberg, 1972; Issacson, 1985; Osipow, 1983).

Donald Super (1957) viewed vocational development as an ongoing, continuous, lifelong process in which the individual expresses self-concept by choosing a particular vocational goal. Accordingly, a person asks himself or herself questions like: "What sort of person do I think I am or would like to be?" The self-concept is thought to evolve and grow with life experiences, with personal needs and resources intertwined with cultural and economic demands.

Career choice is a function of career maturity. If the client is not mature, the counselor needs to take more time to help the client gain an understanding of the impact and scope of a career choice.

Super divided the process of vocational development into five phases: *growth, exploration, establishment, maintenance,* and *decline.* During the *growth stage,* values and self-concept are formulated. Following this, the person experiments with various vocations and tests interests in a variety of ways. In the *establishment stage,* the person tries out various jobs and tests whether the job is representative of his or her uniqueness. During the *maintenance stage,* the person works to adjust and grow in the job. In the *declining stage,* there is a gradual dissociation of viewing personal and work identity as a single entity, and the person plans for withdrawal from the work force.

Super's stages correspond to the age of the individual. The closer the correspondence between the individual's vocational development and the stage expected by society, the greater is that individual's vocational maturity.

Super described four career patterns of vocational development. Some experience a stable career pattern characterized by an early entry into a particular career in which the choice is permanent. Highly trained or skilled persons are likely to be found in this category. By contrast, an unstable pattern is one in which the person tries a series of jobs before settling on a final choice. A multiple trial pattern is one in which the person moves from one entry-level job to another, never gaining a particular identity with any particular choice. In the conventional pattern, the person tries several jobs before securing a stable one.

David Tiedeman and Robert O'Hara (1963) viewed vocational development and career selection within the context of a decision-making model. The theory comprises two periods: *anticipation* and *implementation/adjustment.* Four sequences are found in the first stage: *exploration,* in which activities are based on fantasy, and are not bound by consequences; *crystallization*, in which patterns emerge in the form of alternatives and consequences become known; *choice*, in which there is further clarification and commitment; and *specification*, in which a decision is acted on.

The second stage contains the substages of *induction, reformation,* and *integration*. Induction is described as face to face reality, where information is assimilated and goals decided. During reformation, expectations are modified and some of the purposes of the profession are questioned. Integration is characterized by dynamic equilibrium and satisfaction; in this stage, conflicts and doubts are resolved (Fredrickson, 1982; Tiedeman & O'Hara, 1963).

Social Learning Approach

Anita Mitchell, G. Brian Jones, and John Krumboltz (1979) are career counseling researchers who use behavioral theories, such as Bandura's (1977) Social Learning Theory, to explain how people choose careers. People tend to choose a job that has tasks similar to past successful experiences and to avoid situations in which there is some perceived failure. In essence, the individual chooses a career based on past life experiences, reinforcers, and consequences—both real and vicarious. The career counselor with a behavioral orientation believes that a person questions the payoff for selecting a particular career by asking: "What's in it for me?"

Behavioral career counselors would prefer to have a client visit various work sites to experience actual jobs than employ the use of tests to determine choices. After the site visit, the client would be asked to rank-order all visits by preferences. Counseling then proceeds by a process of selection, elimination, and generalization (Crites, 1981).

Physical Demands and Working Conditions of Jobs

All career counseling theories emphasize the importance of matching the traits and needs of clients with the demands of particular jobs. The counselor must also consider any special needs the client may have with respect to the physical demands of a job or the working conditions. These factors include strength requirements, such as the amount of weight lifted, carried, pushed, or pulled, and environmental conditions of jobs. This material is described in *Selected Characteristics* (1981).

The five degrees of physical demands are as follows:

- **Sedentary Work**. Maximum lifting is 10 pounds. There is occasional carrying of such articles as small tools and supplies. The worker sits for the greater part of the day. Walking and standing are required only occasionally.

- **Light Work**. Maximum lifting is up to 20 pounds. Frequent lifting or carrying of objects is up to 10 pounds. A worker in this category is expected to be able to stand or walk for six hours in an eight-hour workday.

- **Medium Work**. Maximum lifting is up to 50 pounds. Frequent lifting or carrying is up to 25 pounds.

- **Heavy Work**. Maximum lifting is up to 100 pounds. Frequent lifting or carrying is up to 50 pounds.

- **Very Heavy Work**. Lifting exceeds 100 pounds. Frequent lifting or carrying is over 50 pounds.

Other working considerations include the work environment, be it inside, outside, or both, involving hazards, fumes, climate, and humidity. In addition, other physical demands, such as bending, stooping, climbing, kneeling, handling, fingering, balancing, talking, hearing, seeing, and smelling, need to be considered when providing career counseling for special populations.

Job Development Practices

Job development practices consist of two major approaches. In the *client-centered* approach, the client assumes the major responsibility for obtaining a job. The client secures job leads, contacts employers, and does all the mechanical tasks involved in job hunting. *Selective placement* is a trait-factor approach in which the counselor is more active in helping the client secure employment. The counselor not only contacts potential employers but may also accompany the client to the job interview to interpret any special needs the client may have. The counselor who works with clients who have deficient cognitive or interpersonal skills would be more likely to use the selective approach (Salomone, 1971).

There are various job-seeking techniques to help clients acquire a job. One of the best known job-seeking techniques is the job-finding club developed by Azrin, Flores, and Kaplan (1977). Clients participate in a group counseling modality, discussing job-seeking strategies (e.g., interview mannerisms or names of contact persons at individual companies) and sharing job leads. Azrin and Philip (1979) described the job-finding club as having a behavioral focus, exploring obvious needs to acquire a job. The results of Azrin and Philip's research (1979) demonstrated that disadvantaged and disabled persons who participated in a job-finding club had greater success in landing a job than did clients with similar backgrounds who did not participate in a job club.

Minnesota Theory of Work Adjustment

Lofquist and Dawis (1969) combined a behavioral and trait approach to the study of work adjustment and job satisfaction (Osipow, 1983). They found a person is more likely to stay on a job and experience greater motivation to work when individual traits and abilities match environmental demands. These researchers cite job tenure as one way to predict job satisfaction.

Work adjustment is related to the concept of "correspondence," described as a continuous and dynamic process by which a person seeks to achieve and maintain some balance between individual needs and abilities, and the needs demanded by the work environment (Dawis & Lofquist, 1969). When there is correspondence, the worker is satisfied. By contrast, "satisfactoriness" refers to the conditions whereby the employer is satisfied with the performance of the worker.

The theory has been made operational by many instruments, such as the Minnesota Importance Questionnaire, the Minnesota Satisfaction Questionnaire, the Minnesota Satisfactoriness Scales, and the Job Description Questionnaire (Osipow, 1983).

Herzberg's Two-Factor Theory

Fredrick Herzberg (1955) also made some interesting observations in his research on job satisfaction. His conclusions add another dimension and a further understanding that the career counselor may find helpful.

Herzberg identified a *Two-Factor Theory*, dividing job factors, regarded as motivators, into two groups. One group consisted of *motivational factors*, or *satisfiers*, while the other consisted of *maintenance factors*, or *dissatisfiers*.

Achievement, recognition, advancement, responsibility, the work itself, and growth possibilities—all intrinsic factors—are examples of motivators. These result in job satisfaction. By contrast, company policy, administration, supervision, peer relations, pay, job security, and working conditions—all extrinsic factors—are examples of "hygiene" factors and are dissatisfiers.

Herzberg noticed that the lack of hygiene factors has the potential to promote dissatisfaction but, when present, does not advance satisfaction. He concluded that satisfiers and dissatisfiers are not mirror images, but rather separate entities, and that for the worker to be satisfied, both must be present. The counselor may use Herzberg's research to emphasize to clients the importance of looking at various intrinsic factors that a job or career may offer and not focus exclusively on extrinsic factors, especially salary, when selecting a particular career.

OCCUPATIONAL INFORMATION AND RESOURCES

Major federal sources of occupational information and resources include:

- *Dictionary of Occupational Titles* (*DOT*) (1977), the most comprehensive and widely used career information resource, in which groups of occupations are based on their similarities. More than 20,000 titles are described. All jobs have a nine-digit code. The first three digits describe an occupational category. The middle three digits describe a worker's tasks along a *Data, People, Thing* continuum, along which more complex tasks have a lower numerical assignment. Numbers range from 0 to 6 for *data* (and other intangibles such as words); 0 to 8 for *people* (humans or animals); and 0 to 7 for *things* (inanimate objects, such as machines, tools, equipment, and products). For example, a *DOT* code of . . . 147 would indicate: a job involving a great deal of math and computation; some work with others or the public; and very little work with machines. The middle three digits of the *DOT* classification code are helpful for career counselors in identifying transferable skills and related occupations when developing options for persons contemplating a career change or requiring one (e.g., due to a disability). The last three digits alphabetize the order of titles found within the six-digit code groups. The 4th edition of the *DOT* was published in 1977 and was updated by a supplement in 1982. This resource added occupations that were inadvertently omitted from the 1977 publication, included some additional information, and broadened the data base of job titles.

- *Guide for Occupational Exploration* (*GOE*) (1979) was developed by the U.S. Employment Services to provide job seekers with information concerning fields of work that match their interests and abilities. Occupations are grouped by interests, abilities, and traits needed for successful work performance. Data are organized into twelve interest areas and sixty-six work groups. A six-digit coding system permits this resource to be a comparison resource for the *DOT*. A narrative description discusses skills, competency, and physical strength factors.

- *Occupational Outlook Handbook (and Quarterly) (OOH)* (1988–1989) is updated every two years. The most readable of all resources, the *OOH* contains detailed job descriptions of nearly two hundred jobs in nineteen occupational clusters. Information includes the nature of the work, required skills, working conditions, employment opportunities, training and advancement notations, earnings, related occupations, and tools or equipment needed.

- *Standard Occupational Classification Manual (SOC)* (1980) arranges all DOT codes in homogeneous groups on the basis of work performed. Occupations are clustered according to similar worker functions. This characteristic can be especially helpful in identifying transferable skills to related occupations. The *OOH* is organized into SOC divisions.

- *Standard Industrial Classification Manual (SIC)* (1972) classifies each industry by its principal product or service and details the type of firms within industries. Companies in particular geographical areas are also grouped.

- *State Occupational Information Coordinating Committees (SOICCs)* and the *Career Information Delivery System (CIDS)* are statewide data banks that provide career information, trends, and other labor market information.

CAREER COUNSELING TESTS

Since the inception of the career development movement, career counselors have been using tests to assist their clients (Parsons, 1909). Counselors use tests for prediction, diagnosis, monitoring, and evaluation (Cronbach, 1970). Testing is provided in a variety of settings, by various counseling professionals, and for a multitude of reasons. The information in this section is limited to a cursory overview. For a more comprehensive review of this material, the reader is directed to the following commonly used testing resources: *Psychological Testing* (Anastasi, 1988); *Appraisal Procedures for Counselors and Helping Professionals* (Drummond, 1988); *Assessment of Children's Intelligence and Special Abilities* (Sattler, 1982); and *Tests and Assessment* (Walsh & Betz, 1985).

Before reviewing test information, the counselor must address concerns in relation to test taking, as well as the interpretation of results. These include: the appropriateness of various tests, whether the data can be trusted, that effort and motivation to take a test could be a major factor for outcome, that some tests require speed or are based on norms that may not be representative of the test taker, and that test anxiety may interfere with results (Anastasi, 1988).

The counselor must also be cautioned not to be overreliant on test results, as they can be misleading and can result in stereotyping. For example, some tests have a cultural bias that gives white middle-class persons an advantage over those who belong to a minority group (Anastasi, 1988).

In addition, professional ethics guide the administering, scoring, and interpretation of tests. States vary according to required professional competencies. However, many publishers screen test givers and describe the background required to be a qualified tester. At all times, the client must be informed as to the purpose and disposition of any given test (Anastasi, 1988; Drummond, 1988).

The various types of tests covered in this section include: achievement tests; aptitude tests; interest inventory tests; and personality, values, and intelligence tests. Examples of various tests follow. The reader is reminded that this review is very limited, as there are hundreds of tests to choose from. For a comprehensive review of most standardized tests, refer to the *Mental Measurement Yearbook* by Buros (1978).

- **Achievement Tests** measure the degree of knowledge or skills that a person has acquired through academic or experiential training.

- The **Wide-Range Achievement Test** is one of the most widely used achievement tests. It measures the development of basic academic achievement in three basic educational skills: Reading, Spelling, and Arithmetic. There are two levels: Level 1 is designed for children up to eleven years of age; Level 2 is designed for test-takers who are twelve to seventy-five years of age. It is hand scored and takes from fifteen to thirty minutes to administer. This test is helpful in diagnosing learning disabilities.

- **Aptitude Tests** are used to predict future performance on tasks that may or may not be similar to test items.

- The **Differential Aptitude Test** is used to help students plan whether to go to college. Results also identify programs in which the student may have the greatest success. It consists of a battery of eight subtests. It takes approximately three hours to complete.

- **General Aptitude Test Battery (GATB)** is administered at state employment offices for the purpose of measuring major aptitudes required for occupational success. The GATB consists of twelve timed subtests. Sections 1 through 7 have 434 multiple-choice questions and takes 48 minutes. Sections 8 through 12 require special apparatus to test motor coordination, finger dexterity, and manual dexterity. It is for persons who have at least a ninth grade reading level. The total test takes two and one-half hours to complete. For the nonreader, a counterpart of the GATB is the Non-Verbal Aptitude Test Battery.

- The **Minnesota Rate of Manipulation Tests** are designed to measure finger, hand, and arm dexterity. The five tests consist of placing, turning, and displacing, with either one or both hands. Each subtest takes less than ten minutes. The tests are targeted for persons who have reached adolescence or older.

- The **Scholastic Aptitude Test (SAT)** provides an estimate for future performance or the likelihood of success in college. There are two major sections: verbal and quantitative.

- **Interest Inventory Tests** are the least threatening of all tests. They are used to learn or confirm activities that are enjoyed and to translate likes and dislikes into occupational groups.

- The **Career Assessment Inventory** has two versions. The Enhanced Version involves careers requiring up to four years of college. It has an eighth-grade reading level. The Vocational Version involves careers that require little or no post secondary education. It has a sixth-grade reading level. Both versions are based on Holland's personality types, take thirty to forty minutes, and must be computer scored.

- The **Kuder General Interest Survey** uses a forced-choice system in which clients must select one interest that is liked best and one that is liked least. A broad base of interest areas are presented.

- The **Ohio Vocational Interest Survey** contains 253 items arranged on a five-point scale ranging from "Like very much" to "Dislike very much." There are twenty-three scales related to the DPT code found in the *DOT*.

- The **Self-Directed Search** helps clients explore potential careers on their own, as the test is self-administered, self-recorded, and self-interpreted. Descriptions are based on Holland's personality types. It takes forty to fifty minutes and is targeted for individuals aged fifteen years and older. This test is helpful for people who have low reading levels.

- The **Strong Vocational Interest Inventory** is the best-known of all interest inventories. It has had a proven reliability for more than fifty years. It provides occupational themes, interest scales, and occupational scales. It is based on Holland's personality types. It contains 325 items and, although untimed, is expected to take from thirty to sixty minutes to complete. It must be machine scored.

- **Personality, Values, and Intelligence Tests** are concerned with affective and personality problems and the identification of special needs.

- The **Bender Visual Gestalt Test** is designed to screen brain dysfunction and to assess psychopathology for children who are at least four years old; it is also used for adults. This test has a nonverbal response mode, which makes its suitable for use with children who are hearing impaired or who have low intelligence.

- The **Guilford-Zimmerman Temperament Survey** provides a nonclinical description of personality and temperament. It is geared for persons over sixteen years of age for the purpose of measuring adjustment problems or to pinpoint sources of conflict. It contains three hundred items in a yes/no format. The test takes thirty to sixty minutes to complete and must be computer scored.

- The **Minnesota Multiphasic Personality Inventory (MMPI)** is one of the most widely used clinical instruments to assess psychological and psychiatric difficulties of adults and adolescents. The MMPI provides scores on ten clinical scales, ranging from depression to social introversion. It may be hand or machine scored and is available on audiotape for use with the visually impaired.

- The **Myers-Briggs Type Indicator** is based on Jung's theory of types. It identifies four bi-polar scales that can be reduced to a four-letter code or type and can be used for testing personality dispositions and preferences for upper elementary students and adults.

- The **Raven Progressive Matrices** are nonverbal mental ability tests that measure problem-solving abilities. These tests are geared for children who are at least five years of age and for adults. This untimed test takes approximately forty-five minutes.

- The **Rorschach Test (Ink Blot)** is designed to evaluate basic personality structure and to detect possible psychopathology. It is one of the most widely used of all projective tests by psychologists and psychiatrists in mental health care settings for evaluation and treatment planning.

- The **Sixteen Personality Factor Questionnaire** places an emphasis on identifying academic, emotional, and social problems. It is targeted for persons sixteen years and older. Items have a seventh-grade reading level. There are 187 items. Although untimed, the test takes approximately forty-five to sixty minutes to complete. It must be computer scored.

- The **Thematic Apperception Test** is used to reveal an individual's perception of interpersonal relationships. It contains thirty-one pictures. Test takers are asked to make up a story or description for each card. The test is geared toward persons ten years or older and is untimed. It may be administered individually or in groups.

- The **Wechsler Adult Intelligence Scale: Revised (WAIS-R)** is an intelligence test that has also been used to aid in psychiatric diagnosis. The test is composed of eleven tests, divided into six verbal and five performance subtests, from which separate verbal and performance IQ's are computed. Scores are converted to scaled scores and then to IQ's for the Verbal, Performance, and Full Scale, where the mean equals 100, and the Standard Deviation is 15. The Wechsler Intelligence Scale for Children: Revised consists of twelve tests, similarly subdivided and scored as the WAIS-R.

- **Work Samples** are standardized well-defined work activities that measure what is already learned. Test takers use tools or materials found in actual jobs. This type of testing is used for people not easily assessed by means of traditional testing. For example, the person who has some mental deficiency or physical disability may be referred to a work sample to assess residual functioning capacity (Bolton, 1982).

Many commercial systems test physical abilities such as work tolerance, dexterity, speed, mobility and motivity. Examples include the Singer, Valpar, or McCarron–Dial Work Evaluation System.

- **Situational Assessment** is similar to a work sample simulation. The main difference is that the test taker performs actual work. This type of vocational evaluation is found mainly at sheltered workshops.

A wide range of computer-assisted testing has been developed that can help the client make effective and efficient use of helping clients learn about themselves and how they relate to the world of work.

ABILITY TO INTERPRET TEST RESULTS

In order to interpret test results, the counselor must have an ability to understand the basis of research findings. The following items are critical for this understanding:

- **Analysis of Variance (ANOVA)** is a technique of statistical analysis that attempts to answer the question: "Is there an overall indication that the experimental treatments are producing significant differences among the means of the various groups?" A *One-Way Analysis of Variance* refers to statistical analysis of various categories or levels of a single treatment variable. A *Two-Way Analysis of Variance* involves two treatment variables. *Analysis of Covariance* is a statistical procedure that determines what proportion of the variance of the criterion existed prior to the experiment. It combines the techniques of prediction and the analysis of variance to identify and control the effects of one or more variables.

- **Chi Square Analysis** is a statistical procedure employed to find the significance of differences between two or more groups of subjects, objects, or events that fall into defined categories by comparing observed frequencies with expected frequencies. The *F Ratio* is the ratio of two independent *chi squares*, each divided by its degrees of freedom and used to analyze two population variances.

- **Coefficient of Correlation (r)** measures the degree of relationship between two sets of measures for the same group of individuals. A correlation coefficient ranges from .00 (denoting complete absence of relationship) to 1.00 (denoting perfect correspondence); it may be either positive or negative. The *Pearson r correlation coefficient* is the one most frequently used in test development and educational research.

- **Control Group** refers to a group of subjects who do not experience any experimental manipulation in a research project. Their responses are used as a basis of comparison for the *Experimental Group*, the group of subjects who receive special experimental conditions or procedures, for the purpose of seeing whether the experimental manipulation contributed to some change in behavior.

- **Crystallized Intelligence** refers to intelligence acquired through experience and education. This type of intelligence is not expected to diminish with age. It is in contrast to *Fluid Intelligence*—the inherited dimension of intelligence that includes problem-solving and thinking ability, which is thought to diminish with age.

- The **Halo Effect** is the tendency of a rater to let other ratings in a different area influence the outcome of some non-observed variable.

- **Independent Variables** are used to select or group subjects such as age, sex, socioeconomic status and cannot be changed by experimental manipulation. This is in contrast to *Dependent Variables*, variables influenced by experimental conditions.

- **Intelligence** has no single definition. An *Intelligence Quotient (IQ)* is thought to be computed by the following formula: mental age (determined through psychological testing), divided by chronological age, times 100.

- The **Likert Scale** is an attitude scale that asks individuals to rate the intensity of their agreement or disagreement with certain descriptors.

- **Longitudinal Research** views the same individuals over a long period of time. This is in contrast to *Cross-Sectional Research*, in which several sample of subjects are studied over a shorter period of time. Educators prefer the latter research design, as it requires less time and cost, permits rapid data collection, and controls for less attrition among subjects.

MEASUREMENT SCALES

Measurement scales consist of the following four groups.

- A **Nominal Scale** classifies variables or observations by qualitative descriptors. For example, men or women are grouped, with respondents answering yes or no to a particular question, or person-centered versus cognitive therapists are identified by category.

- An **Ordinal Scale** rank-orders variables according to some arbitrary measurement. For example, runners may finish, ranking first, second, third, and so on.

- An **Interval Scale** has equal intervals between quantitative units but no true zero. For example, Fahrenheit or Celsius scales and many psychological tests use an interval scale.

- A **Ratio Scale** has equal units of measurement and a true zero point. Height/weight tables or time are examples.

- **Measures of Central Tendency** refers to the typical or average score in a particular distribution. There are three measures: the mean, median, and mode.

- The **Mean** is the arithmetic average taken by summing a set of scores and dividing by the number of scores. This measure is most affected by extreme scores, as all scores must be taken into account.

- The **Median** is the midpoint, which cuts a distribution in half, where one-half the group of scores will fall below the median and one-half above it. It is synonymous with the fiftieth percentile.

- **Mode** refers to the most frequently occurring score. It does not offer any insight in understanding the meaning of a score.

- **Multiple Regression** refers to a statistical procedure employed for the purpose of predicting one criterion from one or more criteria.

- **Nonparametric Methods** do not require any knowledge of population parameters, nor do they make any assumptions about the shape of the distribution. Nominal and ordinal rankings are examples.

- **Normal Distribution** refers to a distribution of scores or measures distributed symmetrically about the mean. When depicted in graphic form, it has a distinct bell-shaped appearance. In a normal distribution, a plus or minus of one standard deviation equals 68.26 percent of the sample population; a plus or minus of two standard deviations equals 95.44 percent; and a plus or minus of three standard deviations equals 99.72 percent of the sample population. The assumption that many educational and psychological variables are distributed normally has been a useful tool for test development and interpretation. If the distribution is not normal, it is referred to as a *skewed distribution*. The direction of the tail tells whether it is a positive or negative skew.

- **Norms** are used to standardize tests. They indicate average performance and the varying degree of deviation above and below the average. A norm-referenced test presents score interpretation based on a comparison of individual performance with that of other individuals in a specific group.

For a test to be reliable or valid, it is essential to have a comparison of scores with a reference group. The problem with some tests is that norms are arrived at by testing a particular population (often those most accessible, such as students) and the group norm has limited transferability to other populations.

- **Parametric Tests** make use of the normal probability method where statistical analysis typically follows.

- **Percentile Rank** indicates an individual's relative position in a sample. It is the percentage of persons in a standardized sample who fall below a given score.

- **Raw Scores** are meaningless and of little use. A reference point or norms are needed to understand what a particular test score means.

- **Reliability** answers whether the test will hold up over time. Reliability is usually estimated by some form of reliability coefficient (or by the standard error of measurement). A perfect correlation is plus or minus 1.0; 0 to .20 shows little correlation, where .60 shows a high correlation.

- **Split-Half Reliability** refers to using one test but dividing the test into comparable halves, getting two scores. For example, *Kuder-Richardson* formulas permit estimation of reliability from a single administration of a test, without the labor involved by dividing the test into halves.

- **Test-Retest Reliability** refers to consistency with test results when the same people repeat the test on a second occasion.

- **Standard Deviation** is a measure of the variability that describes the dispersion of scores derived at how far above or below the mean, the score falls.

- **Standard Error** estimates the magnitude of the "error" in a score, the amount by which an obtained score differs from a hypothetical true score.

- **Standard or z Score** represents the location of an individual's score within a set of scores. It is the distance from the mean expressed in terms of standard deviation units.

- **Standardized Tests** are carefully constructed with specific procedures for administering, scoring, and interpreting.

- **Stanines** describe a 9-point scale with a mean of 5 and a standard deviation of 2. These tests were developed by the U.S. Air Force during World War II and were found helpful for computer-punched cards, as all scores have a single digit.

- **t-Test** is a statistical measure used to test a hypothesis about the means of two samples where it is assumed the sampling distribution of the means are normally distributed.

- **Transformed (T) Scores** have a mean score of 50 and a standard deviation of 10. It permits normalized standard scores to be expressed into any convenient form for reasons of convenience, comparability, or ease of interpretation.

- **Type I Error** arises when a "true" null hypothesis is mistakenly rejected, whereas a *Type II Error* arises when a "false" null hypothesis mistakenly fails to be rejected.

- **Validity** refers to whether the test measures what it is supposed to measure and how well it does this.

- **Content Validity** determines whether the test covers a representative sample of behavior to be measured.

- **Face Validity** pertains to whether, on superficial examination, the test looks valid to the person taking it.

- **Criterion-Related Validity** is a concurrent and predictive validity that measures the effectiveness of a test to predict particular behaviors of an individual in specified circumstances (e.g., the criterion for predicting college grades may be measured by the score received on the SAT).

- **Construct Validity** refers to the extent a test measures a theoretical construct.

- **Internal Validity** refers to whether the experimental treatment caused the effect; *External Validity* describes whether test results can be generalized to others.

To test your understanding of career information, resources, tests, and testing, answer the following:

1. Why is it important for all counselors to become familiar with theories of career development?

2. What major socioeconomic trends can influence career choice?

3. Describe three major career counseling theories in which personality theory is believed to heavily influence choice.

4. Describe how occupational resources may be of assistance to career counselors.

5. Describe the reasons for recommending an achievement, aptitude, or interest inventory test.

6. Describe why a work sample or situational assessment may be the preferred testing means.

7. Why would interest inventory tests be less threatening than personality tests?

8. Why is it necessary for counselors to understand test statistical measures?

9. Why is Maslow's Hierarchy of Needs repeatedly found in career counseling literature?

10. What special-interest groups could especially benefit from an intelligence test when selecting a career?

SELECTED REFERENCES

The following references are suggested for further study:

Anastasi, A. (1988). *Psychological Testing* (6th ed.). New York: Macmillan.

Drummond, R. J. (1988). *Appraisal Procedures for Counselors and Helping Professionals.* Columbus, OH: Merrill.

Fredrickson, R. H. (1982). *Career Information.* Englewood Cliffs, NJ: Prentice-Hall.

Holland, J. L. (1973). *Making Vocational Choices: A Theory of Careers.* Englewood Cliffs, NJ: Prentice-Hall.

Issacson, L. E. (1985). *Basics of Career Counseling.* Boston: Allyn & Bacon.

Neff, W. (1985). *Work and Human Behavior* (3rd ed.). New York: Aldine.

Osipow, S. J. (1968). *Theories of Career Development.* New York: Appleton-Century Crofts.

U.S. Department of Labor (1977). *Dictionary of Occupational Titles* (4th ed.). Washington, D.C.: U.S. Government Printing Office.

_____ (1979). *Guide for Occupational Exploration.* Washington, D.C.: U.S. Government Printing Office.

_____ (1981). "Selected Charateristics of Occupations." Defined in the *Dictionary of Occupational Titles.* Washington, D.C.: U.S. Goverment Printing Office.

Psychosocial and Medical Aspects of Common Disorders

Section IV

Psychosocial and Medical Aspects of Common Disorders

KEY CONCEPTS

Angina
Anoxia
Arteries
Ataxia
Athetosis
Autonomic Nervous System
Blood Platelets
Braille
Carcinogens
Central Nervous System
Ciliated Cells
Congenital
Delirium Tremens
Diuretics
DSM-III
Dyspnea
EEG-EKG-ECT
Embolism
Erythrocytes
First-Degree Burn
Glomerulus
Hemarthroses
Hemiplegia
Hemodialysis
Hyperglycemia
Hypochondrias
Hypoglycemia
Inherited

Laminectomy
Legal Blindness
Leukocytes
Merck Manual
Metabolism
Monoplegia
Multidisciplinary
Myelin Sheath
Nephron
Neuroses
Organic Brain Syndromes
Overprotection
Paraplegia
Paresis
Personality Disorders
PET
Plasma
Psychoses
Quadriplegia
Second-Degree Burn
Spinal Vertebrae
Stages of Adjustment
Stress
Teletypewriter
Third-Degree Burn
Thrombosis
Veins

PREVIEW QUESTIONS

1. How does acute pain differ from psychogenic pain?

2. For what disability might a TENS unit be prescribed?

3. What medical problems require hemodialysis?

4. What is the number one crippling disease in the United States?

5. What disease causes the most deaths in the United States?

6. Is diabetes a hyperglycemic or hypoglycemic condition?

7. What is the technical name for Lou Gehrig's disease?

8. What common medication can be prescribed for relief of pain as well as for thinning of blood?

9. What is a common complication of stroke?

10. What single habit can contribute to the development of emphysema?

PSYCHOSOCIAL AND MEDICAL ASPECTS OF DISABILITY

Introduction

This section is an overview of common medical problems that the counselor may encounter when working with people who have special needs. The disorders were selected by reviewing textbooks, which professors of rehabilitation counseling have cited as resources for teaching courses on the medical and psychosocial aspects of disability (Liberty & Sampson, 1987).

This section is organized by systemic areas and partly according to the classification system established by the *Merck Manual of Diagnosis and Therapy* (referred to as the *Merck Manual*) (Berkow, 1987). No attempt is made to thoroughly detail the medical condition or complications of the trauma or disorder. Rather, this section outlines in a simple format the major points of a disabling condition.

We begin with an overview of the systemic unit and disease or disorder. This is followed by a discussion of the etiology of the condition and the method of diagnosis. The treatment and prognosis of the disorder is presented next, followed by functional limitations and vocational implications.

The reader is directed to the *Merck Manual* for more information on medical conditions (Berkow, 1987). This reference book offers a comprehensive and detailed discussion of many of the medical disorders commonly seen by doctors. Other major references include the *Disability and Rehabilitation Handbook* (Goldenson, 1978); *Handbook of Severe Disability* (Stolov & Clowers, 1981); *Health and Medical Manual* (Szuhay, 1987) and *Medical Information for*

Human Service Workers (Hylbert, 1979). Most of the information found in this section was taken from these sources.

The Etiology of a Disease or Medical Disorder

The etiology (or cause) of a disability originates from any of four major sources: *congenital, degenerative, acquired* (adventitious), or the source may be *unknown*. Congenital disorders are present at birth and are either attributed to a chromosomal or genetic problem passed on from either one or both of the parents, or there can be a problem during the pregnancy or during the birth process such as Down's syndrome, where an extra chromosome produces a unique abnormality. If the etiology involves degenerative changes, it is typically the result of the normal aging process. Arthritis is an example. An acquired medical problem is the result of an accident, infection, or disease, such as polio. The etiology of many diseases is unknown, although often a viral agent is suspected. This makes the problem more difficult to treat; and people who are afflicted with this type of disorder may be more vulnerable to medical or quasi-medical quackery.

Treatment and Prognosis

It is important to recognize that treatment and prognosis of most medical problems are the result of a multidisciplinary team working together to minimize the trauma and address the holistic nature of a person's problem. The specialized physician is typically the person who heads up the team, although it is usually the family physician who first sees the client. In addition to the physician, the medical team may also consist of various allied health professionals such as the *physical therapist*, who works to assist the client gain or regain the use of gross motor functioning, or the *occupational therapist*, who attends to helping the client with fine motor functioning. The professional counselor on the team will address emotional, familial, vocational, and other concerns that are ancillary to the medical problem. The involvement of medical specialists and the allied health professionals depends on medical and psychosocial needs.

Treatment and prognosis are a function of the outcome of various diagnostic tests. Some of the more common tests are identified in the text. General information regarding the progression or prognosis of the disorder is also addressed.

Medications are also part of the treatment plan and are prescribed to either keep symptoms in abeyance or to rid the person of the disease. The counselor needs to be aware that many medications have side effects. Some examples include drowsiness, impaired vision, gastrointestinal distress, impaired cognition, reduced energy level or physical strength. *The Physician's Desk Reference (PDR)* is a valuable resource that describes many commonly used prescription drugs.

Functional Limitations and Vocational Implications

Functional limitations refer to the restrictions imposed on the client as a result of the disease or medical disorder. Wright (1980) identified fourteen functional limitations when working with a client. Some examples include mobility, the ability to move from one place to another; motivity, the ability to control bodily movements for specific tasks, such as bending over and picking something up; communication and other sensory abilities; and/or the ability to use the mind for cognitive and affective tasks (Wright, 1980). As work is a vital part of life, vocational implications must be addressed by the rehabilitation counselor.

Stages in Adjusting to a Disability

Adjustment to any problem, regardless of the source, depends on a number of personal characteristics, past learning history, available community and interpersonal resources, and any other unique circumstances (Wright, 1980). In addition, adjusting to a major trauma has been documented as following a series of stages (Kerr, 1961).

The stages of adjustment are not discrete categories; rather, they overlap and movement may or may not be continuous. The person may vacillate from stage to stage, entering one stage according to no predictable time line, and entering another stage in a similar manner. Family members may also experience similar stages in adjusting to the permanence of a disability.

The first stage is *shock*. The person may be unaware of the extent of the trauma and be relatively free from anxiety. Eventually there will be a realization that the condition is permanent and with this awareness, *denial* may be experienced. Denial can either be healthy, where the person permits himself or herself time to mourn and come to grips with what may be a major lifestyle change, or it may be neurotic, where the person uses denial as a defense mechanism to avoid the reality of the situation. The person may bargain with "God," may "doctor-shop" with the hope the diagnosis is incorrect, may try to "pass" as normal, or use other defense mechanisms to avoid the acceptance of the condition. When none of these works, the person may become depressed.

When the depression passes, the person is able to acknowledge and accept the problem, and rehabilitation efforts become directed at adapting to the situation.

The Family

The family is a powerful factor in the process of psychologically adjusting to a disability. The family can be a source of support and encouragement and a vital motivation for the person to get on with his or her life. By contrast, family members can be so overwhelmed that they try to escape and deny the problem or may overprotect the person to the point that the person acquires a dependent affect.

The family's reaction to the disability depends on the family member who is affected. While overprotection may be more a problem for the child, denial may be more a problem if the person who has the disability is the mother or father. With the latter, there may be psychosexual problems in adjusting to a disability. The counselor can provide the family with an opportunity to voice sexual concerns, explore ways to enjoy the sexual experience, if this is desired, and also help discuss feelings of sexual attractiveness, and how this impacts upon the person's self-concept and desired lifestyle (Stolov & Clowers, 1981; Wright, 1980).

Attitudes Toward Disabilities

Negative attitudes by others are a problem for the population who have a disability. Attitudes are a complicated phenomenon influenced by societal stereotypes, early childhood experiences, guilt, fear, and lack of knowledge concerning the disability. For example, the person who is mentally retarded may be thought of by others as having a psychiatric impairment.

A well-known attitude measurement instrument, the *Attitude Toward Disabled Persons Scale* (Yuker, Block, & Young, 1966) has provided researchers with a technique to better understand why persons with a handicapping condition may be feared, stigmatized, or rejected. Anthony (1982) found a combination of information about the disability, plus contact with disabled persons, is the most powerful strategy to change negative attitudes to positive ones.

Medical Terminology

Medical personnel use many abbreviations to economize the process of communication. The counselor must develop knowledge and familiarity with various medical nomenclature to read and understand medical reports and feel comfortable in interacting with the physicians and other allied health professionals. A list of common medical abbreviations may be found in the beginning of the *Merck Manual* (Berkow, 1987). Numerous other abbreviations may be found at particular institutions and may be unique to that facility.

Many medical words look formidable and can overwhelm or intimidate the professional counselor. If you keep in mind the notion that almost all medical terms can be divided into three components—the root, prefix, and suffix—medical terminology can be somewhat demystified.

The root is the central part of the word. The prefix is the modifying term that precedes it, and the suffix is the modifying term that follows the root (Szuhay, 1987). For example, in the word "hydromeningitis," *hydro-* refers to water, *-menin-*, membranes, and *-itis*, inflammation.

Pain

Another consideration that needs to be discussed is acknowledgment of pain. There are two major types of pain: *acute*, in which the onset has some organic basis; and *chronic*, where the source of the pain may be either real or psychogenic.

Acute (real) pain can often be relieved by traditional medical intervention, such as medication, physical therapy, or surgery. Chronic pain often fails to respond to treatment.

If the source of the pain is considered *psychogenic*, it may be referred to as "conditioned" pain, which is perpetuated by some reinforcers, such as attention, relief from duties, or drugs or alcohol. This is in contrast to *psychosomatic* pain, which is not organic but psychologically based. Professional counselors will often work more with the person who has chronic pain of an operant nature, whereas the psychiatrist will work with the person who is reported to have psychosomatic pain (Stolov & Clowers, 1981).

SKELETAL SYSTEM AND CONNECTIVE TISSUE DISORDERS

The skeletal system is made up of bones, joints, cartilage, ligaments, muscles, and tendons. Bones form the structure for the body. Joints are where two or more bones meet. Cartilage is the fibrous connective tissue found throughout the body. Ligaments are cordlike structures that serve as a connecting device. Muscles are categorized in three ways: *striated*, used for voluntary movement; *smooth*, for involuntary movement; or *cardiac*, muscles that form the heart. Tendons are stretchable structures that permit the muscles to contract and relax.

The *orthopedist* is the physician who cares for persons with skeletal system disorders. A *physiatrist* is a physician who has expertise in body mechanics and who works closely with the physical and occupational therapists. Either or both of these specialized physicians may head up the medical team.

The source of a skeltal system disorder may vary and range from a congenital problem, such as spondylolisthesis, a mechanical abnormality of the lower lumbar spine, which creates a sliding and slipping of the facets in the socket, to a systemic disease, such as arthritis. The cause could also be adventitious or accidental, the result of a motor vehicle or occupational accident, resulting in pain and or spinal cord injury.

Back Injury or Back Pain

The spinal column is the weakest portion of the human skeleton. As upright creatures, humans can easily place a strain on the back over a period of prolonged sitting or standing. The lower portion of the back is the most frequently insulted, typically through improper body mechanics while lifting, pushing, pulling, turning, stooping, or squatting, and especially while carrying a heavy object.

Back pain is a controversial and ubiquitous problem. Worn joints, herniated disc (also referred to as a slipped or ruptured disc), and pinched nerves are the most common causes of lower back problems. A herniated or ruptured disc occurs when the disc flattens out and the gelatinlike material within bulges or protrudes, sometimes also pressing on a nerve, causing pain.

Etiology and Diagnosis

There is no single cause for back pain. It may result from a congenital abnormality, a disease or trauma, or part of normal aging. Symptoms that accompany back pain include stiffness and limited range of motion.

There are many ways to diagnose back problems. However, because of the subjective nature of the disorder, diagnostic procedures may be inconclusive. The physician initially begins to understand the problem through observation and self-report by the client.

X-rays (radiographs) and other imaging devices may be ordered. In a discogram, radiopaque liquid is injected directly into the spine. If the liquid leaks out, the disc is thought to be ruptured. A myelogram involves the injection of radiopaque material into the subdural space surrounding the spinal cord and nerve roots; this dye outlines the structures so that their movement can be monitored. A Computed Axial Tomography (CAT) Scan, currently called a Computed Tomograph (CT), is the least invasive, least painful, and usually the most accurate of procedures. Magnetic Resonance Imaging (MRI) is a newer imaging technique whose scanning mechanism provides additional valuable information.

Treatment and Prognosis

The initial treatment for back pain is limitation of activity or taking muscle relaxants. Conservative physical therapy treatments may be tried. These include the use of hot or cold packs, ointment rubs, back braces, traction, physical exercise, and relaxation, flexibility, and strengthening techniques. Physical therapists and chiropractors provide body mechanic instructions for exertional activities, such as lifting, bending, stooping, and standing.

If conservative treatments fail, acupuncture—the insertion of needles at certain points of the body—may be recommended. TENS units (Transcutaneous Electric Nerve Stimulation), involving the application of a mild electric current to certain sites on the body, may be prescribed. If these treatments prove unsuccessful, surgery or an epidural block may be recommended.

If surgery is needed, a laminectomy can be performed. The protruding portion of the disc, a gel-like substance, is removed. The surgeon must make sure nothing is pressing on the nerve, or the pain will remain. The recovery period may take as long as one year. The back may also be fused at this time, or subsequent surgery can be performed. Chemonucleolysis is the process whereby a protein-like substance, chymopapain, is injected into the disc to dissolve it; this intervention has a shorter recovery period but carries the risk of a fatal allergic reaction.

Some patients are told by their physicians that they must learn to live with pain and that there is no medical procedure to relieve their pain. These persons may be referred to a pain clinic. The treatment consists of conditioning and hardening exercises, biofeedback and relaxation techniques, and group and individual counseling.

Functional Limitations and Vocational Implications

The person in pain may have difficulty concentrating or staying in any one position for a prolonged period of time. Lifting more than twenty pounds, carrying, bending, or stooping may be contraindicated. As stress is a contributing factor for pain, a job environment that is more relaxed than stressful is recommended. Secondary gains, such as attention and financial benefits, may be a disincentive to vocational training and placement.

Spinal Cord Injury

The spinal cord is the largest nerve fiber tract in the body. Its function is to carry motor, or movement, impulses either down from the brain or up to the brain. If the spinal cord is severed, sensory functioning is impaired.

A knowledge of the configuration of the spine can be useful in understanding the counseling implications for people with spinal cord injuries. The spine is made up of thirty-three or thirty-four vertebrae (bones), which are separated and cushioned by oval pads called discs. These act to absorb shocks. The vertebrae are divided into five sections. The cervical (neck) region contains seven vertebrae (C1–C7). The thoracic (mid-back) contains twelve vertebrae (T1–T12). The lumbar (lower back) region contains five vertebrae (L1–L5): the sacrum (back of the pelvis) and the coccyx (tailbone). Each disc is designated by the vertebrae above and below it. The L4–L5 disc, is the region where complaints of lower back problems are most likely to originate.

If a person suffers a lesion high in the spinal cord, such as in the cervical area, the person will be subject to greater disability than if the lesion is lower. For example, complete severance of the spinal cord at T1 or above will involve limited use of all four extremities, and the person will probably be a quadriplegic, with loss of bowel and bladder control. Injuries in the lower thoracic level will result in paraplegia in which the person is wheelchair bound with a greater chance of gaining independence with bowel and bladder functioning (Stolov & Clowers, 1981).

Etiology and Diagnosis

Once the spinal cord is severed, it loses the ability to regenerate. When trauma occurs, medical management attends to any edema (swelling) or hemorrhaging, as this could contribute to further damage. Due to edema, there are times when the medical team may be unsure of whether the spinal cord is totally severed.

The vast majority of spinal cord injured (SCI) persons are young men from eighteen to twenty-one years of age. The causes of SCI include vehicle or diving accidents, gunshot wounds, industrial accidents, cancer, or tumors (Wright, 1980).

Treatment and Prognosis

Muscle relaxants, pain medication, and strengthing exercises may be prescribed. Complications caused by extended bed rest, loss of sensation, and lack of mobility may result, which include other body systems. A major problem is the formation of a decubitus ulcer(s). The person is at risk of infections and pneumonia. After the acute phase, depression and withdrawal are common. Counseling services are recommended. Vocational counseling and placement services should be vigorously pursued once clients are trained to use adaptive devices because of the young age of many affected persons.

Functional Limitations and Vocational Implications

As with all disorders, limitations depend on premorbid skills, intellect, interests, methods of learning, education, the availability of significant others, and the geographical location in which the person resides. Endurance, architectural barriers, and wheelchair accessibility are added problems. There may also be a need for attendant care to help with personal hygiene needs. Those who have cervical lesions may need ventilatory assistance. Quadriplegics and paraplegics have difficulty with bodily heat regulation and lack sensory awareness, so working in a climate-controlled area must be a consideration.

Amputation

Amputation means complete loss of a portion of a limb below a certain point. Common places are at the joints, such as above or below the knee or above or below the elbow. Since biblical times, amputation has been viewed as a sign of sin; for example, the thief deserves to have his or her hand amputated. As a result, the amputee may experience stigma.

Etiology and Diagnosis

An amputation of a limb may be secondary to complications of a disease such as cancer or diabetes. It may also be the result of some trauma, as in a motor vehicle or occupational accident. The limb may also be missing at birth, such as with the thalidomide babies, whose mothers took the drug thalidomide during pregnancy.

Treatment and Prognosis

The younger a person is who loses or lacks a limb, or a part of the limb, the easier it is to adjust to the disability. However, the young child may be overprotected or isolated, resulting in interpersonal deficiencies or lack of a competitive nature. Family counseling may be recommended to address these issues.

For the older person who suffers a sudden trauma, the shock of the missing limb may be psychologically overwhelming. Treatment should address coping with loss. The person should be allowed to grieve. Honest appraisal of the situation usually helps. The sensation of phantom limb should be described as normal and not a sign of emotional disturbance.

Functional Limitations and Vocational Implications

A prosthesis, or artifical limb, minimizes the extent of the handicapping condition that results from the loss of a body part. Training with an adaptive device is essential for restoring independence; yet it may be met with resistance, as this confirms for the patient the permanence of the problem.

In considering the work environment, one must take into account physical abilities. Many jobs can be modified to meet the unique medical needs of the person. The work area should be climate controlled to prevent irritation of the stump by perspiration, expansion, or contraction.

Rheumatic Diseases

Rheumatic diseases are the number one crippling disorder in the United States. They include more than one hundred arthritic conditions in which the joints are inflamed and in which there is swelling, redness, stiffness, or pain.

Women are more likely to be affected than men. The primary treating physician is a rheumatologist (Stolov & Clowers, 1981).

Rheumatoid arthritis is a total body disease, that is, it is systemic. It may be stress related and can occur at any age. There appears to be a genetic predisposition to the disease. The joints are tender, swollen, and stiff. Other "sick signs" (headache, fever, general malaise) may be present. The disease is symmetrical, which means that both sides of the body are affected. Small, visible, subcutaneous lumps, called rheumatoid nodules, may develop under the skin, causing deformity. Juvenile rheumatoid arthritis is referred to as Still's disease.

Ankylosing spondylitis refers to an inflammatory reaction of the small joints of the spine, followed by repair and healing with new bone formation, resulting in the fusion of the spine. As the nerves become damaged, pain subsides. The etiology is unknown, but since a genetic marker identifies the disease, it may be familial. The disease has been referred to as a malfunction in the body's immune system. The disease affects teenagers or young adults and affects ten times more males than females. It is also known as Marie-Strümpell's disease.

Osteoarthritis is also known as degenerative joint disease. It is a localized disease that may be familial and age related, usually affecting persons older than sixty years. There is pain in the weight-bearing joints; obesity is a factor that exacerbates this disease, since the joints must bear extra weight.

Osteoporosis is a condition in which the bones become brittle and weakened, resulting in fractures of the hip, wrist, spine, or other bones. It affects one of every four postmenopausal women and is causally related to a decrease in estrogen levels, poor calcium intake, and limited exercise of the weight-bearing bones. Smoking and alcohol may also contribute to osteoporosis. There is a genetic predisposition for the disease. It is found more in women who are fair skinned with ancestors from Northern Europe. The disease is less of a problem for men, as males lose a lesser amount of the sex hormone (testosterone) as part of the aging process. The "dowager's hump" is the condition referred to commonly as a hunchback and the result of advanced osteoporosis.

Paget's disease is a condition characterized by destruction of bones, followed by hyperactive abnormal bone formation, usually in the pelvis, legs, skull, vertebrae, clavicle (collarbone), or humerus (upper arm). The cause of the disease is unknown but may be genetic or viral in origin. No cure or specific therapeutic regimen has been found. Treatment is directed at controlling pain and limiting orthopedic deformities. Diagnosis is often discovered incidentally on the basis of X-ray and laboratory tests.

Gout is an intensely painful condition that affects men more frequently than women. The joints, particularly the big toe, become inflamed. The cause can be traced to the body's inability to break down uric acid, a by-product of protein. Diet helps control the disease.

Bursitis is a lesser type of an arthritic condition. The fluid in the sacs around the joints, usually in the shoulder, become inflamed. Tennis elbow also refers to a bursitic condition.

Rheumatic fever is a disease that follows streptococcal infection. This is an episodal, rather than a chronic, condition. With the availability of antibiotics, damage to the heart valves, which is a frequent complication, can be controlled.

Systemic lupus erythematosus is an incurable, chronic, immune system disorder. It is an inflammation of connective tissues throughout the body. Antibodies attack healthy tissue. It can strike at any age but seems to affect particularly women between the ages of thirteen and forty. The disease mimics a host of other illnesses, such as multiple sclerosis, rheumatic fever, rheumatoid arthristis, muscular dystrophy, and leukemia. There can be a long periods of remission. Stress is thought to exacerbate symptoms (Berkow, 1981).

Etiology and Diagnosis

The etiology of arthritic conditions is often unknown but may include viruses or bacteria, allergy, hormonal imbalance, or dysfunction in the nervous or metabolic systems. Diagnosis is by a blood test, X-rays, and other imaging techniques. Common arthritic complaints include joint pain, skin problems, kidney malfunction, frequent infections, and extreme fatigue.

Treatment and Prognosis

Most arthritic conditions are painful and progressive but usually not life-threatening. In many instances, there may be long periods of remission. The prognosis varies from person to person but the general rule is the younger the person, the poorer the prognosis.

Aspirin and other sodium salicylates, and bed rest, are initially prescribed. Heat may alleviate symptoms. In advanced stages, gold salt intramuscular injections, steroids, or quinine may be prescribed, but adverse side effects must be considered. For example, when being treated with gold injections, the patient's urine must constantly be examined for protein. If too much protein is excreted, the kidneys may suffer damage.

Exercise is a controversial treatment for victims of arthritis. Some physicians recommend exercise to keep the synovial fluids around the joint lubricated. Other physicians believe exercise wears away and does additional damage to the joints. The physical therapist may help the person develop a proper exercise program. Plastic joints have also replaced damaged joints in the hip, knee, or wrist areas and have met with good success.

Functional Limitations and Vocational Implications

Arthritic symptoms often take an unpredictable course, making it difficult to plan activities. Pain is usually present. Persons may demonstrate a hostile or angry personality and resent the disease, as it controls their life. Dependency on others may become a problem. Because of the controversy regarding treatment, persons who have an arthritic condition may be easy prey for medical quackery.

The arthritic diseases typically result in a limited range of motion and a loss of strength and of gross or fine motor functions. An inability to get around (mobility) or to grasp or pick up items (motivity) may present functional problems. Manual labor or stressful work should be restricted. Severe deformity may result in isolation and limit vocational opportunities. As extreme temperature can exacerbate symptoms, the person should work in a climate-controlled environment.

NEUROLOGICAL DISORDERS

The nervous system is the primary mechanism by which the body communicates with itself so that body activities may be performed. It is divided into two divisions: the *central nervous system* (CNS), which includes the brain and the spinal cord and voluntary functions; and the *autonomic* (or peripheral) *nervous system* (ANS), which includes smooth muscle organs and involuntary functioning, such as stability of the skin and function of the various glands. Neurological problems occur more frequently as a result of damage to the CNS or to the membranes covering the spinal cord or to the fatty substance that encases and protects the neurons (nerve cells).

A neuron is the structural and functional unit of the nervous system, in which electrical activities conduct nerve impulses. Neurons are composed of axons and dendrites. The region connecting these two structures is referred to as the synapse. The myelin sheath is the fatty material that surrounds and insulates the neuron and improves the rate at which impulses travel. The transmission of impulses is accomplished by means of a neurochemical transmitter called acetylcholine, which is necessary for processing and storing information.

The brain serves as the control panel to sort out neurological messages. It includes the brain stem, the hypothalamus, the cerebrum, and the cerebellum.

The brain stem acts as the pathway between the spinal cord and other parts of the brain. It is where reflex actions such as coughing, sneezing, or swallowing may be found. The hypothalamus is located at the base of the brain. It is the control center for certain hormones, metabolism, sleep, sex drive, and other basic sensations. It is considered the major link between the psyche (mind) and the soma (body). The cerebrum is the largest portion of the brain; it controls higher functioning activities such as emotions, intelligence, and judgment. The cerebellum is the second largest part of the brain; it plays an important role in the coordination of voluntary muscular movements.

The brain must have a continual supply of oxygen and glucose in order to function. Without adequate nutrition, brain cells die. These cells are unable to replace themselves, so any injury to the brain is permanent. However, in the event of a brain injury, the uninjured portion of the brain may take over and compensate for lost functions.

Damage to the nervous system may result in a number of physical problems. *Monoplegia* involves paralysis of one extremity. *Hemiplegia* is a condition that affects one side of the body. *Paraplegia* involves paralysis of the lower extremities. *quadriplegia* involves paralysis of all four extremities. *Paresis* refers to an incomplete or partial paralysis. *Ataxia* describes an irregular or staggering gait and a disturbance in equilibrium. Tremors are repetitive muscle contractions, whereas rigidity is the absence of reflex actions; spasticity refers to stiffness and tightening of muscles. *Athetosis* describes uncontrolled and continuously unwanted movements, especially in the hands and fingers.

General diagnostic procedures for determining the extent of a neurological problem and damage to the brain includes: an electroencephalogram (EEG), which measures and records brain waves; a Computerized Axial Tomography (CAT) scan, imaging of the body's soft tissues, the brain, spinal cord, and their bony enclosures; spinal tap; reflex testing; Magnetic Resonance Imaging (MRI), a sophisticated type of imaging in which the head or body is placed in a strong magnetic field; and the Babinski test. The neurologist is the specialized physician who treats neurological disorders (Berkow, 1987; Goldenson, 1978).

Alzheimer's Disease

Alzheimer's is a disease of the brain in which brain cells are believed to decay faster than those of a normal brain. The disease begins slowly and insidiously. It is irreversible, chronic, and progressive, and it results in a form of dementia. It appears most frequently in people over seventy years of age. Early symptoms include memory loss, apathy, and difficulty with spatial orientation and judgment.

Etiology and Diagnosis

The etiology of Alzheimer's disease is unknown. Possible causal factors may be related to an abnormal gene, faulty metabolism, a change in the synthesis of the neurotransmitter acetycholine, emotional upsets, or other physical illnesses. Abnormal amounts of aluminum have been found in the brains of some persons with Alzheimer's disease (scientists are working on the possibility that years of eating food from aluminum cans or cooked in aluminum pots may be a factor). It is diagnosed by a process of exclusion, made by ruling out other possible causes for memory loss or neurological problems. The person becomes forgetful, misplaces things, takes longer than usual to complete activities, or repeats already answered questions. Changes in personality, mood, and behavior have also been observed. Death often results from respiratory complications or pneumonia.

Treatment and Prognosis

As the cause of Alzheimer's disease is unknown, there is no prevention or cure for the disease. Medical treatment attends to the reduction of symptoms and an emphasis on making the person as comfortable as possible. Tranquilizers may be prescribed to lessen anxiety and permit a normal sleeping pattern. Proper nutrition, exercises, and physical therapy may also be prescribed. Alzheimer's patients can be helped psychologically with emotional support and with certain practical aids, such as labeling of household items (to reduce the anxiety attached to forgetting their names).

In the final stages of the disease, it may be necessary for the individual to be bedridden. This may result in feelings of helplessness, adding both physiological and psychological stress both to the person with the disease and to the family or caretaker. Many families find help in support groups.

Functional Limitations and Vocational Implications

As Alzheimer's disease progresses, there is increased mental deterioration and disorientation to time and place. There may be an inability to write, understand, or use language. Physiological, involuntary functions may become so impaired that the person may forget to chew or swallow food, and choking may result. As physical health deteriorates, there is increasing susceptibility to other problems.

As persons who contract Alzheimer's disease are typically elderly, they are retired from gainful employment; therefore, the ability to work is not critical. For the person who needs or desires to work, it may be possible to perform a routine, concrete job in which there is little need for independent decision-making.

Amyotrophic Lateral Sclerosis

Amyotrophic lateral sclerosis (ALS) is also referred to as Lou Gehrig's disease, named after a former player for the New York Yankees who contracted the disease in the prime of his career. The disease is progressive, with motor nerve cells and their axons degenerating to the point that the muscles atrophy.

Etiology and Diagnosis

The etiology is unknown but may be familial. Males are affected more frequently than females. The onset generally occurs after the victim reaches the age of forty. Symptoms include extreme fatigue, severe muscular cramps, muscle twitching, and loss of reflexes to the point where full paralysis is experienced. Eventually there is a loss of voluntary breathing, and a respirator will be needed to support life.

Treatment and Prognosis

The disease is progressive, and the person will eventually end up wheelchair bound and dependent on others for daily living needs. Death is most likely to occur within five years of contracting the disease because of the wasting away of muscles.

Functional Limitations and Vocational Implications

As intelligence remains intact in persons who develop ALS, the white collar worker may be able to continue to work. However, the muscle weakness and fatigue associated with the disease prevent the person who does blue collar or manual work to remain in his or her former position. Jacob Javits, a senator from New York State for more than two decades, suffered from ALS, yet he was able to continue research and writing activities for almost five years after the onset of the disease, working until his physical condition deteriorated to a nonfunctional status.

Carpal Tunnel Syndrome

This neurological disorder causes pain and tingling in hands, arms, and shoulders to the point that carrying even light objects becomes difficult. It results from nerve damage in the forearm muscles of the wrist and those that flex the hand.

Etiology and Diagnosis

There is pain and weakness in the hand, wrist, palm, and thumb. The condition is seen more often in women and is associated with occupations that require wrist flexion. Electromyography and nerve conduction tests help confirm the extent of nerve involvement.

Treatment and Prognosis

Once the cause of carpal tunnel syndrome is determined, a treatment plan can be developed. Physical therapy is often recommended, while surgery is chosen as a last resort.

Functional Limitations and Vocational Implications

The range of motion of the wrist and hand may be impaired, and pain may be a chronic problem. If the person's job requires extensive use of wrist or hand motion, re-employment in another job may have to be considered. As extreme temperature changes may adversely affect the person who has carpal tunnel syndrome, working in a temperature-controlled environment may be in the patient's best interests when considering re-employment.

Cerebral Palsy

Cerebral palsy (CP) refers to disorders of muscle movement that result from some damage to the brain during the birth process or early developmental years. Symptoms depend on the location and extent of brain damage and may range from limited intelligence to restricted mobility. The person may also suffer from spasticity and be at risk of respiratory infections, seizures, and language and communication deficits.

Etiology and Diagnosis

The diagnosis of CP is based on clinical findings that assess the patient's voluntary muscular motion. Anoxia, lack of oxygen at birth, is often the primary cause of CP. Any other event that restricts the child's brain from receiving adequate amounts of oxygen or nutrition can also lead to CP.

Treatment and Prognosis

Cerebral palsy is not a progressive disorder. Whatever problems are initially identified will remain, and the extent of the limitations will remain throughout life. Both physical and occupational therapists work with the child who has CP to minimize physical problems and permit as much independence in daily living activities as possible.

Functional Limitations and Vocational Implications

The child who has CP is usually identified as having special education needs. Vocational counseling and the decision as to whether the person is able to be gainfully employed or will need sheltered employment can be assessed early on by the educational team. Because spasticity reduces the ability to perform controlled movement, any job that is exertional or that requires accuracy with fine motor tasks is generally contraindicated. The child who has CP may have led a sheltered life, overprotected by the family; therefore, social skills should be assessed so that employment may be successful. Having a counselor as part of the medical team could be helpful both for the child and for his or her parents.

Cerebrovascular Accident (Stroke)

Stroke is thought to be the third leading cause of death in the United States (heart disease is first, followed by cancer). A stroke occurs when an area of brain tissue dies because its blood supply has been cut off or decreased. Damage can occur anywhere in the brain. As brain cells die, the functions they control, such as speech, muscle movement, or cognition, die with them or are impaired.

The cause of a stroke may be a *thrombosis, hemorrhage,* or an *embolism.* A thrombosis is a blood clot that forms in the blood vessel and reduces or restricts blood flow, causing death to brain cells beyond that point. A hemorrhage may be related to high blood pressure. It is caused by a rupture of a blood vessel or an *aneurysm*—the ballooning out of a vessel because of some weakness in the vessel wall. An embolism is a blood clot that has formed elsewhere, broken off, and traveled up the bloodstream, blocking nutrients to the brain.

Etiology and Diagnosis

Most strokes occur because the arteries leading to the brain are clogged with fatty materials (plaque), usually caused by atherosclerosis, also known as hardening of the arteries. Through the years, plaque builds up on the inner linings of blood vessels, becoming so thick that it shuts off the blood supply.

There may be advance warning of an impending stroke in the form of a mini-stroke known as a *transient ischemic attack* (TIA). A TIA signals that the blood flow to the brain has been temporarily interrupted. This local and temporary deficiency of blood is known as ischemia. The attack usually lasts less than thirty minutes, after which the person returns to normal. A TIA may be a warning of an impending major stroke. An arterial angiogram can be performed to identify the extent of the narrowed blood vessel.

Since each side of the brain controls the opposite side of the body, the stroke victim is affected by an incomplete or partial paralysis (hemiparesis) of the upper and lower extremities on the side opposite the side of the brain that was damaged.

The right side of the brain controls motor functions and the expression of emotions and nonverbal cues for details. A stroke affecting the right side will cause left side paresis and some difficulty with expressive tasks, perception, and organized movements. The person may have a staggering gait or great difficulty ambulating without falling. There is also a tendency for the patient to overestimate abilities. The left side of the brain controls language; a stroke on this side produces aphasia and deficits with speech, writing, or language tasks.

Treatment and Prognosis

Aspirin and other blood thinners, such as coumadin or heparin, are prescribed to prevent other clots from forming or becoming larger. Edema (swelling) is always present with strokes. As a result, several months of observation may be required before permanent damage can be assessed.

Functional Limitations and Vocational Implications

The physical therapist and occupational therapist are vital professionals on the medical team; both work to help the person regain as much independent living functioning as possible. Because short-term memory can be more of a problem than long-term memory, the speech pathologist is also vital to the team; prosthetic devices such as lists or calendars can be devised to help the person improve memory. As common complications of a stroke are depression, anger, and the exaggeration of premorbid personality characteristics, the earlier a counselor is included in the stroke team, the better the opportunities to contain problems. Return to gainful employment is possible, depending on the extent of the insult to the brain.

Cystic Fibrosis

Cystic fibrosis (CF) is an inherited disorder in which many of the mucus-secreting organs in the body are damaged by a proliferation of abnormal thick mucus that blocks glands and ducts. Rarely do persons with cystic fibrosis live past the age of twenty.

Etiology and Diagnosis

Cystic fibrosis is believed to be the result of an inborn error of metabolism that occurs when two carriers of the faulty gene conceive. There is no test to identify the CF gene before the birth of a child. By two years of age, the child shows symptoms, which include respiratory and gastrointestinal problems. The diagnosis of the disorder is aided by finding elevated sodium and chloride levels in the sweat.

Treatment and Prognosis

There is no cure for CF, so treatment is directed at alleviating symptoms. The child may be placed on a special diet and may benefit from the assistance of a respiratory therapist who helps the child keep the airways free of mucus. Because the family must devote considerable time and resources to keep the child comfortable and alive, supportive family counseling has been found helpful.

Functional Limitations and Vocational Implications

As the child who has cystic fibrosis rarely lives to be a working person, there is more concern with educational services and less with vocational planning.

Epilepsy

Epilepsy is described as a disorderly discharge of nervous tissue or an abnormal electrical discharge of brain cells within the central nervous system. It is more a description of symptoms than an actual disease. Epilepsy is caused by abnormal chemistry at the neurotransmitter level or a sodium-potassium imbalance. The disruption starts in one area of the brain, referred to as the focal point, and spreads throughout the brain like an "electrical storm." The pattern for seizures is dependent on the point of origination and varies widely from person to person.

Before a seizure, some people have a warning, called an *aura*. Auras vary and can take the form of numbness, spots before the eyes, dizziness, smacking of lips, or some other aimless, repetitive motor task. Any pattern that discerns the time lapse between the aura and the seizure is important to know. There is typically a loss of memory for events that happened during a seizure.

To facilitate a clearer understanding of a seizure disorder, an international classification system that identifies seizures as either partial or generalized has officially replaced the older nomenclature of grand mal or petit mal. A *partial seizure* begins with a specific motor or sensory impairment, such as a jacksonian seizure, in which the point of origination is in the motor cortex of the brain, spreading in an orderly fashion to other parts of the brain. A *generalized seizure* can be minor or major, with or without loss of muscle tone. The person may or may not lose consciousness with either type of seizure.

Etiology and Diagnosis

The etiology of epilepsy is considered to be either symptomatic, which implies a probable cause for the seizure has been identified, or idiopathic, in which the disorder can be traced to a birth trauma or other injury. Some children experience seizures as they go through puberty and outgrow the seizure disorder with hormonal balance.

Seizures can be related to excessive alcohol intake and may occur during the withdrawal phase. Emotional stress is linked to seizures, and some women have found seizures to cluster around the time of menstrual periods. Diagnosis of a seizure disorder is by an electroencephalogram (EEG) and a blood test.

Treatment and Prognosis

The first choice of treatment is benign neglect. If a seizure occurs, persons around must remain calm, recognizing that most seizures last only a couple of minutes. The person experiencing the seizure should not be restrained, but any object that could cause injury should be removed. It may help assist the person to lie down, so that he or she does not fall and incur some injury. When the person is lying down, the head should be turned sideways. It was previously believed that some object should be placed in the mouth so that the tongue would not be swallowed or bitten off. This has been found to be more harmful than helpful, and current recommendations are that nothing should be placed in the mouth.

Anticonvulsant medications control most seizure disorders. Dilantin and phenobarbital are often prescribed.

Functional Limitations and Vocational Implications

Although medications can control most seizures, there are side effects that limit a person's functioning and vocational choice. For example, reflex action may be dull when the person is taking phenobarbital. Seizures are unpredictable, so persons should not work around moving machinery or heights. Stress can be a precipitating factor, making routine jobs preferable. After a seizure, the person is metabolically fatigued so he or she may need to sleep. All of these are important vocational considerations; therefore, it may be in the person's best interest to have an indoor, low-exertion, low-stress job.

Guillain-Barré Syndrome

Segments of the myelin sheath become progressively destroyed (demyelination) with Guillain-Barré syndrome, causing nerve impulses to slow down to the point of paralysis. After the disease runs its course, the myelin sheath slowly regenerates, and full muscle strength and functioning may return.

Etiology and Diagnosis

The etiology of Guillain-Barré syndrome is unknown, but a viral agent may be responsible. Lower limbs are affected first, followed by weakness ascending to the trunk and upper limbs and the muscles supplied by the cranial nerves. Numbness, paresis, or paralysis follows. Residual weakness may be a complication after the disease has run its course, especially in children.

Treatment and Prognosis

Because Guillain-Barré syndrome can cause respiratory problems, medical treatment is directed at minimizing breathing problems. Heat helps relieve pain and physical therapy helps maintain joint movement. The person may require orthopedic appliances to permit mobility. Speech therapy may also be needed.

Guillain-Barré syndrome affects persons in different ways. Some people regain total functioning, while others are left with residual weakness either of a general or localized nature. If recovery has not occurred within one year, it is more probable that symptoms will remain.

Functional Limitations and Vocational Implications

The counselor must recognize that fatigue may be a problem for the person wanting to return to work. Heavy manual work is contraindicated.

Huntington's Disease or Chorea

Huntington's disease is a slowly progressive, inherited, degenerative disease that affects adults over thirty years of age. Physical strength is affected; in the later stages of the disease, decreases in intellectual functioning as well as dementia and personality changes may be seen.

Etiology and Diagnosis

The etiology is unknown, but Huntington's disease has a genetic link. If one parent has the gene or the disease, there is a chance it will be passed on to the children. The diagnosis is made on the basis of family history, with any psychiatric disturbances noted, and by clinical observation for motor abnormalities.

Treatment and Prognosis

The functioning of persons with Huntington's disease becomes progressively impaired. The prognosis is not favorable. Because of limitations with daily living needs, many people eventually become institutionalized.

Functional Limitations and Vocational Implications

Huntington's disease is associated with an elevated anxiety state. The person may be able to manage the anxiety or may need psychiatric intervention. Typically the person is unable to work as a result of physical weakness and psychiatric and cognitive problems.

Multiple Sclerosis

Multiple sclerosis (MS) is a neurological disorder found most frequently in people who have lived their first fifteen years of life in the northern half of the United States or Europe. It affects women between the ages of twenty and forty more frequently than any population group.

The major pathogenic process of the disease is demyelination of the myelin sheath, the fatty substance surrounding the neurons. Neurological problems vary according to the body site affected.

Etiology and Diagnosis

The etiology of MS is unknown. Stress or infection may trigger the destruction of the myelin sheath and lower the resistance of the immune system. The cause may also be familial. When the myelin sheath is destroyed, it is later replaced by scar tissue, which can block the normal flow of nerve impulses.

An early sign of MS is impaired, blurred, or double vision (dyplopia). The person may also experience fatigue and gait disturbances and may also have difficulty controlling bladder functioning. Diagnostic tests include lumbar puncture, CAT scans, MRI, and blood tests.

Treatment and Prognosis

Multiple sclerosis is marked by periods of remission, during which symptoms are partially resolved, and by exacerbations, when symptoms worsen. There is no specific treatment or cure. Physical therapy, massage, drug therapy, and acupuncture may all be tried as a way to eliminate or control symptoms. Due to the unpredictable nature of the disease, supportive counseling may help prevent a hopeless attitude.

Functional Limitations and Vocational Implications

As fatigue may bring on symptoms, strenuous physical exercise or activities should be avoided. Spasticity is a common problem that may restrict ambulation and confine the person to a wheelchair. The unpredictability of the disease makes it difficult to determine functional assets and limitations, but a job that is stress free and of a sedentary nature may be best.

Muscular Dystrophy

Muscular dystrophy (MD) is a general condition that refers to a family of hereditary diseases that cause weakening of the muscles, resulting in an inability to walk independently. The most common type of MD is Duchenne's syndrome, which occurs only in males; the symptoms are identifiable before the child is five years old. Some children are afflicted with cognitive deficits and mental retardation.

Etiology and Diagnosis

The etiology of MD is unknown, but a genetic marker confirms the presence of the disease. Laboratory tests that analyze various enzymes also confirm the diagnosis.

Treatment and Prognosis

The physical therapist will design range of motion exercises to keep the muscles strong. An occupational therapist may teach the child to use adaptive devices to increase independent functioning with daily living activities. A special educational plan will also need to be developed. As much stress may be placed on the family as well as on the child who has MD, counseling should be available.

Functional Limitations and Vocational Implications

The child who has MD typically does not live past twenty years of age; therefore, vocational planning is limited.

Myasthenia Gravis

Myasthenia gravis is a progressive disease found more commonly in young adult women between the ages of twenty and forty. There is an abnormal amount of voluntary muscle weakness, which is greater after physical activity.

Etiology and Diagnosis

Myasthenia gravis is an auto-immune disorder. Its etiology is unknown, but there is a decrease in the amount of acetylcholine, which initiates muscle contraction. The most common symptoms are ptosis (drooping of the eyelids), diplopia (double vision), weakness in the throat muscles, and fatigue following exercise. Diagnosis is made by laboratory tests.

Treatment and Prognosis

The course of myasthenia gravis is varied. The person may go into a period of remission for months, or the disease may spread rapidly from muscle to muscle. Medications are prescribed to interfere with the auto-immune pathogenesis. As the thymus gland may be involved, a thymectomy may be performed to arrest progression of the disease. Eventually, the person will experience respiratory difficulties, leading to pneumonia. The heart and other muscles become so stressed that death may result from cardiac failure.

Functional Limitations and Vocational Implications

Muscular activity needs to be limited, and only light activities of short duration will be successfully performed. Intelligence remains intact, so the person can work at a sedentary, low-stress job. The unpreditable nature of myasthenia gravis may make long-term vocational planning difficult.

Parkinson's Disease

Parkinson's disease is a progressive neurological disorder involving loss of muscle control. The disease produces tremors, muscular rigidity, fatigue, loss of balance, and sometimes dementia. A characteristic "masked face," giving the person an expressionless aspect, accompanies this disease. In the past, Parkinson's disease was referred to as "shaking palsy."

Etiology and Diagnosis

The cause of Parkinson's disease is unknown, but symptoms are the result of some deterioration to the portion of the brain where dopamine, a chemical needed to transmit nerve signals and responsible for motor movements, is produced. Parkinson's is rarely seen in persons younger than forty years of age. With increasing life span, this disorder may become more prevalent.

Treatment and Prognosis

Parkinson's disease is a slow degenerative process. Eventually the muscles lose their spontaneity. Speaking, eating, and voluntary movement become labored.

The most common drug for treatment of Parkinson's is L-dopa (levodopa). This drug can provide temporary relief from symptoms but, within a few years, loses its therapeutic effect. Scientists have discovered that the adrenal gland (above the kidneys) produces a hormone chemically similar to dopamine. They have attempted to transplant tissue from this gland into an area of the brain that regulates body movement to increase dopamine production. The use of fetal tissue has also been tried, but ethics have stopped this research in the United States.

Functional Limitations and Vocational Implications

As intelligence remains intact during the early stages of the disease, sedentary, low-stress work may continue. Shaking may be a problem for fine motor tasks. A cold working environment should be avoided, as should an environment in which there are irritating substances (such as chemicals), both of which tend to aggravate respiratory difficulties.

Poliomyelitis

Poliomyelitis (polio) is an acute viral infection of the spinal cord, followed by a residual paralysis of muscles. At one time it was called infantile paralysis, as it was thought that small children were at greater risk. With the availability of the Salk and Sabin vaccines, the incidence of polio has greatly decreased.

Etiology and Diagnosis

A virus is believed to be the agent responsible for contracting polio. Historically, summer and fall have been the seasons of highest incidence.

Treatment and Prognosis

Therapy is nonspecific and depends on the extent of paralysis. Physical and occupational therapy help the person increase and maintain independent functioning. It was recently found that after a number of years, symptoms may reappear and worsen. This is thought to be because of the wear and tear on the muscles weakened by the disease, which becomes more pronounced with normal aging.

Functional Limitations and Vocational Implications

Polio is not a progressive disease. Once the condition has stabilized, long-term planning can be initiated. Because independent ambulation may be a problem and the person may need to rely on assistive devices, such as leg braces, nonexertional work is recommended.

Spina Bifida

This condition is also known as an open or split spine. It is a birth defect in which the vertebrae in the spine of the developing fetus does not close normally during the first trimester of pregnancy. There is some indication that this condition may be familial.

Many children with spina bifida are born with a hydrocephalic condition in which the head is enlarged due to trapped water in the skull. Left untreated, brain damage could result, causing some degree of mental retardation.

Etiology and Diagnosis

The reason for the failure of the vertebral canal to close normally around the spinal cord in not known. Amniocentesis can diagnose the problem in utero.

Treatment and Prognosis

In utero surgery can now correct this condition, and any damaging effects can be greatly minimized. However, as the child is at greater risk of infection or meningitis, antibiotics may be prescribed after birth. The child who is born with spina bifida may suffer from weakness of the lower extremities and limitations with independent bowel and bladder functioning, due to a loss of sensation. A regular exercise program and physical therapy can help develop muscle strength and minimize problems.

Functional Limitations and Vocational Implications

Special educational services can address the special needs of the child at an early age. Since the disease is not progressive, long-range vocational planning can be developed, taking into consideration any residual functional limitations. Exertional work will probably be contraindicated.

CIRCULATORY SYSTEM, CARDIOVASCULAR DISORDERS, HEMATOLOGY, AND ONCOLOGY

The function of blood is to supply cells and tissues with oxygen and nutrients, transport waste products to excretory organs, help equalize and regulate body temperature, regulate the acid-base balance and salt content of all tissues, and transport hormones necessary for regulation. The blood is composed of a number of elements: *Red blood cells* (RBC's), or erythrocytes, have as one of their primary functions the transportation of oxygen to all cells and tissues. They are concave and disk shaped and must be flexible enough to pass through tiny capillaries. *White blood cells* (WBC's), or leukocytes, are colorless, have a longer life span, and are larger than RBC's. The primary function of WBC's is to protect the body against invading or foreign substances introduced by disease or injury. *Plasma* is the watery part of the blood. Blood *platelets* are responsible for clotting. The *lymph* is a clear transparent fluid that is transported by means of the lymphatic system, a secondary circulatory system; it is protected from invading bacteria by the lymph nodes.

Diseases of the blood can be caused by problems in the composition of the blood or problems in the transport of the various constituents of the blood that the body may need. For example, if the RBC count and WBC count are not in the correct proportion, leukemia could result. If the blood is blocked from reaching vital organs such as the heart, a heart attack could result.

The blood must have a mechanism by which it can be propelled throughout the body. This is the function of the heart and vessel network, referred to as the circulatory system. It consists of the heart, arteries, veins, and capillaries.

The heart is responsible for pumping the blood throughout the arteries and veins. Arteries carry bright red blood, oxygenated by the lungs, away from the heart. Veins carry darker, deoxygenated blood back to the heart. (An exception is the pulmonary artery, which carries deoxygenated blood to the heart, and the pulmonary vein, which carries newly oxygenated red blood to the heart.) The capillaries branch into the veins that lead back to the heart.

Symptoms of irregularities of the blood, or of a problem with the amount of blood pumped, or of any of its many other functions include general "sick signs," such as fatigue, lethargy, weakness, apathy, poor memory, or depression. There can also be shortness of breath (dyspnea), tachycardia, an accelerated heartbeat, or fibrillations, which is a type of quivering that results from rapid incomplete contractions.

Anemias

Anemia refers to an abnormal low RBC count. There are a variety of types, each having a particular and unique, often unrelated cause.

In thalassemia, or Cooley's anemia, a recessive gene seen more in people of Greek or Italian-American ancestry, causes the child to develop the disorder. The child appears healthy at birth but develops symptoms before two years of age; these include paleness, listlessness, irritability, and retarded growth. The victim rarely lives past the age of thirty.

Sickle cell anemia is an inherited disease found more commonly in people of African ancestry. The RBC's take on an unusual form, becoming sickle or crescent shaped, and are unable to pass comfortably through the blood vessels, depriving the organs and tissues of needed ogygen. Attacks can be very painful, and life span is shortened as a result of other systemic complications.

Leukemia is a disease of the blood characterized by an overproduction of abnormal WBC's which compete with the production of the RBC's. When this happens, there is interference with oxygen transport and clotting. Men over forty years of age are at greater risk, as are children from four to fourteen years of age.

Etiology and Diagnosis

Although Cooley's anemia and sickle cell anemia are very different, both are present at birth, and the result of an inherited genetic problem. The etiology of leukemia is unknown, but a viral agent is suspect.

Most anemias are manifested similarly, producing fatigue, lethargy, and other "sick signs." Diagnosis for all conditions is by a blood test.

Treatment and Prognosis

The treatment for anemic conditions is multifaceted. A nutritional protocol may be recommended. Physical and occupational therapy may provide supervised exercises and any needed adaptive devices for independent living. Medical attention is directed at relieving as many symptoms as possible. Because symptoms may be exacerbated by stress, a professional counselor may be recommended for both the client and family.

Functional Limitations and Vocational Implications

Persons who have some form of anemia need to restrict physical demands, as their energy level will not sustain exertional activities. In addition, there is a greater risk of infection and other systemic complications. For the child with an anemic condition parental overprotection may be a problem that could result with the child having poor social skills.

Arteriosclerosis

Arteriosclerosis is a general term describing a number of diseases of the blood vessels. Atherosclerosis refers to the thickening of the arteries due to an accumulation of lipids (fats). This medical problem is also referred to as coronary artery disease.

When the arteries become clogged with fatty substances, the heart fails to receive the necessary supply of nutrients and oxygen. This restricts the flow of blood to the heart, causing a myocardial infarction (heart attack). Coronary atherosclerosis is the leading cause of cardiac distress.

Etiology and Diagnosis

The exact cause of this disease is unknown, but predisposing factors include hypertension, high blood cholesterol or triglycerides, cigarette smoking, physical inactivity, type A personality, (see *Myocardial Infarction*), obesity, or diabetes. Men over forty years of age are at greatest risk. A diet high in fat and refined sugar adds an additional risk factor.

There is no warning until the valve passageway becomes so narrow (stenotic) that tissues are left undernourished and a coronary thrombosis (blood clot) obstructs the flow of blood to the heart. Diagnosis includes the use of angiography, in which radioactive dye is injected into the heart chambers and arteries.

Treatment and Prognosis

A change in diet and a modification of living habits may help. Stress is to be avoided. Diuretics may be prescribed.

Acquired Immune Deficiency Syndrome (AIDS)

Although acquired immune deficiency syndrome (AIDS) is not found in the *Merck Manual* (Berkow, 1987) in this category, because of the complex nature of the disease and its effect on the circulatory and other related systems, this medical problem is included here.

AIDS is a medical problem of a progressive and incurable nature. The body's immune system is attacked, rendering the person more vulnerable to infection than normally experienced. The incidence of AIDS is spreading at an alarming rate in large urban areas.

Individuals affected with the AIDS virus fall into three categories: An asymptomatic carrier does not show signs or symptoms and remains so for a number of years. A person with *AIDS-Related Complex* (ARC) syndrome shows symptoms that include weight loss, night sweats, diarrhea, chronic fatigue, and swelling of the lymph nodes in the armpits and groin. In full-blown AIDS, the individual's immune system is unable to protect the body against invading microorganisms.

Etiology and Diagnosis

Diagnosis of AIDS is made on the basis of a blood test, in which the presence of human immunodeficiency virus (HIV) antibodies in the bloodstream indicates a person has been exposed to the virus. Certain groups of people are at risk of developing AIDS. They include homosexual or bisexual men, male and female intravenous drug users, sexual partners of persons carrying the AIDS virus, children who acquired AIDS at birth from infected mothers, and persons who have received transfusions of contaminated blood. Casual contact with an HIV infected person is not thought to transmit this disease.

Treatment and Prognosis

There is no known cure for AIDS. Drugs such as AZT, azidothymidine, or a-interferon, and radiotherapy may slow down the progression of the disease. The person is weakened by infections and death results often from either pneumonia or Kaposi's sarcoma (a type of cancer).

Functional Limitations and Vocational Implications

If the disease does not become full blown, normal activities may continue. Unfortunately, people who have a known AIDS condition suffer much discrimination in their personal life and in the work force. There is much misinformation and fear of being exposed to the disease, as well as a stigma in being at risk. Toll-free hotlines have been established nationally for general information, counseling, testing, and assistance.

Cancers

Oncology is the study of cancer. More than one hundred different diseases are classified as cancer, typically described as an unusually rapid and uncontrollable proliferation of abnormal cells. Cancer can develop in any tissue of any organ and can appear at any age. The exact mechanism that transforms a normal cell into a cancer cell is unknown.

Cancer is the most feared of all diseases. One in four persons will have some type of cancer during his or her lifetime. Early detection is the best way to control the spread of any cancer.

Etiology and Diagnosis

Although the specific etiology of many cancers is unknown, certain cancer-causing agents, known as *carcinogens*, play a role in the development of the disorder. For example, overexposure to ultraviolet rays can cause skin cancer. A diet high in saturated fats and low in dietary fiber can be a predisposing factor to the development of colon cancer. People who are heavy pipe smokers are at risk of developing cancer of the mouth, while cigarette smokers and people who work around asbestos and coal dust are at risk of developing lung cancer. The use of the hormone estrogen may be a factor in the development of cancer of the uterus.

Cancer is not contagious. Certain types of cancer seem to have a genetic link. Warning symptoms include a change in bowel or bladder habits, unusual bleeding, a sore that does not heal, a lump in the breast or elsewhere, indigestion or difficulty in swallowing, an obvious change in a wart or mole, and/or a nagging cough or hoarseness.

Treatment and Prognosis

The prognosis for most cancers depends on how early the diagnosis was made. The earlier the diagnosis, the better the chance for a cure. Treatment is by surgery, chemotherapy, radiotherapy, and a nutritional protocol.

Functional Limitations and Vocational Implications

There are side-effects to cancer treatment that may result in functional limitations. For example, chemotherapy may bring about nausea, vomiting, loss of appetite, and fatigue, and loss of hair. Anxiety and fear of death may be debilitating to both the affected person and the family. As a result, the American Cancer Society has made available individual and group counseling and hot lines to provide emotional support and information.

There are no specific vocational implications, as different types of cancer involve different restrictions. Since intelligence remains intact in most cancers, the person who works at a cognitive task will in all likelihood be less affected than the person who does manual work.

Hemophilia

Hemophilia is a congenital, inherited disorder that prevents the blood from clotting properly. Hemophiliacs have been referred to as "bleeders." The disease is caused by a recessive, gender-linked gene and is either transmitted by the mother to her male offspring, or carried by a daughter to the next generation.

Diagnosis

A blood test confirms the presence of hemophilia. Family history provides additional information.

Treatment and Prognosis

There is no cure for hemophilia. Hemorrhaging can occur throughout life, and the recurrent bleeding into the joints (hemarthroses) can cause swelling and pain. Transfusions may be needed, presenting the victim with the additional complication of contracting AIDS from contaminated blood. As there may be anxiety concerning death, counseling may be needed for both the person and the family.

Functional Limitations and Vocational Implications

Strenuous activities are restricted for the person who has hemophilia. Mobility may also be limited. The child may grow up overprotected, and this may result in deficient social skills, possibly limiting vocational options.

Hypertension

High blood pressure, also known as hypertension, occurs commonly in middle-aged or elderly men and women. It is the leading cause of stroke. It can cause damage to the heart, brain, kidneys, and arteries. It increases the risk of heart attacks, congestive heart failure, and kidney failure.

Etiology and Diagnosis

Hypertension is not technically a disease, but rather a description of a state of elevated blood pressure which is measured by a systolic/diastolic number. *Systolic* pressure describes the moment when the blood is ejected from the heart, and the heart muscle contracts. *Diastolic* describes the moment when the blood enters and fills the heart, and the heart is at rest. The device used to measure blood pressure is called a sphygmomanometer; it consists of an inflatable cuff that is wrapped around the upper arm.

Blood pressure varies with each individual. It tends to elevate with age and activities. High blood pressure is seen more frequently in persons of African heritage. Normal pressure is considered to be about 120/80.

Treatment and Prognosis

Left untreated, high blood pressure can lead to kidney disease. The person is placed on diuretics and other medications. The intake of coffee, sodium, saturated fat, or alcohol should be reduced or eliminated. Obesity may be a contributing factor, so weight should be controlled. Smokers and women using oral contraceptives are at increased risk.

Functional Limitations and Vocational Implications

Hypertension is an invisible problem. There are no physical restrictions or problems with ability or agility. The person can select any suitable vocation and can work in a job environment of their choice.

Myocardial Infarction

A myocardial infarction is more commonly known as a heart attack. It is accompanied by pain due to inadequate blood flow to the heart. When the blood flow of the major coronary arteries is blocked, a blood clot forms (coronary thrombosis) resulting in a myocardial infarction, or heart attack.

Etiology and Diagnosis

Angina pectoris or intense chest pain results when a coronary artery is too narrow to let needed nutrients through. The pain typically radiates down the left arm. Feelings of pressure, weight, and tightness are experienced. Nausea, vomiting, and a cold clammy sweat may be additional symptoms.

Diagnosis is by an electrocardiogram (EKG), which records electrical activity of the heart, or by a blood test in which the activity of an enzyme known as SGOT (serum glutamic oxalacetic transaminase) is analyzed. Another diagnostic procedure is cardiac catheterization or a cardiac angiogram in which dye is injected.

A Type A personality, who is time-conscious, goal-oriented, and competitive, is believed to be at greater risk of having a heart attack, than the Type B personality, who is more easy-going and relaxed.

Treatment and Prognosis

Heart disease is a progressive condition. The rate varies from person to person. Vasoconstrictors such as epinephrine are given to increase blood pressure. Nitroglycerin is prescribed to alleviate pain. In addition to medications, surgery and a change in lifestyle may be recommended to correct the condition. In extreme cases, heart transplant is also possible.

As a heart attack can be life-threatening, this condition is a source of anxiety for both the heart attack victims and their families. Family members may become so overprotective that a "cardiac neurosis" may develop, with resulting hypochondriasis. Spouses may become so fearful and anxious that sexual activity decreases. Therefore, counseling may be helpful.

Functional Limitations and Vocational Implications

The American Heart Association has devised a functional classification system for the identification of recommended activities. A class I rating indicates the presence of cardiac disease, but the person is asymptomatic with ordinary activity. A class II rating indicates slight limitations of activity. The person is comfortable at rest but, with ordinary physical activity, symptoms appear. A class III rating indicates that even with less than ordinary activity, symptoms appear, obligating the person to limit activities. A class IV rating is the most severe. The person is confined to bed, as any activity produces discomfort. (An earlier system classified activities by letters A–E, with A the least severe, and E the most severe.)

Peripheral Vascular Disorders

Peripheral vascular disorders are also referred to as arteriosclerosis of the extremities. One example is thromboangiitis obliterans, known also as Buerger's disease, a blockage of small peripheral arteries in the hands, fingertips, and feet. Men between the ages of twenty and forty-five and cigarette smokers are at greatest risk. Raynaud's disease is similar to Buerger's disease but more frequently affects young women.

Obliterative arterial disease is a severe form of a peripheral vascular disorder. It involves a slow progressive obstruction of the blood vessels in the lower part of the body, such as the abdomen, legs, or buttocks. If there is a complete loss of nutrients, gangrene may result and amputation may be required.

Thrombophlebitis is a medical problem in which the veins, usually in the legs, become inflamed. If clots form and break off, they could float to the heart, and lodge in the coronary or pulmonary arteries, causing cardiac distress.

Etiology and Diagnosis

Many of the peripheral vascular disorders are secondary to other circulatory or systemic problems. The onset is more frequently gradual and stress may be a contributing factor. Diagnosis can be made by clinical observation. Angiography or venography may also be used, especially if surgery is recommended.

Treatment and Prognosis

Medications are prescribed to ease the condition. A physical therapist may work with the person and develop an exercise program to minimize symptoms.

Functional Limitations and Vocational Implications

The person with a peripheral vascular disorder must take care to remove all factors that exacerbate the problem. Prolonged sitting or standing is contraindicated, as are physically strenuous activities. The person must work in a temperature-controlled environment, as extremes can aggravate the condition.

PULMONARY DISORDERS

Pulmonary disorders describe any condition that involves the lungs. The function of the lungs is to regulate breathing through inspiration, the taking in of air (oxygen), and expiration, the letting out of air (carbon dioxide).

As air passes through the nasal cavity, it leads to the pharynx, out the larynx (voice box) to the trachea, to the chest, where it passes into two chambers, the right and left bronchi, and then to the lungs. Ciliated (hairlike) cells prevent foreign bodies from entering the lungs.

The lungs are covered by a thin membrane, the pleura. Pleurisy is an inflammation of the fluid that lies between the membranes and the lungs.

Pneumonia is a common respiratory complication; one that can be fatal for many other systemic diseases and medical problems. An outbreak of a type of pneumonia among members of the American Legion in Philadelphia in 1976 led to pneumonia being called legionnaire's disease, which is now recognized as one of the most common forms of pneumonia.

Pulmonary impairment can result from allergies, exposure to irritating substances, such as pollen, household dust, or chemicals. It can also be an aftermath of other medical problems such as infections. In addition, industrial hazards, such as dusts or noxious fumes, can be the causal agent of pulmonary diseases.

The primary symptom of a pulmonary disorder is shortness of breath, or *dyspnea*. A grading system from I to V indicates the severity of dyspnea. A grade I rating indicates the presence of symptoms only with severe exertion; it is only mildly restricting, while a higher grade indicates more severe symptoms and dyspnea with minimal exertion, which may even be present when resting.

Chest imaging techniques, such as X-rays, CAT scans, MRI, and ultrasound of the lungs, are the most common diagnostic tools for pulmonary problems. A spirogram is a pulmonary function test that measures the maximum amount of inspiration and expiration blown in and out of a tube while a computer analyzes data.

Chronic obstructive pulmonary diseases (COPD) is a generalized descriptive term used to describe various disorders of the lungs. Bronchial asthma, emphysema, occupational lung diseases, and tuberculosis are among the COPD reviewed in this section.

Bronchial Asthma

Bronchial asthma is characterized by shallow rapid breathing, cough, and shortness of breath. It can be an acute or a chronic problem with asthmatic attacks lasting minutes to hours or days to weeks. Attacks can come and go without warning, leaving a person totally fatigued and overwhelmed.

Etiology and Diagnosis

Asthma can be present at birth or can occur at any age; the causal agent can be an infection or allergic reaction to some environmental agent. Breathing becomes labored and shallow. Coughing, wheezing, dyspnea, and the production of thick sputum are typically present. Asthma tends to be familial and stress-related. Seasonal temperature changes may bring on an attack.

Diagnosis is made on the basis of family history, laboratory tests, and results of imaging devices. In the past, asthma had been labeled a psychosomatic disorder, but more recent research has refuted this claim.

Treatment and Prognosis

Medical treatment is directed at relieving symptoms. Oxygen and antibiotics may be given. Allergy shots can be taken to minimize the number of attacks and relieve their intensity. Treatment also consists of the use of bronchodilators and steroids. Breathing exercises and training in relaxation or biofeedback may be prescribed. Sleep may be a problem, and the choking and gasping that may accompany asthma can be frightening. If asthma is not well controlled, emphysema can result. Children may eventually outgrow asthma. However, the effects of parental overprotection can be a problem in later years.

Functional Limitations and Vocational Implications

During and after an asthma attack, a person becomes greatly fatigued and activity must be restricted. Oxygen and hospitalization may be needed. As stress can bring on an attack, a person with asthma should avoid a high-stress environment, as well as irritants or a climate that is damp or cold. For example, work as a florist, farmer, or chemist is contraindicated. Vocational choice should be directed at nonexertional positions.

Emphysema

Emphysema is a destruction of the walls of the lungs. At first, small black holes appear; as the disease progresses, the holes become larger and tear the membranes, and this interfers with the normal exchange of carbon dioxide and oxygen. Breathing becomes labored and impaired. The lungs try to compensate for the decrease in viable lung tissue by enlarging. This forces the chest cavity to increase in size, giving persons who have advanced emphysema a barrel-chested appearance.

There are two main types of emphysema disorders. Type A, also known as type PP for "pink puffers," is characterized by a tendency toward thinness. There is progressive dyspnea and a scanty cough. In Type B, or type BB for "blue bloaters," victims look healthy except for a bluish discoloration of the lips and fingernails (cyanosis) and a tendency to collect excessive amounts of fluid in the body. They have chronic bronchitis, a hacking cough, and are constantly spitting up phlegm.

Etiology and Diagnosis

The cause of emphysema is unknown, but chronic bronchitis or irritating factors, such as cigarette smoking, exposure to environmental irritants, or chest infections may be the contributing factors. Medical evaluation is by chest imaging and spirogram.

Treatment and Prognosis

Damage to the lungs is irreversible. Treatment is directed at alleviating symptoms. Antibiotics are prescribed to prevent infection. General health must be maintained to keep symptoms in abeyance.

Respiratory therapists are vital allied health professionals who are part of any team assigned to the person who has emphysema. They help educate the patient to minimize symptoms. The person is taught to tap his or her chest (chest percussion) to aid in decongestion. A diet high in fluid intake is encouraged, to prevent dehydration and produce more liquid secretions. Intermittent positive pressure breathing (IPPB) facilitates inhalation through the use of a mouthpiece.

Medications such as antibiotics and steroids may be prescribed. Aerosols, mists containing medications, are also used. The patient is warned against the tendency to overuse and become dependent on aerosols, as they can irritate the bronchial tubes.

Functional Limitations and Vocational Implications

The person with advanced emphysema will be short of breath. Activities must be restricted in general and avoided altogether in cold weather. Depression caused by a fear of death can result in overprotection by family members.

Work that is fatiguing is contraindicated. Factory work involving exposure to dust or fumes and construction work should also be eliminated.

Occupational Lung Diseases

Occupational lung diseases are directly related to exposure to irritating properties in the work environment. Often symptoms do not appear until late in the disease process, complicating the prognosis.

Examples include silicosis which can be caused by working in a metal-mining, foundry, sandstone, granite-cutting, or pottery-making industry. In coal miners, black lung disease, or anthracosis, may result from exposure to dust. Asbestosis is the consequence of inhalation of asbestos fibers found in mining, milling, and manufacturing or in the application of asbestos products.

Etiology and Diagnosis

Diagnosis of any of the occupational lung diseases is confirmed by X-rays and other imaging devices. The etiology can be typically traced to a particular career or lifestyle.

Treatment and Prognosis

Treatment is aimed at the relief of symptoms. The prognosis depends on the length of exposure to the hazardous substances.

Functional Limitations and Vocational Implications

Dyspnea is the result of exertion, so the person is unable to tolerate strenuous exercises or activities. If the person is able to return to some type of job, a controlled environment, where the work is sedentary or light, is recommended.

Tuberculosis

Tuberculosis (TB) was originally called consumption and found among the malnourished and impoverished population. The incidence of TB has been greatly reduced in developed countries thanks to early diagnostic tests and the pasteurization of milk. However, recently there has been a resurgence of TB in urban areas, among the homeless, alcoholics, and drug abusers.

Etiology and Diagnosis

Tuberculosis is contagious when the bacteria becomes airborne by a cough. Diagnosis is based on x-ray findings and laboratory tests.

Treatment and Prognosis

At one time the TB patient was isolated in a sanitarium, as there was a fear in spreading the disease. Today drugs render the infected person noninfectious. If left untreated, TB can involve gradual loss of lung tissue and cause other medical complications.

Functional Limitations and Vocational Implications

Tuberculosis can now be controlled to the point symptoms can abate and residual functioning is normal. Physically or mentally stressful jobs should be avoided.

ENDOCRINE DISORDERS

The endocrine glands regulate metabolic functioning by hormones. Either an excess or a lack of hormones will produce abnormal metabolic functioning, in which growth and development, reproduction potential, and energy utilization may be adversely affected.

The major endocrine glands include the pituitary, abnormal functioning of which can result in dwarfism or giantism; the thyroid, of which hypofunctioning can result in Gull's disease, and hyperfunctioning in Grave's disease; the adrenals, of which hypofunctioning can result in Addison's or Cushing's disease; and the pancreas, of which abnormal functioning produces diabetes. The endocrine glands also play a major part in the development of the gonads, or sex glands, and if malfunctioning, there may be other problems. Discussion in this section is limited to diabetes mellitus, the most common endocrine disorder.

Diabetes Mellitus

Diabetes mellitus (diabetes) is a chronic disorder of metabolism that affects all body systems. In this disease of the insulin-producing cells of the pancreas, a lack of insulin to the blood supply results in impaired utilization of carbohydrates and glucose. Without insulin action, blood sugar levels rise dangerously high (hyperglycemia). Fat is broken down for energy, forming ketones, which change the acid-base balance of the blood. This can lead to ketoacidosis, which if left untreated, can lead to hallucinations or a diabetic coma. Complications include heart disease, diabetic retinopathy, and damage to other blood vessels.

Hypoglycemia is the exact opposite of diabetes and yet the precursor of it. An excess of blood sugar drives blood sugar levels below normal, triggering a craving for sweets. Other symptoms, such as dizziness, headaches, fatigue, poor circulation in the extremities, insomnia, or crying spells, may be experienced. In an attempt to relieve symptoms, the person ingests more sugar. This stops the discomfort temporarily but leads to further craving for sugar, causing the person to experience highs and lows and interfering with smooth metabolic functioning.

Etiology and Diagnosis

There are two main classes of diabetes: type I, or juvenile diabetes, in which the body is unable to produce or use insulin, and type II, or adult-onset diabetes. Type I is the more severe form of the disorder, requiring daily injections of insulin to maintain life. Type II diabetes is less threatening and is found mainly in adults who are overweight. The body has the ability to produce insulin but is unable to use it effectively. This form can often be controlled with a strict diet, although oral insulin may also be required. There is a genetic predisposition to either form.

Diagnosis is by urinalysis or a blood test known as a glucose tolerance test. There are some warning signals to signify that the body has lost some of its ability to use glucose. *Polydipsia* is characterized by a high level of glucose spilling into the urine, making the person feel extremely thirsty and leading to an excessive need to urinate, referred to as *polyuria. Polyphagia*, excessive hunger, is another symptom, as are blurred vision and loss of weight or strength.

Treatment and Prognosis

There is no cure for diabetes. Numerous complications may include: narrowing of the arterial blood vessels, producing thrombosis, which could result in a myocardial infarction or a stroke; the development of gangrene in the extremities; gastrointestinal distress; sexual impotence; and bladder infections. Diabetic retinopathy is the leading cause of blindness in the United States.

Treatment is by diet, weight control, exercise, and insulin. Stress management techniques are also believed to be helpful for the diabetic, as stress is related to hormonal changes.

Functional Limitations and Vocational Implications

The person who has diabetes is at risk of developing other systemic problems. Stress-free work, without rotating shifts (so the person can eat at regular and predictable times) is recommended. In addition, work in a temperature-controlled environment is best, as extreme temperatures often impair circulation.

There is a psychosocial reaction to being dependent on a substance (in this case insulin) for life. Some stigma may be imposed by others, as the diabetic may have to inject himself or herself at particular intervals throughout the day.

GASTROINTESTINAL DISORDERS

The major function of the gastrointestinal (GI) system is to metabolize food substances into a form that can be used by the body to carry out life-sustaining activities. The GI tract includes the mouth and tongue, esophagus, stomach, small and large intestines, and rectum. Ancillary organs include the liver, gallbladder, and pancreas. Problems with any of these structures can result in a GI disorder. Although GI disorders have unique characteristics, they share a similar etiology, symptoms, and treatment. Some of the more common disorders are discussed under a single general category here.

Gastrointestinal Disorders

Crohn's disease is a condition in which there is chronic inflammation of the small bowel. It most frequently attacks persons of Jewish ancestry, and Europeans, and it is seen more often in whites than in nonwhites. It is characterized by a thickening and inflammation of all layers of the intestinal wall.

Diverticulosis affects many people over fifty years of age. It is an inflammation of the lower or sigmoid colon and is more common in men than in women. Many attacks are mild and clear up by themselves. At one time, patients were advised to eat a soft diet and avoid roughage such as bran. Today high-fiber diets are recommended as a preventive measure against diverticulosis.

Irritable bowel syndrome, or spastic colon, is a disorder in which intestinal contractions propel food and waste along the GI tract, causing cramps and other GI distress. Women are more likely to suffer than men.

Ulcerative colitis is a chronic disease characterized by inflammation of the inner lining of the colon and rectum. The entire colon or only the last segment of the colon, the sigmoid, may be involved. In most cases, the attacks are intermittent and come and go without warning.

Etiology and Diagnosis

The etiology of most GI disorders is unknown. Causal theories range from genetics, infections, or faults in the body's immune system; stress may also be a contributing factor. Symptoms are varied but generally include abdominal pain, constipation or diarrhea, bloating, nausea and vomiting, and in some cases, rectal bleeding. Laboratory tests help confirm the presence of the disorder. Included in these tests are X-rays and other imaging devices, family history, clinical interviews, and observation.

Treatment and Prognosis

There is no cure for GI disorders. The course of most GI diseases is unpredictable. Drugs can offer relief from symptoms of pain and discomfort, and bed rest and tranquilizers may be prescribed. Surgery may be recommended in some cases. Emotional support and dietary changes may also be helpful.

Functional Limitations and Vocational Implications

When symptoms are not present, normal activities may be carried out and there are no functional limitations. When symptoms are present, the person is typically homebound and unable to work. If the person has a highly stressful job, a career change may be necessary.

RENAL DISORDERS

The kidneys act as a filtration system designed to rid the body of materials that are no longer needed. Two kidneys are located in the back of the abdomen on either side of the body, each composed of about one million separate functioning units called nephrons. The head of each kidney is called the glomerulus. It is through this mechanism that blood filtrate is converted (approximately every thirty minutes) to urine, which passes into the ureter and then to the bladder. In addition to filtering the blood, the kidneys are involved in controlling blood pressure, red blood formation, metabolism of insulin, and regulation of the acid and base balance of sodium and potassium.

Kidney problems can be chronic or acute, reversible or irreversible. They can result from an infection or obstruction, or be secondary to other diseases such as diabetes and hypertension. They can occur at any age and may be related to a familial or genetic influence.

A clinical examination may confirm the presence of kidney problems, as retention of excess salt causes puffiness of the extremities and face. Other general diagnostic procedures include blood and urine analysis, radiographic procedures such as X-rays, ultrasound, CAT or MRI scans, and biopsy. *End-stage renal disease* has far-reaching medical and psychosocial implications that can be generalized to other renal problems; this section is therefore limited to a review of this disorder.

End-Stage Renal Disease

If the kidneys shut down, toxic substances build up in the blood and an ammonia-like substance (urea) builds up in the body. If left untreated, death will result.

Etiology and Diagnosis

Edema (swelling) is an early warning sign that the kidneys are not functioning properly. Hematuria (blood in the urine) is another signal. Laboratory findings confirm the presence and extent of the disease.

Treatment and Prognosis

Diuretics are prescribed to rid the body of excess fluid. Antibiotics are prescribed to reduce inflammation.

A person only needs one kidney to sustain life. In the event that both kidneys fail, a kidney transplant can be performed. To avoid the complications of transplant rejection, the ideal donor would be an identical twin. The next best donor is a sibling who has a similar blood makeup. A last resort is to receive a kidney from an unrelated person. This is possible, and it may be life-saving, but immunological problems are more likely to occur.

Hemodialysis is an mechanical detoxifying process that can take over the work of the kidneys. A fistula or shunt is constructed in the forearm, which connects the body to plastic tubes from the artificial kidney. The patient's unfiltered blood is pumped through a solution in which impurities and normal blood constituents are diffused and discarded. The cleansed blood is then returned to the person. The process typically takes three to four hours at each session and is done three times a week. The machine can be placed in the home, although it is more common for the person to travel to a dialysis center or hospital.

Functional Limitations and Vocational Implications

A person on dialysis has limited mobility. Chronic pain may be a factor. There may be complications such as recurrent bleeding into the joints, causing swelling (hemarthrosis). This can lead to degenerative joint disease and other complications.

There is a psychosocial overlay to dialysis. A reduction in energy, and sexual functioning, the loss of independence, and the threat of the loss of life may be factors precipitating depression.

Hemodialysis is both expensive and inconvenient. Family members may be overwhelmed by the cost in time, money, and energy; counseling may be helpful.

If the person is able to work, a part-time situation may be most practical. Heat intolerance can be a problem because of a failure to perspire normally; nonexertional work in a temperature-controlled environment is recommended.

BURNS

Burns are typically associated with an accident. Persons working with electricity or around heat or fumes are most vulnerable. Burns may also be the result of a motor vehicle crash or other accident.

Etiology and Diagnosis

There are three classifications for burns. First-degree burns are confined to the outer layer of the skin (epidermis) and are the most superficial type of burn. The circulation of the blood is unaffected and complications may be few. Second-degree burns are deeper and affect the blood vessels and nerve endings. The area is red, swollen, and blistered, and circulation is affected. Third-degree burns are the most severe. The nerve endings have been destroyed and circulation is impaired. The skin has a charred and blackened appearance.

Treatment and Prognosis

The person who experiences residual pain in the burn area is considered luckier than the person who experiences little or no pain; lack of pain signifies the nerve endings have been destroyed and rehabilitation will be more lengthy.

Hospitalization is required for all major burns. Trained personnel must monitor vital signs and be on guard against pneumonia or renal failure. The victim is also at increased risk of infections. The period of hospitalization is very stressful both for the patient and the family. The burn victim may experience excruciating pain both from the burn and the frequent cleansing required; unfortunately, pain medication must be kept to a minimum so that the extent of damage can be determined. It is difficult for family members to sit by and recognize that pain is a hopeful sign.

Skin grafting describes the process in which healthy portions of the person's skin are removed and applied to areas in which the skin is burned. At a later date, reconstructive or plastic surgery may be performed.

Scarring can be kept to a minimum by the person wearing elasticized, skinlike garments made by the Jobst Company. They protect the raw skin against infection, sun, temperature changes, and other environmental agents.

Functional Limitations and Vocational Implications

The physical therapist and occupational therapist work to assist the person to avoid stiffening of the joints. The recuperation period is lengthy; return to work will depend on the type of job: indoor temperature-controlled conditions and a nonexertional activity will expedite the ability to return to work.

BLINDNESS

Legal blindness is defined as 20/200 in the better eye with corrective lenses. Those who have total loss of vision and those who have some limited visual field are considered legally blind. Blindness can be the result of a congenital problem (e.g., rubella during the first trimester of the fetus's life), a developmental problem (cataracts), complications from a disease (e.g., syphilis or cancer), or an accident. In adults, the leading cause of blindness is diabetic retinopathy.

The ophthalmologist is the physician who works with eye problems. An optometrist is not a medical doctor but rather functions to test the loss of a visual field.

The major problems for persons who are blind are limited mobility and limited opportunities to be independent. Many assistive devices have been developed to address these needs. They include the use of Braille, tape recorders, talking books, finger spelling, and a cane or a seeing-eye dog. Rehabilitation engineers continue to develop other electronic devices to increase discrimination and the use of other senses that may aid the person to experience greater autonomy. Glaucoma will serve as an example to further explain blindness.

Glaucoma

Glaucoma results from pressure within the eye. The disease may be asymptomatic until irreversible damage has occurred. At first, there is loss of peripheral vision, then central vision. Left untreated total blindness may result.

Etiology and Diagnosis

The etiology of glaucoma is unknown but it may be secondary to other medical problems. Diagnosis is made with a tonometer by measuring intraocular pressure and by clinical history.

Treatment and Prognosis

Glaucoma is treated by medication to control pressure. Surgery may be recommended, depending on the cause and extent of the disease. Early diagnosis is critical for a favorable prognosis.

Functional Limitations and Vocational Implications

The person who has glaucoma or blindness can be employed in any of a variety of jobs, in which the employer will have to agree to minor job modifications. Transportation may be a major handicapping problem that will need to be addressed. Inside work of a nonexertional nature is recommended.

HEARING IMPAIRMENT

Hearing impairment refers to any reduction or sensitivity to sounds. Deafness is the extreme inability to discriminate conversational speech. Total deafness is rare.

An otologist or an audiologist evaluates the extent of hearing loss using an audiometer. Hearing in each ear is measured in decibels and expressed as frequencies known as cycles per second, or Hertz, plotted on a graph called an audiogram. The speech pathologist is the professional who works with the person to minimize adverse and limiting effects of the hearing impairment.

Etiology and Diagnosis

Deafness is classified as either conductive deafness or sensorineural deafness. In conductive deafness, problems with the outer or middle ear cause a failure in the transmission of sound waves. An example is *otosclerosis*, in which a spongy growth of bone develops in the middle ear. Sensorineural deafness involves the inner ear such as Menière's syndrome, where the person experiences vertigo (dizziness) and tinnitus (ringing or tinkling sounds in the ear).

Hearing impairments can be the result of illness such as measles, mumps, meningitis, or inner ear infection. They can be caused by the development of rubella during the first trimester of pregnancy (with mental retardation often a second handicapping condition), or it can have a genetic basis.

Treatment and Prognosis

The time of life that hearing becomes impaired is a critical factor in assessing the extent of a handicapping condition. For example, if the loss was present at birth, or during early intellectual development, the result will be more traumatic than if the person acquired deafness later in life from trauma or disease, as speech will be more difficult to acquire.

226

Functional Limitations and Vocational Implications

Isolation is a major problem for the person who has a hearing impairment. The teletypewriter, or TTY, is a machine on which messages can be typed and transmitted by telephone to a receiving machine that types the messages. Close-captioned television programs are also available. These technological advances have greatly minimized isolation problems, decreasing the extent of functional limitations.

Hearing aids and other assistive devices have also helped reduce any functional limitations imposed by a hearing impairment. At one time, hearing aids were large and cumbersome. Today the sophistication of electronics has greatly minimized stigma in wearing a hearing aid, and many devices are not at all obvious to others. This, plus the use of manual communication techniques, has helped the hearing-impaired population express their abilities and interests.

With regard to employment opportunities, only minor modifications are needed. One example is that visual cues be made available for safety.

MENTAL RETARDATION

Mental retardation is a condition of subaverage intellectual functioning, existing concurrently with deficiencies in adaptive behavior, having its roots during the developmental period. It is the greatest single cause of disability among children in the United States.

The condition may range from mild to profound. Historically, parents who had a child diagnosed as mentally retarded would be advised to place the child in an institution. Today most children live at home and attend school and, as adults, become employed.

There is a difference between a child who has a learning disability (LD) and one who is mentally retarded (MR). The LD child has normal intelligence but has difficulties in learning. There may be other behavioral symptoms that contribute to the learning problem, including hyperactivity, poor coordination, immaturity, or a poor or short attention span. The LD label is ambiguous. Many children are categorized as LD, because their parents prefer it to the MR label. A need exists whereby the LD term is defined operationally.

Etiology and Diagnosis

There are a myriad of causes of mental retardation, which may include genetics, faulty metabolism, trauma at birth or in the early developmental ages, or disease. For example, Down's syndrome involves an extra chromosome (47 instead of 46); Klinefelter's and Turner's syndromes involve an abnormality in the sex chromosomes. Phenylketonuria (PKU) is the result of abnormal digestion of protein, and cretinism is a severe iodine deficiency; left untreated, these conditions can result in mental retardation.

During pregnancy, problems can arise that lead to mental retardation. Examples include the development of toxemia, an excess of poisons or waste in the mother's blood; rubella or German measles during the first trimester of pregnancy; syphilis, transmitted from the mother; or exposure of the mother to excessive radiation, such as X-rays, during the first trimester of pregnancy.

Children of chronic alcoholic mothers may be born with fetal alcohol syndrome, which includes mental and growth retardation (intrauterine growth retardation), as well as numerous other physical problems. Lead poisoning or a high fever during critical growth periods can also cause mental retardation.

The classification of mental retardation is by a measure of intelligence on some standardized test. The scales most widely used are the Stanford-Binet and the Wechsler Scales. An intelligence quotient (IQ) below 70 or 75 indicates that the person is operating at a deficient level.

Treatment and Prognosis

Mental retardation is a lifelong condition. There is no cure but, depending on the cause, further damage may be controlled by a particular medical or psychosocial program. As soon as mental retardation is suspected, parents should involve the child in needed services and should also be provided counseling to cope with the uncertainty of the label.

A multidisciplinary team consisting of special educators, physical and occupational therapists, and school and rehabilitation counselors can help develop a program and provide understanding regarding the extent of the handicapping condition. An individualized program can be developed with a focus on the child's abilities.

Functional Limitations and Vocational Implications

One problem for the person who has some mental retardation is overprotection from family members. The child can be so sheltered as to be robbed of the opportunity to learn how to get along with others or to gain independence in activities of daily living. Nonhandicapped siblings may resent getting less attention than their handicapped sibling; this can result in family trauma.

Functional limitations vary from person to person, as mental retardation is not the same for all individuals. Most people who have some degree of mental retardation can be trained to work as either a sheltered or competitive employee.

PSYCHIATRIC DISORDERS

Psychiatric disorders describe conditions in which persons are emotionally unstable and overstressed to the point of being unable to carry out the activities required for daily living. Diagnostic procedures are available that discriminate among the various types of mental health disorders.

Three conditions are discussed in this section: Eating disorders gives an overview of anorexia and bulimia. The second, and largest, section summarizes some of the main mental health and affective disorders. Because substance abusers have been considered as having the potential to have a psychiatric problem, substance abuse has been placed in this section as the third category.

Eating Disorders

Anorexia nervosa and bulimia are both characterized by severe weight loss and an intense fear of becoming obese. The anorectic becomes preoccupied with food and eats very little. The bulimic eats in binges, followed by induced vomiting and the use of laxatives and diuretics to purge herself of unwanted calories. Onset is usually during adolescence and is more commonly found in young women from middle and upper socioeconomic families.

Etiology and Diagnosis

The etiology of eating disorders is unknown but is related to societal values equating thinness with attractiveness. Certain personality attributes, such as compulsiveness, perfectionism, and orientation to high achievement and success, are common. Amenorrhea often accompanies eating disorders, caused by a loss of needed body fat required for menstruation; this has lead to eating disorders being described as a way for the young woman to delay the process whereby reproduction is possible.

Treatment and Prognosis

Treatment is aimed at restoring needed body weight. Individual, group, and family counseling are typically needed to learn and understand the source of the problem. Because of a strong tendency to deny the existence of the illness and manipulative behaviors, counseling is more difficult than would appear on the surface. Once the person admits the problem and gains an understanding of how the condition came to be, there can be complete and successful resolution.

Functional Limitations and Vocational Implications

Once the condition is controlled, no functional limitations remain, nor are there any restrictions or special considerations with respect to career or vocational choice.

Mental Illness

There are four general types of mental illness: *psychoses, neuroses, organic brain syndromes,* and *personality disorders.* The person who suffers from psychosis does not deal adequately with reality. He or she may be disoriented to time, place, and person. With neurosis, the person maintains touch with reality but is debilitated by severe anxiety. He or she is unable to fulfill needs and is prevented from successfully dealing with emotions and environmental demands. (Stolovic & Clowers, 1981).

Organic brain syndromes can be either temporary or permanent, depending on the cause, such as head trauma resulting from a fall or motor vehicle accident, or a disease involving the central nervous system or the brain (e.g., encephalitis, stroke, alcohol abuse, or a toxic reaction from a medication).

A personality disorder is the result of some maladaptive pattern of relating, perceiving, or thinking. It can be either treatable or resistant to treatment. For example, the sociopathic personality is an antisocial person who is aware of self-centered behaviors but who is not willing to give them up and be inconvenienced in any way; this type of personality disorder is typically not amenable to treatment, as any problem is viewed as environmental and not residing in the self.

Other personality disorders include *schizophrenia,* which is the biggest catchall label for a personality disorder; *bipolar affective disorders; somatoform disorders;* and *phobias.*

There are many types of schizophrenia. One example is a paranoid type, characterized by visions of persecution, grandeur, or suspicion. Generally, schizophrenia is described as the absence of full affective abilities and a tendency toward chronic deterioration of personality accompanied by problems with communication, behavior, and perception lasting more than six months.

Bipolar affective disorder, also known as manic depression, is another major affective disorder, which is characterized by mood swings manifested as either manic episodes—excitement, hyperactivity, and euphoria—or depressive episodes—feelings of worthlessness and hopelessness, slowed thinking, or extreme guilt.

Somatoform disorders describe conditions in which there is some overt physical problem but no verifiable organic findings to explain these symptoms. Examples include hypochondria, preoccupations with a medical disorder; or chronic pain, where the basis of pain is psychogenic rather than organic. Phobias, described as an obsessive and unrealistic fear of some object or situation, have the potential to lead to a somatoform disorder.

Etiology and Diagnosis

There is no single cause of mental illness. Genetic factors, coupled with certain personality characteristics, and environmental considerations have been used to explain and understand vulnerability or predisposition to a disorder.

The basis for the specific type of mental illness comes from the third edition of the *Diagnostic and Statistical Manual of Mental Disorders*, more commonly referred to as the DSM-III-R. This guide to classic disorders attempts to rely on clinical interviews in which what the person says and does are indicators of functioning. Problems are classified along a mild, moderate, or severe continuum.

Other than clinical interviews by a psychologist or psychiatrist, diagnostic techniques include: brain scans, such as the EEG (electroencephalogram), showing graphic changes in electric potential produced by the brain; the CAT scan; and the spinal tap. The PET scan (Positron Emission Tomography) is a more recent technique, which provides information about the structure and functioning of the brain by measuring the metabolic activity of specific areas of the brain.

Treatment and Prognosis

Prognosis depends on the severity of the illness and the causative factors. A person's premorbid personality before the illness can also be a factor for progress and recovery.

Antipsychotic or psychotropic drugs are typically prescribed to control symptoms. Undesired side effects of most of the drugs include blurred vision, impotence, tremors, tardive dyskinesia (involuntary movement of the face or other parts of the body, such as smacking of the lips), and cognitive impairment.

Other treatments include electroconvulsive shock therapy (ECT), where an electric current is applied to the brain to induce a convulsive type of a seizure; or a lobotomy, a brain operation. Individual, group and family counseling, and hypnosis have also been found helpful.

Functional Limitations and Vocational Implications

Mental health disorders have an unpredictable nature. Many clients are able to live and work independently or live in group homes where there is minimal supervision, with symptoms under control for a long period of time. Unfortunately, with added stress, symptoms may reappear and total services may once again be needed.

When symptoms are present, the ability to think, emote, and act appropriately is grossly impaired to the point that the person is unable to carry out needed activities of daily living. Feelings of low self-esteem may further complicate the problem. An evaluation is necessary to determine needed services and develop a realistic career goal. Generally a structured work environment and tasks that are organized help the person with a psychiatric disorder to maintain employment are essential. Examples of this type of work include routine clerical or factory work, where needed interaction with co-workers is at a minimum.

Substance Abuse

The use of chemical substances such as alcohol and drugs is an escalating problem in the United States. As a society, we tend to deliver mixed messages that both encourage users yet ostracize abusers. In some social groups, it is fashionable and social to use mood-altering substances, and those who do not join in may be left out and considered unsociable. The problem is seen in all age and occupational groups, but the choice of a particular substance may be more representative in one population than another. For example, the older person may be more at risk of abusing cocaine, while the school-age person may be more involved with either alcohol or marijuana. For either group, there is a risk that more than one drug may be abused.

A major problem with abusers is that they may have sociopathic tendencies (see *Mental Illness*). Yet, for successful treatment the person must admit there is a problem and have a willingness to change. In addition, cooperation must be elicited from others in the abuser's system, such as family, friends, or employer.

Alcohol is a short-acting drug that depresses the central nervous system (CNS). All CNS depressants foster physiological tolerance, such that the person needs greater and greater amounts of the substance to experience the same effect. The larger amounts and continued use of alcohol result in physical, psychological, sensory, and muscular dysfunctioning.

Cirrhosis of the liver is a problem for the chronic and long-term user of alcohol; scar tissue builds up to the point that the liver is impaired and unable to metabolize nutrients vital for healthy functioning. The person has a swollen abdomen and jaundice, a yellowing of the skin. As the liver loses the ability to function, the brain eventually becomes unable to receive needed nutrients, and irreversible brain damage may result.

Korsakoff's psychosis, result of advanced alcoholism, is marked by a gradual decline in intellectual ability resulting from progressive brain destruction. Memory problems are noted, in which large blocks of time become erased and the learning of new behaviors may be limited.

Fetal alcohol syndrome occurs when the alcoholic mother has passed alcohol through the umbilical cord to the unborn fetus during critical stages of development. This can cause the child to be born with facial and limb irregularities, heart defects, low birthweight, and mental retardation.

In addition to these complications, many other problems can result from alcohol abuse, including pancreatitis, gastro-intestinal problems, or impotence.

Drugs that are abused include opioid types, such as heroin; barbiturates, such as sedatives and tranquilizers; cannabis; marijuana; cocaine; amphetamines; hallucinogens; and others. The choice of a drug depends on the desired effect and can range from having a calming effect (sedatives) to having a feeling of euphoria and heightened activity (hallucinogens).

Tolerance is a similar problem for the drug abuser as it is for the alcoholic, even though the etiology of the tolerance may be from a psychological, rather than a physiological, basis. Where one begins and the other leaves off is a confounding problem, and psychological addiction can be just as much of a problem for the addicted person.

Etiology and Diagnosis

There is much disagreement among professionals as to the etiology of substance abuse. Hypotheses include a genetic predisposition, the result of an inadequate personality, or an environment in which drinking or using drugs was learned by imitating others.

Treatment and Prognosis

The person must agree to be detoxified before treatment can begin. A number of behavioral techniques, such as hypnosis, group and individual counseling, and aversive conditioning, have helped the substance abuser break the habit. The person must be willing to take responsibility for his or her own actions, or the treatment program will not be successful.

Delirium tremens describes the condition in which there is some aversive reaction to withdrawal, a condition that can be life threatening. The person may convulse, have seizures or hallucinations, or could fall into a hypoglycemic coma as a result of a rapid drop in blood sugar levels. This is why the chemical abuser must be detoxified under medical supervision. To maintain a sober or drug-free state, support groups such as Alcohol Anonymous and Narcotics Anonymous have helped the substance abuser remain free from substance dependence.

Functional Limitations and Vocational Implications

If the person has stopped abusing before the body suffers permanent damage, functional limitations are either minimal or nonexistent. On many occasions, persons have hit bottom before admitting to a problem; many times the person has either lost his or her job, or faces going to jail before help is sought. Employee assistance programs are available in many companies throughout the United States to prevent this from happening.

Substance abuse tends to be a "revolving door" problem for many people. The person gives up the substance, only to start using it again, and the detoxification process has to be repeated. Stress can precipitate reliance on substances. Counseling can help guard against this phenomenon. The person is also encouraged to seek a job in a low-stress, structured environment.

To test your understanding of the medical and psychosocial aspects of disabilities, answer the following questions:

1. Why does medical terminology exist?

2. Why would someone want to remain in pain?

3. Why is back pain such a common and complicated problem?

4. Why should a person who has epilepsy avoid alcohol?

5. Why may families resist documenting the presence of Alzheimer's disease?

6. Why should body weight be controlled?

7. Why is cancer such a feared disease?

8. Why was asthma once thought to have a psychogenic origin?

9. Why may tuberculosis be on the rise in the United States?

10. How is an elevated stress level hazardous to one's health?

11. Why would blindness be considered the most limiting of all disabilities?

12. Why do parents who are expecting a child experience both anxiety and joy?

13. Why are some people with mental illness able to work, while others are not?

14. Why may a hearing-impaired person be deficient in social skills?

15. Why may alcohol treatment not be successful?

SELECTED REFERENCES

The following references are suggested for further study:

American Psychiatric Association (1987). *Diagnostic and Statistical Manual of Mental Disorders* (3rd ed.). Washington D.C.: Author.

Berkow, R. (Ed.). (1987). *The Merck Manual of Diagnosis and Therapy* (15th ed.). Rahway, NJ: Merck Sharp & Dohme.

Goldenson, R. M. (Ed.). (1978). *Disability and Rehabilitation Handbook*. New York: McGraw-Hill.

Hylbert, K. W. (1979). *Medical Information for Human Service Workers* (2nd ed.). State College, PA: Counselor Education Press.

Stolov, W. C., and Clowers, M. R. (1981). *Handbook of Severe Disability*. Washington, D.C.: Rehabilitation Services Administration, U.S. Department of Education.

Section

V

Test Bank

TIPS ON TAKING A MULTIPLE-CHOICE TEST

1. The night before the examination, get a good night's sleep. Eat breakfast the morning of the examination, so that your energy level will be adequate. Arrive at the testing facility at least thirty minutes in advance, so you will not feel rushed or anxious about being late.

2. Once in the examination room, put away all your study materials and relax. Do some self-talk to increase your confidence.

3. Read each question thoroughly. Notice such words as "always" and "never," and carefully consider the exclusive nature of these modifiers.

4. Do not read more into a question than is already there.

5. Watch for double negatives.

6. Budget your time. Make a quick survey to see how many questions you will be expected to answer within a given time period. For items on which you have doubts, make a mark in the margin and proceed to the next item.

7. Don't leave questions unanswered.

8. Don't change answers unless you are sure you are changing an incorrect response to a correct one.

9. Try recalling by associating with other information. Other questions may also provide clues.

10. Do not look for patterns in responses.

11. Anticipate the correct answer before reading the choices.

12. If time permits, check over your responses. Do not feel pressured to finish when others do.

(The major reference for this information was from Shertzer, 1985, pp. 46–48.)

TEST BANK

History, Legal and Professional Ethics, and Service Delivery

1. A client informs the counselor in confidence that he or she is planning to burn down the neighbor's barn. The counselor's obligation is:

   a. to record the information in the client's file

   b. to report the information to involved parties and to the authorities

   c. to inform his or her supervisor

   d. both (b) and (c)

2. A counselor is sexually attracted to a client. Which answer is ethically sound?

   a. The counselor should be honest and inform the client and see what happens next.

   b. The counselor should refer the client to another counselor without any explanation.

   c. The counselor should refer the client but first explain the situation.

   d. The counselor should act in a professional manner and deny the attraction.

3. A code of ethics:

   a. is a legally binding document

   b. varies widely among specialized counselors

   c. has boundaries determined by state legislation

   d. governs professional conduct

4. All codes of ethics state the counselor's primary responsibility is to the:

   a. profession

   b. agency

   c. client

   d. supervisor

5. The supervisor of a counseling agency drinks alcohol on the job to steady nerves. As a subordinate, you should:

   a. not say anything

   b. report the supervisor to a higher authority

   c. counsel the supervisor and assist him or her to schedule an appointment with the Employee Assistance Counselor

   d. confront the supervisor before taking any action

6. If the counselor does not feel competent to deal with a particular problem a client has, the counselor should:

   a. immediately terminate the relationship

   b. discuss referral to another agency with the client

   c. offer co-therapy to the client

   d. refocus the client to discuss an area that is comfortable

7. You have worked with a particular client for more than one year and there has been practically no progress. You should:

   a. refer the client to another counselor

   b. be patient and wait for the client to initiate the desired changes

   c. request psychometric testing

   d. try a new counseling strategy or technique

8. Is it necessary for counselors to continue their education?

   a. No, as college training is intended to be comprehensive.

   b. No, it would take away from time spent serving clients.

   c. Yes, as it is essential to incorporate new research and data into an existing knowledge base.

   d. Yes, or clients will be more likely to file a malpractice charge.

9. Counselors in training often tape-record their sessions so that they may be provided supervision. When taping:

   a. the tape recorder should be out of sight so that it is not a distraction

   b. the client must first agree to the taping

   c. the client must be informed who will listen to the tape

   d. all of the above

10. Privileged communication is whatever a client tells a counselor during a counseling session. The counselor is obligated not to share the information with anyone else unless:

    a. there is clear and imminent danger to others

    b. the client is a minor

    c. the client lacks a definite well-laid-out plan to harm another person or property

    d. all of the above

11. You are a drug and alcohol counselor in a public school system. A 14-year old student asks to see you to discuss a substance abuse problem. You are obligated to tell:

    a. the principal

    b. the homeroom teacher

    c. the parents

    d. none of the above

12. While on the way home from work, the school counselor notices a transaction in which one of his or her students is buying marijuana. The counselor is ethically bound to:

    a. stop the transaction

    b. notify the police

    c. call the student to the office the following day

    d. do nothing

13. Your client informs you he or she is not taking prescribed medication because the side effects are unpleasant. As the counselor you:

    a. do nothing

    b. refer the client to the doctor to discuss the problem

    c. refuse to see the client until the prescription is followed

    d. ask for permission to consult with the doctor

14. As a private practitioner, you are seeing a particular client for career counseling. You learn inadvertently that the client is also seeing a psychiatrist. Under ethical guidelines, you may:

    a. continue to see the client without contacting the psychiatrist

    b. continue to see the client but ask to contact the psychiatrist

    c. contact the psychiatrist before proceeding

    d. pretend you are unaware the client is also seeing a psychiatrist

15. Regarding ethics and advertising:

    a. Professional advertising is unethical.

    b. There are currently no standards for advertising.

    c. Only counselors who are state licensed may advertise.

    d. none of the above

16. The National Board for Counselor Certification is intended to certify:

  a. rehabilitation counselors

  b. generic counselors

  c. mental health counselors

  d. career counselors

17. Family counseling is typically referred to professional group agencies because:

  a. caseloads may be too large

  b. it may be difficult to get the family together

  c. professional training may be inadequate

  d. all of the above

18. Public outcry over the establishment of group homes may be explained in part by the belief that:

  a. property values will go down

  b. crime will decrease

  c. too many people are living under one roof

  d. all of the above

19. Recidivism refers to:

  a. a revolving door phenomenon in which clients continuously return for services

  b. the alcoholic withdrawing from the substance

  c. evaluation procedures

  d. the development of a counseling plan

20. Client success in a plan depends on:

  a. client motivation

  b. community resources

  c. cooperation of the family

  d. all of the above

21. Which of the following is not a consideration when making a client referral?

  a. Information should be objective.

  b. The counselor should have a specific request.

  c. The client must be consulted.

  d. The counselor may refer without client approval.

22. Schools require parental approval for counseling minors in all but which of the following situations?

  a. peer pressure

  b. birth control information

    c. suicide

    d. abuse or neglect

23. The Council for Accreditation of Counseling and Related Educational Programs laid the basis for which of the following credentials?

    a. National Certified Counselor

    b. Certified Rehabilitation Counselor

    c. Marital and Family Counselor

    d. Drug and Alcohol Counselor

24. When planning research activities involving human subjects, the following must be attended to:

    a. permission from all family members

    b. explanation of experimental procedures

    c. explanation of statistical measurement

    d. all of the above

25. Counselors engaged in private practice:

    a. must be licensed

    b. must be certified

    c. must be both licensed and certified

    d. none of the above

26. A disability is:

    a. the extent of a handicapping condition

    b. a medical diagnosis

    c. the results of a psychometric assessment

    d. none of the above

27. Social Security Disability Benefits differ from Supplemental Security Income in that the former:

    a. requires a work history

    b. is for persons who have congenital disabilities

    c. has a federal state ratio of 70/30

    d. does not require a work history

28. An advocate is needed for handicapped persons to:

    a. make decisions that are based on sound judgment

    b. influence channels of services

    c. force public agencies to serve the severely disabled

    d. all of the above

29. The main thrust of the Randolph-Shepperd Act was to ensure that:

    a. civilians receive rehabilitation services

    b. vending stands on federal property be operated by the blind

    c. educational opportunities for the deaf be expanded

    d. personal counseling be provided to all rehabilitation clients

30. A handicapping condition is:

    a. the extent of limitations

    b. the degree of mental impairment

    c. the inability to work

    d. a medical diagnosis

31. Rehabilitation in the private sector differs from public rehabilitation in that the former:

    a. emphasizes competitive placement

    b. has larger client caseloads and more paperwork

    c. is uniform throughout the United States

    d. is mandated by legislation

32. State rehabilitation agencies are subsidized by federal funds by:

    a. 80 percent

    b. 75 percent

    c. 60 percent

    d. 50 percent

33. People who are employed in a sheltered workshop typically earn less than the minimum wage per hour. This is because:

    a. the worker has subaverage intellect

    b. the worker works at a slower pace than unimpaired workers

    c. the agency needs to take back a certain portion of wages for counseling services

    d. the worker must make an additional contribution to Social Security

34. _____ occurs when a person's total body image is so pervasive that functioning affects total lifestyle.

    a. Containment

    b. Spread

    c. Denial

    d. Adjustment

35. Which descriptive statement is preferred?

    a. The client is a paraplegic.

    b. The client is confined to a wheelchair.

c. The client has a spinal cord injury.

d. The client is a patient of rehabilitation services.

36. The Civil Rights provision that has had the most profound effect on persons who have some minority status is:

    a. Section 504

    b. Fourth Amendment

    c. Job Partnership Training Act

    d. Public Law 94–143

37. The state agency that serves the greatest number of rehabilitation clients is:

    a. Office of Vocational Rehabilitation

    b. Commission for Visually Impaired

    c. Social Security Agency

    d. Worker's Compensation

38. The major problem encountered by people who are blind is:

    a. safety

    b. accessibility

    c. communication

    d. intimacy

39. The concept of holism refers to:

    a. concentration of the major handicapping condition

    b. an individual's sum is greater than the parts

    c. all phases of rehabilitation must have psychological aspects

    d. rehabilitation clients are more religious

40. Peer counselors are especially needed for individuals who are severely disabled for all of the following reasons except:

    a. opportunity to be sexually active

    b. short supply of professional counselors

    c. high cost of professional counselors

    d. role models

41. _____ is a condition that causes a person difficulties with life adjustment.

    a. Coping

    b. Succumbing

    c. Containment

    d. Enlarging

42. All of the following are targeted rehabilitation goals except:

    a. sheltered employment
    b. self-employment
    c. institutionalization
    d. medical stability

43. An early advocate for persons with mental illness was:

    a. Mary Switzer
    b. Joseph Lister
    c. John Itard
    d. Dorothea Dix

44. _____ established the first school for the deaf.

    a. Benjamin Franklin
    b. Thomas Gallaudet
    c. Dorothea Dix
    d. Beatrice Wright

45. The Smith-Fess Act is also known as the:

    a. Smith-Hughes Vocational Act
    b. Soldier's Rehabilitation Act
    c. Civilian Rehabilitation Act
    d. National Defense Act

46. The Barden-LaFollette Act expanded services to include:

    a. orthopedically disabled
    b. Vietnam veterans
    c. mentally retarded and mentally ill
    d. Civil War veterans

47. Section 502 of the Rehabilitation Act mandates that:

    a. public buildings be accessible
    b. the federal government be a model agency to hire the handicapped
    c. schools and universities be nondiscriminatory in their admission policies
    d. hearing-impaired persons are entitled to an interpreter at public functions

48. Section 501 of the Rehabilitation Act mandates that:

    a. the blind operate vending stands in federal buildings
    b. the federal government be a model agency in its hiring practices
    c. public buildings be accessible
    d. vocational services be expanded to special education students

49. The Education for All Handicapped Children Act mandates that children are entitled to services up to ___ years of age.

    a. 16
    b. 18
    c. 19
    d. 21

50. The Certified Rehabilitation Counselor is:

    a. a state license
    b. a national license
    c. a national certification
    d. state certification

**Answer Key to Section I
is found on page 298.**

Section II

Theories to Guide the Professional Counselor

1. Which of the following researchers has written extensively on moral development?

   a. Piaget

   b. Kohlberg

   c. Frankl

   d. Perls

2. The formation of trust or mistrust begins:

   a. during early school years

   b. the first year of life

   c. during the teenage years

   d. at different times for males and females

3. A child is asked to put away his toys before nap time. His mother says she will reward him with milk and cookies for having a neat room. The stimulus in this situation is:

   a. milk and cookies

   b. putting toys away

   c. mom's attention

   d. the nap

4. The blinking of your eye due to some irritation is known as:

   a. an operant response

   b. a reflexive response

   c. a response controlled by consequences

   d. a response conditioned by previous learning

5. _____ is the conscious or unconscious effort by a client to prevent or delay movement toward maturity within a therapeutic milieu.

   a. Transference

   b. Displacement

   c. Analysis

   d. Resistance

6. An emerging sense of shame and doubt in a child is due to a lack of:

   a. autonomy

   b. initiative

c. friends

d. siblings

7. To which of the following theorists is the understanding of the family constellation an important concept?

   a. Rogers

   b. May

   c. Lazarus

   d. Adler

8. Which of the following is *not* one of Erikson's stages of psychosocial development?

   a. intimacy versus stagnation

   b. integrity versus despair

   c. industry versus inferiority

   d. basic trust versus mistrust

9. One problem in testing Freud's theory is that it rests on:

   a. phenomenology

   b. natural environment

   c. unconscious thoughts

   d. heuristic concepts

10. "Who am I?" is a pressing question for the:

    a. teenager

    b. graduate student

    c. toddler

    d. elderly person

11. The job of the counselor is to provide a therapeutic environment. To do this, Freud would say the therapist must act:

    a. anonymously

    b. interactively

    c. friendly

    d. bored

12. According to Rogers, the job of the counselor is to be:

    a. genuine

    b. confrontational

    c. anonymous

    d. soft-spoken

13. A factor commonly operating in all untreated alcoholics is:

   a. optimism

   b. regression

   c. denial

   d. sublimation

14. To resolve fixation in any psychosexual stage, the client must:

   a. regress back to this period

   b. recognize resolution is impossible and to carry on as well as possible

   c. become self-centered

   d. suspend logical thoughts

15. Marital and family therapists view the locus of pathology as lying with the:

   a. identified patient

   b. family system

   c. parents

   d. children

16. A here-and-now focus is used by all of the following therapists *except*:

   a. Perls

   b. Adler

   c. Freud

   d. Frankl

17. Free association would be used by which of the following therapists?

   a. Berne

   b. Freud

   c. Rogers

   d. Kohlberg

18. _____ therapists do not believe self-actualization is a finite experience.

   a. Existential

   b. Person-centered

   c. Behavioral

   d. Both (a) and (b)

19. Researchers considered to be humanistic include:

   a. Maslow, Skinner, Glasser

   b. Erikson, Freud, Watson

   c. Rogers, Adler, Frankl

   d. Frankl, Ellis, Rogers

20. _____ characterizes the expression of something opposite to one's true feelings.

   a. Repression

   b. Projection

   c. Reaction formation

   d. Conversion reaction

21. If an individual does not develop a sense of integrity in later life, there is a tendency to:

   a. regress to an earlier stage

   b. be optimistic that the future will bring it

   c. blame others

   d. overestimate abilities

22. The "blank slate" of human nature is related to what type of counseling philosophy?

   a. Behaviorism

   b. Cognitive

   c. Humanistic

   d. Eclectic

23. All of the following are developmental tasks of later adulthood *except:*

   a. acceptance of one's life

   b. reduction of energy to a more leisurely lifestyle

   c. disengagement in terms of roles and responsibilities

   d. developing a point of view about death

24. The acceptance of an interpretation and integration of that interpretation into a better understanding of the self is known as:

   a. repression

   b. sublimination

   c. insight

   d. transference

25. "The relationship between the client and the counselor must be one of mutual respect." Which therapist would agree with this statement?

   a. Adler

   b. Harris

   c. Skinner

   d. all of the above

26. When a response continues following reward or reinforcement it is said to be the result of _____ conditioning.

    a. operant

    b. respondent

    c. classical

    d. intermittent

27. _____ is an environmentalist who believes that children learn through imitation.

    a. Bandura

    b. Piaget

    c. Kohlberg

    d. Rogers

28. The crisis of generativity is a crisis in:

    a. meaningfulness

    b. autonomy

    c. despair

    d. inferiority

29. The concept of developing a unique style of life as a way to compensate for basic inferiority feelings is a belief of which therapy?

    a. Logotherapy

    b. Existentialism

    c. Person-centered therapy

    d. Individual psychology

30. Transactional analysis:

    a. has a three-ego-state configuration

    b. holds the belief that the past is more important than the future

    c. holds the belief that life is predetermined

    d. all of the above

31. Which emphasis is a characteristic of reality therapy?

    a. responsibility

    b. exploring the past

    c. dream analysis

    d. lifestyle

32. Transactional analysis is particularly suited for:

    a. the elderly

    b. group counseling

    c. substance abuse counseling

    d. midlife crisis issues

33. The therapy that relies most heavily on objective data and research to support its practice is:

    a. Gestalt

    b. Behavioral

    c. Person-centered

    d. Eclectic

34. A direct confrontational approach is used by:

    a. Ellis

    b. Rogers

    c. Maslow

    d. May

35. Which therapy believes a safe climate is a necessary requisite for a client's self-exploration?

    a. Psychoanalytic

    b. Gestalt

    c. Reality

    d. Person-centered

36. Countertransference occurs when:

    a. the client is attracted to the counselor

    b. the counselor has reactions toward the client that interfere with objectivity

    c. the client is unable to resolve anxiety

    d. the counselor becomes too rigid

37. Piaget described the last stage of cognitive development as:

    a. Preoperational thought

    b. Concrete operational thought

    c. Transactional thought

    d. Formal operational thought

38. The ego defense mechanism that consists of developing certain positive traits to make up for deficiencies is known as:

    a. compensation

    b. projection

    c. reaction formation

    d. denial

39. Kicking the dog after having a bad day at work is a demonstration of:

    a. repression

    b. introjection

    c. displacement

    d. reaction formation

40. Which of the following theorists is identified with the "collective unconscious"?

    a. Jung

    b. Lazarus

    c. May

    d. Perls

41. Which is *not* true of resistance?

    a. It delays closure and resolution of concerns.

    b. It is an inevitable part of Freudian therapy.

    c. Rogers would not directly address it.

    d. The counselor should wait until the client addresses it.

42. Gestalt therapy focuses on:

    a. the here and now

    b. the first five years of life

    c. future plans

    d. critical life stages

43. Which theorist is the author of *Games People Play?*

    a. Frankl

    b. Harris

    c. Berne

    d. Lazarus

44. Which of the following therapists believes a midlife crisis permits undeveloped trust to emerge?

    a. Glasser

    b. Skinner

    c. Hall

    d. Jung

45. A principle that divides the neo-Freudians from traditional Freudians is the former's emphasis on:

    a. developmental stages

    b. ego defense mechanisms

    c. determinism

    d. individual choice

46. Formal psychometric testing is *not* used by:

    a. Ellis

    b. Skinner

    c. Rogers

    d. Glasser

47. Transference occurs when:

    a. the client projects trust from significant others onto the counselor

    b. the client recalls dreams

    c. the counselor makes recommendations that are subliminal

    d. the counselor has not resolved psychological concerns

48. Unconditional positive regard is associated with this (these) therapist(s):

    a. Rogers

    b. Skinner

    c. Jung

    d. both (a) and (c)

49. Which of the following therapists views the role of the counselor as that of a teacher?

    a. Freud

    b. Frankl

    c. Rogers

    d. Ellis

50. To which of the following therapists is reinforcement a key concept?

    a. Skinner

    b. Adler

    c. Dreikurs

    d. Haley

51. A decrease in responding to material that was earlier reinforced is known as:

    a. reaction formation

    b. shaping

    c. extinction

    d. regression

52. Which theorist has not postulated a stage theory of development?

    a. Erikson

    b. Freud

    c. Jung

    d. Ellis

53. The id is:

    a. governed by the pleasure principle

    b. guided by parental injunctions

    c. logical

    d. none of the above

54. The term eclecticism refers to:

    a. the use of a variety of procedures and techniques

    b. the belief that early recollections are not useful

    c. the philosophy that each counselor must try all theories

    d. the efficient use of time

55. The psychoanalytical point of view emphasizes the fact that:

    a. the counselor should challenge the client's perception of self

    b. repressed information causes conflict

    c. inappropriate cognitive habits are acquired in early school years

    d. family constellation must be explored

56. The superego:

    a. is pleasure seeking

    b. is illogical

    c. acts as a conscience

    d. contains "oughts" and "shoulds"

57. Adler maintains that social interest is:

    a. inborn

    b. developed during the first five years of life

    c. unable to develop without an opposite-sex role model

    d. developed during teenage years

58. Which of the following theorists is known for his use of reciprocal inhibition?

    a. Lazarus

    b. Perls

    c. Wolpe

    d. Piaget

59. Preconscious material is:

    a. only retrievable after years of psychotherapy

    b. not retrievable at all

c. retrievable at will

d. repressed, as it is painful

60. Which of the following therapists would say the underachiever has not taken the responsibility to be self-directed?

    a. Rogers

    b. Skinner

    c. Harris

    d. Glasser

61. The need for a feeling of superiority is a principle of:

    a. Freud

    b. Adler

    c. Berne

    d. Skinner

62. Logotherapy was founded by:

    a. Frankl

    b. Sullivan

    c. Horney

    d. Glasser

63. Counselor anonymity is deemed essential by:

    a. Classical analysts

    b. Adlerians

    c. Jungians

    d. Skinnerians

64. Which of the following theorists is known for including mythology and religion in his theory?

    a. Freud

    b. Hall

    c. Jung

    d. Frankl

65. Ellis believes that dissatisfaction with life is associated with:

    a. low intelligence

    b. lack of early childhood stimulation

    c. caring too much about what others think

    d. lack of bonding at birth

66. In transactional analysis, the adult is thought to be comparable to Freud's:

    a. id

    b. ego

c. superego

d. shadow

67. The counselor's focus during the initial interview is to:

    a. discuss the services of the agency

    b. establish goals with the client

    c. get to know the client by conversing on some neutral topic

    d. establish rapport with the client

68. In Gestalt therapy, change occurs when:

    a. emotions do not rule behavior

    b. free association frees the individual

    c. one becomes what he or she is, rather than trying to be someone else

    d. having the ability to indirectly express desires

69. A major weakness of Freud's theory is that it is:

    a. impossible to test using the scientific method

    b. too old for contemporary problems

    c. too confusing for the novice counselor

    d. lacks guidelines for therapeutic progression

70. The person-centered approach places emphasis on:

    a. exploration of the unconscious

    b. objective test results

    c. unqualified acceptance of client statements

    d. exploration on unfinished business

71. Adler believes humans strive to:

    a. satisfy sexual desires

    b. overcome inferiority

    c. have immediate gratification

    d. understand unconcious motives

72. A person who is suffering from feelings of despair and hopelessness has not achieved a sense of _____ in the _____ stage.

    a. identity; later adulthood

    b. generativity; early adulthood

    c. intimacy; middle age

    d. integrity; later life

73. _____ occurs when the counselor sincerely grasps what the client is experiencing.

    a. Modeling

    b. Empathizing

    c. Clarifying

    d. Sympathizing

74. Existentialists believe that:

    a. individuals' actions are determined by genetics

    b. reinforcement changes behavior

    c. persons are endlessly remaking themselves

    d. both (a) and (c)

75. According to Pavlov, which type of reinforcement is most effective?

    a. immediate

    b. delayed

    c. continuous

    d. simultaneous

76. _____ occurs when an unconditioned stimulus evokes a conditioned response.

    a. Generalization

    b. Differentiation

    c. Extinction

    d. Neutrality

77. Adler believed the _____ is generally the most outgoing.

    a. first-born in a large family

    b. second-born

    c. youngest

    d. only child

78. Punishment:

    a. is an effective long-term shaping mechanism

    b. has the potential to stop unwanted behaviors

    c. is more effective than intermittent reinforcers

    d. none of the above

79. According to Rogers, human beings strive to:

    a. attain pleasure

    b. avoid pain

    c. repress uncomfortable moments

    d. actualize themselves

80. Existentialists believe past events in life are:

    a. important for understanding growth and development

    b. determinants for future opportunities

    c. important, as they affect present situations

    d. unimportant

81. A counselor working with the homeless would be more concerned with:

    a. lower order needs

    b. anxiety

    c. anger

    d. self-esteem

82. Which researcher cites reasons why persons may adopt particular behaviors by watching role models on television?

    a. Bandura

    b. Maslow

    c. Rogers

    d. Perls

83. Assertiveness training is basically a _____ model.

    a. client-centered

    b. learning styles

    c. affective

    d. behavioral

84. A counselor who follows an eclectic approach:

    a. lacks a theoretical base

    b. is more than likely a marital and family therapist

    c. works with uncooperative clients

    d. uses various techniques

85. When a counselor explains inconsistencies to the client, which technique is being employed?

    a. paradoxical directive

    b. confrontation

    c. reflection

    d. summarization

86. In rational emotive therapy, clients are encouraged to:

    a. restructure cognitions

    b. perform personal experiments to see if beliefs are consistent with reality

    c. go through hypnosis

    d. both (a) and (b)

87. When a client identifies with something the counselor has said, it is thought to be a:

    a. catharsis

    b. countertransference

    c. sublimated exercise

    d. none of the above

88. A direct approach that addresses dysfunctional behaviors within a short time period would most likely be:

    a. psychodynamic

    b. behavioral

    c. affective

    d. existential

89. Genuineness is a critical component for which type of counselor?

    a. cognitive

    b. affective

    c. behavioral

    d. all of the above

90. Saying in slightly different words what the client has previously stated is an example of:

    a. modeling

    b. integrating

    c. paraphrasing

    d. summarizing

91. Which one of the following persons is most closely affiliated with Adler's philosophy?

    a. Frankl

    b. Dreikurs

    c. Lazarus

    d. Ellis

92. The Gestalt counselor is:

    a. authoritarian

    b. confrontational

    c. analytical

    d. passive

93. Rational emotive therapy can best be characterized as:

    a. experiential

    b. affective

c. cognitive

d. psychodynamic

94. The empty-chair technique is credited to:

    a. Berne

    b. May

    c. Frankl

    d. Perls

95. Which of the following may be considered to be the most threatening for both the client and the counselor?

    a. silence

    b. interpretation

    c. questioning

    d. reflecting

96. Which of the following is *not* likely to be a reason why clients shift topics in conversation?

    a. They forgot what they were saying.

    b. They question whether the material is relevant.

    c. To seek relief because the material is too painful to proceed.

    d. To make sure the counselor is listening.

97. A major concept in rational emotive therapy is:

    a. emotions are beyond the control of the individual

    b. thoughts and emotions are two discrete processes

    c. emotions lead to internalized statements that may be self-defeating

    d. behavior is a function of rational thoughts

98. Which type of counseling is more a philosophy than a specific technique?

    a. Existentialism

    b. Rational emotive therapy

    c. Multimodal therapy

    d. Freudian therapy

99. Maslow's hierarchy of needs, from low to high, are:

    a. safety, love, belonging, esteem, self-actualization

    b. physiological needs, safety, love, esteem, self-actualization

    c. love and belonging, safety, esteem, self-actualization, integrity

    d. physiological, love, safety, self-actualization, esteem

100. _____ believes there is no such thing as mental illness.
    a. Glasser
    b. Rogers
    c. May
    d. Lazarus

**Answer Key to Section II
is found on page 299.**

Section III

Career Counseling Theories, Occupational Resources and Tests, and Ability to Interpret Test Results

1. _____ believes that the choice of a career is to resolve unconscious motives.

   a. Super
   b. Bordin
   c. Ginzberg
   d. Holland

2. The concept of joining individual differences with job analysis is known as:

   a. trait and factor theory
   b. personality type theory
   c. client-centered theory
   d. none of the above

3. The "investigative" person would prefer to:

   a. teach others
   b. persuade others
   c. help resolve interpersonal problems
   d. engage in intellectual activities

4. A client scored 55 on a test. This score:

   a. indicates that the person failed
   b. indicates that the person scored higher than the mean
   c. is not enough information to determine meaning
   d. both (a) and (b)

5. This type of person welcomes the opportunity to express emotions more readily than others:

   a. artistic
   b. conventional
   c. enterprising
   d. investigative

6. An underemployed worker is:

   a. underpaid
   b. one who accepts a lower skill level employment than qualified for

    c. the victim of an economy with low employment

    d. the victim of rampant inflation

7. The conventional person likes to work in an environment where there are:

    a. rules

    b. no rules

    c. extensive use of physical skills

    d. extensive use of interpersonal skills

8. Client-centered job placement occurs when:

    a. the counselor secures job leads

    b. the client secures job leads

    c. clients are typically low functioning

    d. sheltered employment is the goal

9. The influence of early parent-child interaction in choosing careers is an important concept in the theory developed by:

    a. Roe

    b. O'Hara

    c. Super

    d. Tiedeman

10. Vocational maturity is a concept expressed by:

    a. Super

    b. Krumboltz

    c. Ginzberg

    d. Ginsburg

11. A common way to measure intelligence is:

    a. mental age minus chronological age

    b. mental age divided by chronological age $\times$ 100

    c. chronological age divided by mental age $\times$ 100

    d. mental age multiplied by chronological age $\times$ 100

12. The notion of irreversibility and career choice is credited to:

    a. Ginzberg

    b. Roe

    c. Super

    d. Holland

13. Which percentage represents all of the scores which fall above or below one standard deviation from the mean?

    a. 34.13

    b. 68.26

    c. 95.44

    d. 99.72

14. Which researcher is known for his work with job clubs?

    a. Azrin

    b. Hoppock

    c. Brill

    d. O'Hara

15. In a job interview a client who has a handicapping condition should:

    a. not address any limitations

    b. present abilities and special qualifications to do the job

    c. cite affirmative action reasons for hiring the disabled

    d. all of the above

16. Satisfaction and satisfactoriness can be evaluated by:

    a. vocational maturity

    b. job tenure

    c. amount of education a worker has

    d. a correspondence between chronological and vocational age

17. The term "environmental press" is credited to:

    a. Murray

    b. Maslow

    c. Hoppock

    d. Terkel

18. Standard scores (z) can best be described as test scores that:

    a. form a symmetrical bell-shaped curve

    b. were developed by the U.S. Air Force during World War II

    c. were developed to rid negative scores

    d. are expressed in terms of standard deviation units

19. With a supply/demand theory of career choice, the counselor's role is primarily to:

    a. help the client explore unconsious needs

    b. help the client explore early childhood experiences

    c. function as an economic counselor

    d. function as an affective counselor

20. The Kuder is a(n):

    a. occupational interest survey

    b. aptitude test

    c. achievement test

    d. personality test

21. A major resource for occupational information is the:

    a. General Aptitude Test Battery

    b. *Dictionary of Occupational Titles*

    c. Rorschach

    d. Census Report

22. Which researcher believes the person who elected to be a surgeon or a butcher is acting in a way where unacceptable impulses may be gratified?

    a. Brill

    b. Roe

    c. Thoresen

    d. Lofquist

23. One person scored a 95 on a test. Another person scored a 75 on the same test. In order to determine whether the difference between the two scores was due to chance, you would have to know the:

    a. standard deviation

    b. standard error of measurement

    c. mean

    d. z score

24. A person scored an 85 on a test. This means the person:

    a. passed the test

    b. scored in the upper quartile

    c. answered 15 questions incorrectly

    d. not enough information is provided

25. A theorist who views career choice to be a function of reinforcers and learning experiences follows which type of counseling model?

    a. Cognitive

    b. Affective

    c. Behavioral

    d. Eclectic

26. A T-Score is used

    a. to account for extreme scores

    b. for intelligence testing

    c. to avoid negative values

    d. all of the above

27. An accountant would have a major orientation as a(n) _____ type of person.

    a. investigative

    b. enterprising

    c. social

    d. realistic

28. Understanding the family environment is important to which career counseling theorist?

    a. Roe

    b. Krumboltz

    c. Ellis

    d. O'Hara

29. Which score is used before any statistical measures are applied?

    a. z score

    b. stanine score

    c. raw score

    d. standardized score

30. If two examiners give the same test to the same person and obtain similar results, we say the test is:

    a. valid

    b. objective

    c. true

    d. reliable

31. When comparing two testing groups, it was found the reliability coefficient was .78 for the entire group. It could be assumed that the reliability coefficient for one of the groups was:

    a. lower than .78

    b. .78

    c. lower than the mean

    d. not enough information is provided

32. The "Hawthorne effect" suggests that:

    a. production rates may be increased by attention

    b. close supervision distracts workers

    c. an increase in salary will increase production

    d. union membership is needed for workers to believe they have fair representation

33. *The Dictionary of Occupational Titles* describes more than _____ job titles.

    a. 20,000
    b. 50,000
    c. 75,000
    d. 100,000

34. _____ is when a test measures a theoretical base.

    a. Construct validity
    b. Criterion-related validity
    c. Face validity
    d. none of the above

35. In Super's "Establishment" stage, it would be expected that the individual would:

    a. change jobs
    b. be promoted
    c. find a vocational choice unsatisfactory
    d. dissociate from the work force

36. *The Occupational Outlook Handbook:*

    a. describes jobs by geographical areas
    b. is the most readable of all employment resources
    c. is updated annually
    d. uses the DPT code to arrange job titles

37. Which of the following is the most meaningful measure of central tendency?

    a. mean
    b. median
    c. mode
    d. percentile rank

38. *The Guide to Occupational Exploration:*

    a. is a companion volume for the *DOT*
    b. is updated every two years
    c. has a nine-digit occupational code
    d. was the first employment resource to be developed

39. Both Holland's _____ and _____ personality types seek to avoid close interpersonal relationships in the workplace.

    a. realistic; investigative
    b. realistic; social

c. investigative; artistic

d. artistic; conventional

40. A major criticism of standardized testing is:

a. lack of reliability and validity

b. improper use

c. insufficient score interpretation methods

d. poor control

41. A standard deviation is a measure of:

a. variability

b. degree of normality

c. reliability

d. validity

42. All of the following researchers share the view that career development is a decision-making process *except*:

a. Brill

b. Ginsburg

c. O'Hara

d. Super

43. A 50th percentile rank corresponds to the:

a. mean

b. median

c. mode

d. z score

44. The choice of a career was at first thought as an irreversible process by researchers:

a. Roe and Holland

b. Tiedeman and O'Hara

c. Super and Brill

d. Ginzberg, Ginsburg, Axelrad, and Herma

45. When attempting to generalize research findings to other circumstances and subjects, _____ is a critical consideration.

a. internal validity

b. external validity

c. content validity

d. face validity

46. Which phenomena causes interference with objectivity in test interpretation?

     a. random selection

     b. repetitious questions

     c. halo effect

     d. none of the above

47. A standardized test:

     a. has a standard deviation of plus or minus 10

     b. has a mean of 50

     c. is reliable and valid

     d. all of the above

48. When a test yields the same result time after time, it is thought to have:

     a. reliability

     b. validity

     c. no sampling error

     d. separate norms for special populations

49. You would have a client take a(n) _____ test to understand and assess what has been previously learned in a particular subject area.

     a. aptitude

     b. achievement

     c. standardized

     d. personality

50. Murray's Needs-Press theory was a theoretical base for _____ 's career counseling theory.

     a. Holland

     b. Hoppock

     c. Super

     d. Roe

51. The number of different occupations in the United States is estimated to be:

     a. 10,000–15,000

     b. 20,000–25,000

     c. 25,000–50,000

     d. 50,000–60,000

52. The Kuder-Richardson method is an example of:

     a. criterion-related validity

     b. content validity

     c. split-half reliability

     d. test-retest reliability

53. _____ validity pertains to whether or not a test looks valid.

    a. face

    b. criterion

    c. construct

    d. content

54. Experts customarily determine _____ validity.

    a. face

    b. criterion

    c. construct

    d. content

55. Standard scores take into account the _____ .

    a. mean and standard deviation

    b. median and percentile

    c. mode and standard deviation

    d. median and standard deviation

56. A job placement strategy for a person who suffered brain injury in a motor vehicle accident would be:

    a. selective

    b. client-centered

    c. laissez-faire

    d. none of the above

57. Which career counseling theory uses job analysis information to counsel clients?

    a. psychoanalytical

    b. trait and factor

    c. humanistic

    d. developmental

58. Which career counseling theory has been discarded by contemporary counselors as too simplistic an approach?

    a. psychoanalytical

    b. trait and factor

    c. humanistic

    d. developmental

59. The last three digits of the DOT code:

    a. are most helpful to identify transferable skills

    b. designate the order of job titles found in a particular industry group

    c. classify each industry by its principal product of services

    d. identifies career trends

60. When an individual receives a score in the 75th percentile, the score is:

    a. meaningless by itself

    b. 75 percent above others who took the test

    c. 25 percent above others who took the test

    d. equal to the mean of the raw score

61. A high school student is considering several occupational alternatives. Which of the decision-making steps identified by Tiedeman and O'Hara would she be in?

    a. crystallization

    b. reformation

    c. induction

    d. exploration

62. The person who chooses to work as a butcher is using which ego defense mechanism to express unacceptable behaviors?

    a. repression

    b. regression

    c. alternate coping

    d. sublimation

63. In Super's "Maintenance" stage, the individual:

    a. tries out various jobs

    b. adjusts and grows on the job

    c. gradually disassociates from a job

    d. both (b) and (c)

64. Standard scores (z) can best be described as test scores:

    a. expressed in terms of norm-referenced units

    b. expressed in terms of standard deviation units

    c. calculated by dividing the mean by the standard deviation

    d. calculated by regression equations

65. According to Holland, which of the following personality types would be most closely related?

    a. realistic and social

    b. enterprising and artistic

    c. investigative and conventional

    d. enterprising and conventional

66. The TAT requires the subject to:
    a. make up a story about a picture
    b. do quantitative analysis
    c. study inkblots
    d. arrange blocks

67. According to Super, the process of vocational development is:
    a. influenced by early childhood experiences
    b. a function of unconsious forces
    c. becoming aware of basic patterns of needs
    d. developing and implementing a self-concept

68. With increased age, a person would most normally show what type of intelligence change?
    a. fluid
    b. crystallized
    c. both of the above
    d. none of the above

69. The _____ offers very little conclusive testing information.
    a. median
    b. mode
    c. mean
    d. percentile rank

70. Research on Roe's theory:
    a. has lent strong support of her tenets
    b. revealed her theory was practical for special needs students
    c. was partly based on the Rorschach Ink Blot Test
    d. none of the above

71. Super believes a highly trained person would more likely have a(n) _____ career pattern.
    a. stable
    b. unstable
    c. multiple trial
    d. conventional

72. Super describes a "Conventional" career pattern as one where the person:
    a. tries out several jobs
    b. changes jobs but not career fields
    c. has loyalty to a particular and single employer
    d. never finds satisfaction with work

73. Tiedeman and O'Hara describe "induction" as:

    a. vocational activities based on fantasy

    b. emerging career patterns

    c. the questioning of the goals of a profession

    d. the assimilation of information and the reaching of goals

74. _____ theorists believe people look at a job by asking "What's in it for me?"

    a. Psychodynamic

    b. Developmental

    c. Behavioral

    d. Structural

75. The self-directed search is:

    a. self-administered

    b. computer scored

    c. targeted for high school students

    d. targeted for midlife career change

76. When a worker's task involves lifting up to 50 lbs., and frequently carrying up to 25 lbs., the exertional level is considered to be:

    a. sedentary

    b. light

    c. medium

    d. heavy

77. Only state employment employees may administer the:

    a. Strong Vocational Interest Inventory

    b. Wide Range Achievement Test

    c. Minnesota Multiphasic Personality Inventory

    d. General Aptitude Test Battery

78. When a test is designed with a yes/no format, it is considered a(n) _____ type of test.

    a. ordinal

    b. ratio

    c. nominal

    d. interval

79. One way to predict job satisfaction is to consider the:

    a. length of time on job

    b. amount of training required

c. availability of union membership

d. all of the above

80. The standard deviation on the WAIS-R is:

   a. five

   b. ten

   c. twelve

   d. fifteen

81. Which population group would be more likely to have been excluded from the standardization sample for the WAIS-R?

   a. mentally retarded

   b. gifted

   c. high school students

   d. college students

82. Which test is considered to be one of the most widely used personality tests?

   a. Minnesota Multiphasic Personality Inventory

   b. Self-Directed Search

   c. Bender Visual Gestalt Test

   d. Minnesota Importance Questionnaire

83. In which of these resources would users expect to find norms for a particular test?

   a. Mental Measurements Yearbook

   b. Standard Classification Index

   c. The Test Manual

   d. Selected Characteristics of Individuals

84. The SAT is an example of a(n):

   a. aptitude test

   b. ratio type of test

   c. intelligence test

   d. nominal type of measurement

85. *The Guide to Occupational Exploration:*

   a. gives regional predictions and trends

   b. has a six-digit code

   c. organizes data into 20 interest areas

   d. all of the above

86. The term "reliability" refers to _____ of test scores.

   a. consistency

   b. objectivity

    c. variability

    d. dispersion

87. Achievement tests are commonly used to measure:

    a. progress in school

    b. innate traits

    c. personality preferences

    d. none of the above

88. When a person applies for a clerical position and is asked to file a certain number of letters in a 15-minute period, this task is an example of:

    a. projective technique

    b. job analysis technique

    c. job sample

    d. manual dexterity sample

89. An example of a neuropsychological battery is the:

    a. Minnesota Importance Questionnaire

    b. Myers–Briggs

    c. Differential Aptitude

    d. none of the above

90. The vocational version of the Career Assessment Inventory:

    a. contains mostly white collar jobs

    b. contains mostly blue collar jobs

    c. does not have a required reading level

    d. both (b) and (c)

91. In an experimental design, the variable that is manipulated by the research is termed the:

    a. dependent variable

    b. independent variable

    c. covariate

    d. multivariate

92. Categorizing someone as being in a particular socioeconomic status is an example of a _____ measurement scale.

    a. nominal

    b. interval

    c. ratio

    d. ordinal

93. _____ refers to the notion that test results can be generalized.

    a. Internal validity
    b. External validity
    c. Face validity
    d. Construct validity

94. A stanine scale has a mean of:

    a. zero
    b. one
    c. two
    d. five

95. Standardization of a test is concerned with:

    a. establishment of norms
    b. predicting the validity of a test
    c. how to determine an appropriate scoring system
    d. a way to ensure test items relate to some theoretical construct

96. If Test X has a mean of 50, standard deviation of 10, and N of 1000, about how many individuals would score between 40 and 60?

    a. 340
    b. 680
    c. 890
    d. more information is needed

97. An example of a projective test is the:

    a. WRAT
    b. WAIS
    c. Stanford-Binet
    d. Rorschach

98. _____ refers to how well a test measures what it is supposed to measure.

    a. Test/retest criterion
    b. Reliability
    c. Validity
    d. Standardized

99. Test validity refers to _____ items.

    a. consistency of
    b. accuracy of
    c. number incorrectly answered
    d. none of the above

100. Your client has an occupational profile of realistic, conventional, and investigative. Holland would say the client demonstrates a(n) _____ personality type.

    a. compatible
    b. conflicting
    c. androgynous
    d. unsuccessful

Answer Key to Section III
is found on page 300.

Section IV

Medical and Psychosocial Aspects of Common Disorders

1. One recommendation for employment for a person who has paranoid schizophrenia might be as a:

   a. pottery maker

   b. security guard

   c. receptionist

   d. police officer

2. A neuropsychiatric examination may be needed for a person who has:

   a. phantom limb pain

   b. Still's disease

   c. myasthenia gravis

   d. none of the above

3. Dilantin is prescribed for:

   a. Marie-Strümpell's disease

   b. epilepsy

   c. Raynaud's disease

   d. manic-depression

4. A lumbar myelogram that is abnormal indicates:

   a. a herniated disc

   b. nerve root damage

   c. extent of paralysis in upper extremities

   d. none of the above

5. The pulmonary artery carries:

   a. red oxygenated blood

   b. dark deoxygenated blood

   c. blood to the capillaries

   d. blood to the vena cavae

6. Pain medications:

   a. carry the hazard of physical addiction

   b. have a shorter shelf life than other drugs

   c. may produce a change in cognitive functioning

   d. all of the above

7. Respondent pain:

    a. is predominantly found in migraine sufferers

    b. is reflexive

    c. typically occurs on one side of the body only

    d. is a function of reinforcers

8. Phantom pain:

    a. is related to tumors in the cranial cavity

    b. suggests indicated pain medication is insufficient

    c. follows amputation of a missing limb

    d. all of the above

9. Which condition is characterized by abnormal bone formation and orthopedic deformities?

    a. Paget's disease

    b. Spina bifida

    c. Addison's disease

    d. Turner's syndrome

10. Amyotrophic Lateral Sclerosis is:

    a. a progressive disease of children

    b. affects predominantly the elderly

    c. a degeneration of motor nerve cells and their axons

    d. an inherited disorder

11. A person who suffers a lesion at the C7 level will probably be more severely disabled than a person who suffers a lesion at the L5 level.

    a. true

    b. not true

    c. impossible to predict

    d. it depends on the person's age

12. Injuries from repetitive wrist motions result in which of the following disorders?

    a. Crohn's disease

    b. Huntington's chorea

    c. myasthenia gravis

    d. carpal tunnel syndrome

13. A person who has gout would most likely be referred to a:

    a. neurologist

    b. orthopedist

    c. rheumatologist

    d. ontologist

14. A common complication of paraplegia is:

    a. dementia

    b. sarcoma

    c. valium addiction

    d. decubitis ulcers

15. Guillain-Barré syndrome:

    a. is similar to spina bifida

    b. causes intellectual deficits

    c. has symptoms disappear after several months

    d. is found most commonly in young adults

16. An example of an antipsychotic medication is:

    a. salicylates

    b. robaxin

    c. coumadin

    d. thorazine

17. In prescribing medication, physicians need to be aware of:

    a. the person's age

    b. the person's height

    c. the person's weight

    d. all the above

18. The person who suffers from Crohn's disease has:

    a. stomach problems

    b. a hearing disorder

    c. a pulmonary problem

    d. low vision

19. Which of the following is *not* a diagnostic tool for a neurological disorder?

    a. CT scan

    b. EEG

    c. EKG

    d. spinal tap

20. Marie-Strümpell's disease is also known as:

    a. Guillain-Barré

    b. ALS

    c. ankylosing spondylitis

    d. gout

21. Huntington's chorea:

    a. is hereditary

    b. is a disease of the brain

    c. involves mental deterioration

    d. all of the above

22. Ulceration of the skin refers to:

    a. conversion of heat energy for temperature elevation

    b. eruption of skin blemishes

    c. excision of a bony structure

    d. swelling after amputation

23. The family of a disabled person should be involved in rehabilitation:

    a. if the client is young

    b. if the client is elderly

    c. at all times

    d. to preserve client confidentiality, only some of the time

24. Because of the nature of the disease, the rehabilitation counselor will probably not with work persons with:

    a. cystic fibrosis

    b. polio

    c. arthritis

    d. cerebral palsy

25. Quadriplegia is caused by a lesion in the:

    a. lumbar vertebrae

    b. cervical vertebrae

    c. xiphoid region

    d. gluteus maximus

26. When a person is said to be in remission, symptoms:

    a. exacerbate

    b. worsen

    c. subside

    d. cause side effects

27. Education and intelligence remain intact in:

    a. rheumatoid arthritis

    b. multiple sclerosis

    c. polio

    d. all of the above

28. Ketoacidosis is a complication of:

    a. Hodgkin's disease

    b. sickle cell anemia

    c. diabetes mellitus

    d. tuberculosis

29. With diabetes, the patient is:

    a. hyperactive

    b. hypoglycemic

    c. hyperglycemic

    d. both (a) and (c)

30. The most common complication of a CVA is:

    a. atherosclerosis

    b. urinary tract infections

    c. pneumonia

    d. depression

31. Hemophilia is:

    a. transmitted by fathers

    b. transmitted by mothers

    c. found predominantly in males

    d. both (b) and (c)

32. In chronic or advanced alcoholism, individuals typically:

    a. have alcohol with all meals

    b. drink alone

    c. make excuses to explain their drinking

    d. all of the above

33. Which disease is genetically transmitted to offspring, causes mental retardation in children, and leads to a child's early death?

    a. Tay-Sachs disease

    b. Hodgkin's disease

    c. Phenylketonuria

    d. Korsakoff's syndrome

34. A typical first reaction to the confirmation of any disability is:

    a. acceptance

    b. rage

  c. disbelief

  d. overindulgence

35. Prejudice can be as disabling as the disability itself. Which disability group probably experiences the greatest societal prejudice?

  a. mentally retarded

  b. paraplegics

  c. epileptics

  d. those with renal disease

36. The term "carcinogen" is related to:

  a. heart disease

  b. cancer

  c. thyroid disorders

  d. diabetes

37. Type A behavior heart disease personalities include people who are:

  a. hard-driving

  b. overweight

  c. simple

  d. easy-going

38. Persons with right CVA damage tend to:

  a. overestimate their abilities

  b. deny assets

  c. seem to be euphoric

  d. have mask-like facial features

39. A recommendation for a person who has a class II functional limitation for heart disease is that he or she could be employed as a:

  a. census taker

  b. car salesperson

  c. power sander

  d. air traffic controller

40. Hypertension:

  a. begins in childhood

  b. strikes blacks more commonly than whites

  c. is a precursor of diabetes

  d. strikes women more often than men

41. _____ is the major cause of chronic bronchitis.

  a. Obesity

  b. Congenital malformation of the nasal cavity

    c. Pulmonary hypertension

    d. Cigarette smoking

42. The overwhelming majority of deaf adults are usually:

    a. blind

    b. employable

    c. more susceptible to respiratory infections

    d. mentally retarded

43. Blindness is defined as:

    a. 20/400 in the worse eye with corrective lenses

    b. 20/400 in the better eye with corrective lenses

    c. 20/200 in the worst eye with corrective lenses

    d. 20/200 in the better eye with corrective lenses

44. The most severe type of burn is:

    a. first degree

    b. second degree

    c. third degree

    d. topical

45. The specialized physician who cares for persons who have hearing impairments is the:

    a. orthopedist

    b. ontologist

    c. optimist

    d. otologist

46. The leading cause of a myocardial infarction is:

    a. hypertension

    b. cigarette smoking

    c. high cholesterol count

    d. sedentary lifestyle

47. Anthracosis may result from:

    a. alcoholism

    b. living in poverty

    c. thryoid insufficiency

    d. exposure to dust

48. Which of the following occupations would not be contraindicated for the person who has rheumatoid arthritis?

    a. video display terminal operator

    b. fish fileter

    c. aerobic instructor

    d. welder

49. Persons with AIDS typically die from:

    a. Karposi's sarcoma

    b. pleurisy

    c. diverticulosis

    d. contaminated blood

50. Anorexia nervosa is typically considered a(n) _____ disorder.

    a. psychiatric

    b. developmental

    c. non-life-threatening

    d. easily prevented

51. Cerebral palsy is a condition that:

    a. always results in mental retardation

    b. is affiliated with insufficient oxygen at birth

    c. is hereditary

    d. affects only male children

52. A mild case of rubella during the first trimester of pregnancy:

    a. does not seem to damage the fetus

    b. can cause mental retardation

    c. can cause deformities of the arms and legs

    d. may be related to maternal death

53. Dementia is all but which of the following?

    a. caused by organic brain damage or disease

    b. a normal biological progression of old age

    c. may result in malnutrition

    d. often misdiagnosed

54. Gastrointestinal problems can be related to:

    a. diabetes

    b. insomnia

    c. stress

    d. Type B personalities

55. A CAT scan:

    a. measures and records brain waves

    b. measures and records cardiac arrhythmias

    c. tests reflexes

    d. images the body's organs and tissues

56. Which label has served as a "catchall" for many persons who suffer from a psychiatric disorder?

    a. schizophrenia

    b. manic-depression

    c. agoraphobia

    d. antisocial

57. Spinal cord injury is more prevalent among which of the following age groups?

    a. women under 25

    b. men under 25

    c. women over 25

    d. men over 25

58. With which functional problem would the person who has peripheral vascular disease have the greatest difficulty?

    a. mobility

    b. motivity

    c. communication

    d. cognition

59. _____ is a disorder for which medical quackery may be a greater risk.

    a. Cancer

    b. Rheumatic fever

    c. Rubella

    d. Tuberculosis

60. Which disease was originally referred to as "consumption?"

    a. tuberculosis

    b. cerebral palsy

    c. pneumonia

    d. AIDS

61. Which disorder is characterized by episodic disturbances in the central nervous system?

    a. cerebrovascular accident

    b. Huntington's chorea

    c. myasthenia gravis

    d. epilepsy

62. End-stage renal disease is treated by:

 a. medication

 b. physical therapy

 c. hemodialysis

 d. all of the above

63. Obesity is a complicating factor for:

 a. diabetes mellitus

 b. heart disease

 c. emphysema

 d. all of the above

64. In sickle cell anemia:

 a. only males are affected

 b. persons of European heritage are most affected

 c. intelligence is affected

 d. none of the above

65. Fetal alcohol syndrome:

 a. is characterized by a small head and mental retardation

 b. skips a generation

 c. happens only to male babies

 d. all of the above

66. Cirrhosis of the liver results from:

 a. diabetes

 b. alcoholism

 c. goiter

 d. cancer

67. All of the following psychiatric problems have been treated successfully with medication *except*:

 a. schizophrenia

 b. manic-depression

 c. agoraphobia

 d. narcissism

68. Glaucoma can be:

 a. life-threatening

 b. genetic

 c. found more frequently in females

 d. both (a) and (b)

69. A disease of the inner ear is:

    a. Grave's
    b. Still's
    c. Ankylosing spondylitis
    d. Ménière's

70. Anorexia nervosa is a condition:

    a. more commonly found among teenagers
    b. in which the person overeats to the point of becoming sick
    c. both of the above
    d. none of the above

71. The major reference book that describes and classifies psychiatric disorders is:

    a. *DSM-III*
    b. *PDR*
    c. *Tabers Cyclopedia*
    d. *Merck Manual*

72. A class I pulmonary impairment indicates that symptoms are:

    a. mild
    b. moderate
    c. severe
    d. untreatable

73. Children born to drug-abusing mothers are at risk of:

    a. growth retardation
    b. mental retardation
    c. motor retardation
    d. all of the above

74. A quadriplegic would be limited to _____ work.

    a. light
    b. medium
    c. sedentary
    d. clerical

75. Epilepsy:

    a. gets worse as the individual ages
    b. is often confused with mental retardation
    c. can be a factor in head injuries
    d. all of the above

76. The symptoms of Parkinson's disease are caused by an absence of:

   a. glycogen

   b. protein

   c. dopamine

   d. norepinephrine

77. The _____ gland regulates basal metabolic rate.

   a. pituitary

   b. adrenal

   c. beta

   d. thyroid

78. The purpose of biofeedback is to teach people to:

   a. relax

   b. get at unconscious repressed materials

   c. be open to others for advice

   d. both (a) and (c)

79. Your client has been diagnosed as having a peptic ulcer. Rehabilitation should be directed at:

   a. working through stressful situations

   b. conditioning exercises

   c. college training

   d. psychopharmacology

80. Your client has incurred a below-elbow amputation. He has refused a prosthesis. This could be due to:

   a. fear of not being able to learn to use the prosthesis

   b. embarrassment

   c. low intelligence

   d. both (a) and (b)

81. Your client has incurred a head injury as a result of a motor vehicle accident. You should:

   a. refer him or her to a psychological evaluation

   b. provide an interest inventory

   c. consult with a psychiatrist to understand what psychotropic medications will be prescribed

   d. none of the above

82. A client who has not completed high school informs you, a rehabilitation counselor, that he or she would like a job counseling others. Your next step is to:

    a. tell the client this is unrealistic

    b. explore with the client the reasons for this decision

    c. ignore the client

    d. refer the client to the community college

83. Your client has limitations with respect to bending, stooping, and lifting. You can assume this person is:

    a. a woman

    b. a paraplegic

    c. a diabetic

    d. not enough information is provided

84. Your client is a 55-year-old mail sorter who has had a heart attack. Counseling would be directed at:

    a. leisure time and retirement planning

    b. explaining educational opportunities

    c. vocational counseling and job analysis

    d. obtaining a psychological evaluation

85. When a person has an emotional reaction to a disability:

    a. medication needs to be prescribed

    b. the person is reluctant to admit the need

    c. family members should be warned

    d. the person should be hospitalized

86. Functional limitation refers to:

    a. cognitive deficiencies

    b. medical diagnosis and prognosis

    c. transferable skills

    d. how handicapping a disability is

87. Tolerance is a phenomenon whereby:

    a. a greater amount of alcohol is needed

    b. the handicap is not regarded as much of a distraction

    c. medication may only be given intravenously

    d. medication may only be taken orally

88. Another name for juvenile diabetes is:

    a. Still's disease

    b. Marie-Strümpell's disease

    c. Hansen's disease

    d. none of the above

89. People who sustain spinal cord injuries are typically:

    a. adventurous

    b. scholarly

    c. athletic

    d. introverted

90. "Cardiac neuroses" refers to:

    a. fear of having another heart attack

    b. Type A personality

    c. Type B personality

    d. denial of symptoms

91. In adjusting to a disability, _____ precedes _____.

    a. denial; anger

    b. anger; spread

    c. spread; adjustment

    d. anger; shock

92. Another name for degenerative joint disease is:

    a. Grave's disease

    b. osteoporosis

    c. osteoarthritis

    d. Sabin's disease

93. A transient ischemic attack (TIA) is a:

    a. major stroke

    b. mini-stroke

    c. precursor to multiple sclerosis

    d. reaction to chemotherapy

94. Which of the following groups is at greatest risk of contracting AIDS?

    a. female IV drug users

    b. marijuana smokers

    c. crack users

    d. all of the above

95. At one time, persons who had this disorder were believed to be "possessed" by demons:

    a. blindness

    b. diabetes

c. epilepsy

d. cerebral palsy

96. Leukemia results in:

   a. dyspnea

   b. an overproduction of red blood cells

   c. an overproduction of white blood cells

   d. none of the above

97. Birth defects are positively correlated with:

   a. mothers who are under 15 or over 40 years of age

   b. German measles contracted by the mother during the first three months of pregnancy

   c. poverty

   d. all of the above

98. A paraplegic woman who is about to give birth to a child:

   a. will not be given anesthesia

   b. must be given a cesarean section

   c. may be able to have the baby delivered via the normal vaginal birth process

   d. had to have conceived the child by in vitro fertilization

99. Dyspnea refers to:

   a. poor circulation

   b. shallow breathing

   c. shortness of breath

   d. inability to sleep

100. A(n) _____ is a blood clot that travels to the heart, lungs, or head.

   a. thrombosis

   b. embolism

   c. leukocyte

   d. glycolipid

Answer Key to Section IV
is found on page 301.

A N S W E R K E Y T O S E C T I O N I

1. d	11. d	21. d	31. a	41. b
2. c	12. b	22. d	32. a	42. c
3. d	13. d	23. a	33. b	43. d
4. c	14. b	24. b	34. b	44. b
5. d	15. b	25. d	35. c	45. c
6. b	16. b	26. b	36. a	46. c
7. a	17. d	27. a	37. a	47. a
8. c	18. a	28. b	38. a	48. b
9. d	19. a	29. b	39. b	49. d
10. a	20. d	30. a	40. a	50. c

ANSWER KEY TO SECTION II

1. b	21. c	41. d	61. b	81. a
2. b	22. a	42. a	62. a	82. a
3. b	23. b	43. c	63. a	83. d
4. b	24. c	44. d	64. c	84. d
5. d	25. d	45. d	65. c	85. b
6. a	26. a	46. c	66. b	86. d
7. d	27. a	47. a	67. d	87. d
8. a	28. a	48. a	68. c	88. b
9. c	29. d	49. d	69. a	89. b
10. a	30. a	50. a	70. c	90. c
11. a	31. a	51. c	71. b	91. b
12. a	32. b	52. d	72. d	92. b
13. c	33. b	53. a	73. b	93. c
14. a	34. a	54. a	74. c	94. d
15. b	35. d	55. b	75. a	95. a
16. c	36. b	56. d	76. a	96. a
17. b	37. d	57. b	77. b	97. c
18. d	38. a	58. c	78. b	98. a
19. c	39. c	59. c	79. d	99. b
20. c	40. a	60. d	80. c	100. a

A N S W E R   K E Y   T O   S E C T I O N   I I I

---

1. b	21. b	41. a	61. d	81. a
2. a	22. a	42. a	62. d	82. a
3. d	23. b	43. b	63. b	83. c
4. c	24. d	44. d	64. b	84. a
5. a	25. c	45. b	65. d	85. c
6. b	26. c	46. c	66. a	86. a
7. a	27. d	47. c	67. d	87. a
8. b	28. a	48. a	68. a	88. c
9. a	29. c	49. b	69. b	89. d
10. a	30. d	50. b	70. c	90. b
11. b	31. a	51. b	71. a	91. a
12. a	32. a	52. c	72. a	92. a
13. b	33. a	53. a	73. d	93. b
14. a	34. a	54. a	74. c	94. d
15. b	35. b	55. a	75. a	95. a
16. b	36. b	56. a	76. c	96. b
17. a	37. a	57. b	77. d	97. d
18. d	38. a	58. b	78. c	98. c
19. c	39. a	59. b	79. a	99. b
20. a	40. b	60. b	80. d	100. b

ANSWER KEY TO SECTION IV

1. a	21. d	41. d	61. d	81. a
2. d	22. b	42. b	62. d	82. b
3. b	23. c	43. d	63. d	83. d
4. a	24. a	44. c	64. d	84. c
5. b	25. b	45. d	65. a	85. b
6. d	26. c	46. a	66. b	86. d
7. b	27. d	47. d	67. d	87. a
8. c	28. c	48. a	68. a	88. a
9. a	29. c	49. a	69. d	89. a
10. c	30. d	50. a	70. a	90. a
11. a	31. d	51. b	71. a	91. a
12. d	32. b	52. b	72. a	92. c
13. c	33. a	53. b	73. d	93. b
14. d	34. c	54. c	74. c	94. a
15. c	35. a	55. d	75. c	95. c
16. d	36. b	56. a	76. c	96. c
17. d	37. a	57. b	77. d	97. d
18. a	38. a	58. a	78. a	98. c
19. c	39. a	59. a	79. a	99. c
20. c	40. b	60. a	80. d	100. b

References

REFERENCES

Adler, A. (1963). *The Practice and Theory of Individual Psychology.* Paterson, NJ: Littlefield, Adams.

Adler, A. (1964). *Social Interest: A Challenge to Mankind.* New York: Capricorn.

Allen, V. B., Sampson, J. P., Jr., and Herlihy, B. "Details of the 1988 AACD Ethical Standards." *Journal of Counseling and Development,* 67 (3), 157–158.

American Association for Counseling and Development. (1988). *Ethical Standards.* Alexandria, VA: Author.

American Psychiatric Association (1987). *Diagnostic and Statistical Manual of Mental Disorders* (3rd ed.). Washington D.C.: Author.

Anastasi, A. (1988). *Psychological Testing* (6th ed.). New York: Macmillan.

Ansbacher, H. L., and Ansbacher, R. (Eds.) (1956). *The Individual Psychology of Alfred Alder.* New York: Basic Books.

Anthony, W. A. (1972). "Societal Rehabilitation: Changing Society's Attitudes toward the Physically and Mentally Disabled." *Rehabilitation Psychology* (19), 117–126.

Arlow, J. A. (1984). "Psychoanalysis." In R. J. Corsini (Ed.), *Current Psychotherapies.* Itasca, IL: F. E. Peacock.

Azrin, N. H., Flores, T., and Kaplan, S. J. (1977). "Job-Finding Club: A Group-Assisted Program for Obtaining Employment." *Rehabilitation Counseling Bulletin,* 2, 130–140.

Azrin, N. H., and Philip, R. A. (1979). "The Job Club Method for the Job Handicapped: A Comparative Outcome Study." *Rehabilitation Counseling Bulletin,* 2, 144–155.

Baker, R. (1955). *Sigmund Freud for Everybody.* New York: Popular Library.

Bandura, A. (1977). *Social Learning Theory.* Englewood Cliffs, NJ: Prentice-Hall.

Bandura, A. (1979). *Principles of Behavior Modification.* New York: Holt, Rinehart, & Winston.

Bandura, A., and Walters, R. H. (1963). *Social Learning and Personality Development.* New York: Holt, Rinehart & Winston.

Barton, W. E., and Barton, G. M. (1984). *Ethics and Law in Mental Health Administration.* New York: International Universities Press.

Baruth, L. G., and Huber, C. H. (1986). *Counseling and Psychotherapy: Theoretical Analysis and Skills Applications.* Columbus, OH: Charles E. Merrill.

Berne, E. (1972). *What Do You Do After You Say Hello?* New York: Grove Press.

Berkow, R. (Ed.). (1987). *The Merck Manual of Diagnosis and Therapy* (15th ed.). Rahway, NJ: Merck Sharp & Dohme.

Bertalanffy, L., von (1968). *General Systems Theory: Foundation, Development, Applications.* New York: Braziller.

Bijou, S. W. (1976). *Child Development: The Basic Stages of Early Childhood.* Englewood Cliffs, NJ: Prentice-Hall.

Bolton, B. (Ed.). (1982). *Vocational Adjustment of Disabled Persons.* Baltimore: University Park Press.

Brammer, L. M. (1969). "Eclecticism Revisited." *Personnel and Guidance Journal,* 48, 193–197.

Brammer, L. M. (1985). *The Helping Relationship: Process and Skills.* Englewood Cliffs, NJ: Prentice-Hall.

Brammer, L. M., and Shostrom, E. L. (1986). *Therapeutic Psychology: Fundamentals of Counseling and Psychotherapy.* (4th ed.). Englewood Cliffs, NJ: Prentice-Hall.

Brill, A. A. (1949). *Basic Principles of Psychoanalysis.* New York: Doubleday.

Brown, D., Pryzwansky, W. B., and Schulte, A. C. (1987). *Psychological Consultation: Introduction to Theory and Practice.* Boston: Allyn & Bacon.

Brown, J. H., and Christensen, D. N. (1986). *Family Therapy Theory and Practice.* Monterey, CA: Brooks/Cole.

Buber, M. (1957). *Pointing the Way.* New York: Harper & Row.

Buros, O. K. (Ed.). (1978). *The Eighth Mental Measurement Yearbook.* Highland Park, NJ: Gryphon.

Carkhuff, R. R., Alexik, M., and Andrews, S. (1967). "Do We Have a Theory of Vocational Choice?" *Personnel & Guidance Journal,* 46 (4), 335–345.

Clausen, J. A. (1975). "The Social Meaning of Differential Physical Maturation." In D. E. Drugastin & G. H. Elder (Eds.). *Adolescence in the Life Cycle.* New York: Halsted.

Corey, G. (1985). *Theory and Practice of Group Counseling.* Monterey, CA: Brooks/Cole.

Corey, G. (1986). *Theory and Practice of Counseling and Psychotherapy.* (3rd ed.). Monterey, CA: Brooks/Cole.

Corsini, R. J. (Ed.), (1984). *Current Psychotherapies.* Itasca, IL: F. E. Peacock.

Craig, W. C. (1980). *Theories of Development: Concepts and Applications.* Englewood Cliffs, NJ: Prentice-Hall.

Crites, J. O. (1981). *Career Counseling: Models, Methods, and Materials.* New York: McGraw-Hill.

Cronbach, L. J. (1970). *Essentials of Psychological Testing,* (3rd ed.). New York: Harper & Row.

Dawis, R. V., and Lofquist, L. H. (1976). "Personality Style and the Process of Work Adjustment." *Journal of Counseling Psychology.* 23, 55–59.

Dembo, T., Leviton, G. L., and Wright, B. A. (1975). "Adjustment to Misfortune: A Problem of Social-Psychological Rehabilitation." *Rehabilitation Psychology,* 22, 1–100.

Dinkmeyer, D. C., Pew, W. L., and Dinkmeyer, D. C. Jr. (1979). *Adlerian Counseling and Psychotherapy.* Monterey, CA: Brooks/Cole.

Dreikurs, R. (1961). *The Adlerian Approach to Therapy.* New York: Free Press of Glencoe, 80–94.

Drummond, R. J. (1988). *Appraisal Procedures for Counselors and Helping Professionals.* Columbus, OH: Charles E. Merrill.

Dusay, J. M., and Dusay, K. M. (1984). "Transactional Analysis." In Corsini, R. J. (Ed.). *Current Psychotherapies.* Itasca, IL: F. E. Peacock.

Egan, G. (1982). *The Skilled Helper: Model, Skills and Methods for Effective Helping.* (2nd ed.). Monterey, CA: Brooks/Cole.

Egan, G. (1986). "The Skilled Helper." In *A Systematic Approach to Effective Helping.* Monterey, CA: Brooks/Cole.

Ellis, A. (1962). *Reason and Emotion in Psychotherapy.* New York: Lyle Stuart.

Ellis, A. (1967). "Rational-Emotive Psychotherapy," In D. Arbuckle, (Ed.), *Counseling and Psychotherapy.* New York: McGraw-Hill.

Ellis, A. (1973). *Humanistic Psychotherapy.* New York: McGraw-Hill.

Ellis, A. (1984). "Rational-Emotive Therapy." In R. J. Corsini (Ed.), *Current Psychotherapies.* Itasca, IL: F. E. Peacock.

Erikson, E. H. (1950). *Childhood and Society.* New York: Norton.

Erikson, E. H. (1964). *Insight and Responsibility.* New York: Norton.

Erikson, E. H. (1968). *Identity, Youth, and Crises.* New York: Norton.

Erikson, E. H. (1982). *The Life Cycle Completed.* New York: Norton.

Festinger, S. (1957). *A Theory of Cognitive Dissonance.* New York: Harper & Row.

Fisher, L., and Sorenson, G. P. (1985). *School Law for Counselors, Psychologists, and Social Workers.* Boston: Houghton Mifflin.

Forsyth, D. R. (1983). *An Introduction to Group Dynamics.* Monterey, CA: Brooks/Cole.

Frankl, V. (1959). *Man's Search for Meaning.* New York: Washington Square Press.

Frankl, V. (1979). "The Will to Meaning." In *Foundations and Application of Logotherapy.* New York: Simon & Schuster.

Fredrickson, R. H. (1982). *Career Information.* Englewood Cliffs, NJ: Prentice-Hall.

Freud, S. (1935). *A General Introduction to Psychoanalysis.* New York: Liveright.

Freud, S. (1960). *Psychopathology of Everyday Life.* A. A. Brill, trans. New York: New American Library.

Frey, D. H., and Raming, H. E. (1979). "A Taxonomy of Counseling Goals and Methods." *Personnel and Guidance Journal,* 58, 26–33.

Ginzberg, E. (1972). "Toward a Theory of Occupational Choice: A Restatement." *Vocational Guidance Quarterly,* 20 (3) 169–176.

Ginzberg, E., Ginsburg, S. W., Axelrad, S., and Herma, J. L. (1951). *Occupational Choice: An Approach to General Theory.* New York: Columbia University Press.

Glasser, W. (1965). *Reality Therapy: A New Approach to Psychiatry.* New York: Harper & Row.

Glasser, W. (1969). *Schools without Failure.* New York: Harper & Row.

Glasser, W. (1984). "Reality Therapy." In R. J. Corsini (Ed.), *Current Psychotherapies.* Itasca, IL: F. E. Peacock.

Glasser, W., and Zunin, L. M. (1973). "Reality Therapy." In R. J. Corsini (Ed.). *Current Psychotherapies.* Itasca, IL: F. E. Peacock.

Goldenberg, I., and Goldenberg, H. (1985). *Family Therapy: An Overview.* (2nd ed.). Monterey, CA: Brooks/Cole.

Goldenson, R. M. (Ed.). (1978). *Disability and Rehabilitation Handbook.* New York: McGraw-Hill.

Groden, G., and Cauleta, J. R. (1981). "Behavior Therapy: A Survey of Procedures for Counselors." *Personnel and Guidance Journal,* 11, 175–180.

Guide to Rehabilitation Counselor Certification (1987). Commission on Rehabilitation Counselor Certification. Arlington Heights, IL: Author.

Hass, K. (1979). *Abnormal Psychology.* New York: Van Nostrand Reinhold.

Hall, C. (1954). *A Primer of Freudian Psychology.* New York: New American Library (Mentor).

Hall, C. S., and Lindzey, G. (1978). *Theories of Personality* (3rd ed.). New York: John Wiley & Sons.

Hall, C. S., and Nordley, V. J. (1973). *A Primer of Jungian Psychology.* New York: New American Library.

Hansen, J. C., Stevic, R. R., and Warner, R. W., Jr. (1986). *Counseling: Theory Process* (4th ed.). Boston: Allyn & Bacon.

Harris, T. (1967). *I'm OK—You're OK: A Practical Guide to Transactional Analysis.* New York: Harper & Row.

Herzberg, F. (1955). *Mental Health in Industry.* Pittsburgh: Psychological Services of Pittsburgh.

Hinsie, L. E., and Campbell, R. J. (1960). *Psychiatric Dictionary.* London: Oxford University Press.

Holland, J. L. (1959). "A Theory of Vocational Choice." *Journal of Counseling Psychology,* 6, 35–44.

Holland, J. L. (1973). *Making Vocational Choices: A Theory of Careers.* Englewood Cliffs, NJ: Prentice-Hall.

Hopkins, B. R., and Anderson, B. S. (1985). *The Counselor and the Law.* (2nd ed.). Alexandria, VA: AACD.

Hoppock, R. (1957). *Occupational Information.* New York: McGraw-Hill.

Hylbert, K. W. (1979). *Medical Information for Human Service Workers* (2nd ed.). State College, PA: Counselor Education Press.

Issacson, L. E. (1985). *Basics of Career Counseling.* Boston: Allyn & Bacon.

Ivey, A. E. (1971). *Microcounseling: Innovations in Interviewing Training.* Springfield, IL: Charles C. Thomas.

Ivey, A. E., and Authier, J. (1978). *Microcounseling* (2nd ed.). Springfield, IL: Charles C. Thomas.

Ivey, A. E., and Simek-Downing, L. (1980). *Counseling and Psychotherapy: Skills, Theories, and Practices.* Englewood Cliffs, NJ: Prentice-Hall.

Jacobson, E. (1938). *Progressive Relaxation.* Chicago: University of Chicago Press.

James, M., and Jongeward, D. (1971). *Born to Win: Transactional Analysis with Gestalt Experiments.* Reading, MA: Addison-Wesley.

Jung, C. G. (1933). *Modern Man in Search of a Goal.* New York: Harcourt, Brace, Jovanovich.

Jung, C. G. (1961). *Memories, Dreams, Reflections.* (A. Jaffe, & C. Winston, trans.). New York: Vintage Books.

Jung, C. G. (1964). "Approaching the Unconscious." In C. G. Jung (Ed.), *Man and His Symbols.* New York: Dell.

Karpman, S. (1968). "Fairy Tales and Script Drama Analysis." *Transactional Analysis Bulletin* (26), 39–43.

Kaufmann, Y. (1984). "Analytical Psychology." In R. J. Corsini (Ed.), *Current Psychotherapies.* Itasca, IL: F. E. Peacock.

Kerr, N. (1977). "Understanding the Process of Adjustment to Disability." In Stubbins (Ed.), *Psychosocial Aspects of Disabilities.* Baltimore, MD: University Park.

Kitchener, R. F. (1978). "Epigenesist: The Role of Biological Models in Development Psychology." *Human Development,* 21, 141–160.

Kohlberg, L. (1969). "States and Sequence: The Cognitive-Developmental Approach to Socialization." In D. A. Goslin (Ed.), *Handbook of Socialization, Theory and Research.* Skokie, IL: Rand McNally.

Kohlberg, L. (1984). *Essays on Moral Development.* Vol. 2: *The Psychology of Moral Development.* New York: Harper & Row.

Kovel, J. (1976). *A Complete Guide to Therapy: From Psychoanalysis to Behavior Modification.* New York: Pantheon.

Krumboltz, J. D., and Thoreson, C. E. (Ed.). (1976). *Counseling Methods.* New York: Holt, Rinehart & Winston.

Lazarus, A. A. (1971). *Behavior Therapy and Beyond.* New York: McGraw-Hill.

Lazarus, A. A. (1976). *Multimodal Behavior Therapy.* New York: Springer.

Levinson, D. (1978). *The Seasons of a Man's Life.* New York: John Wiley & Sons.

Levitsky, A., and Perls, F. (1970). "The Rules and Games of Gestalt Therapy." In J. Fagan and I. Shepherd (Eds.), *Gestalt Therapy Now.* New York: Harper & Row.

Liberty, L. H., and Sampson, D. E. (1987). "Textbooks Used Most Widely in Rehabilitation Counselor Education Programs." *Rehabilitation Education, 1* (4), 295–301.

Lorenz, K. (1965). *Evolution and Modification of Behavior.* Chicago: University of Chicago Press.

Maslow, A. H. (1968). *Toward a Psychology of Being.* (2nd ed.). Princeton, NJ: Van Nostrand Reinhold.

Masters, W. H., and Johnson, V. E. (1966). *Human Sexual Response.* Boston: Little, Brown.

May, R., and Yalom, I. (1984). "Existential Psychotherapy." In R. J. Corsini, (Ed.), *Current Psychotherapies.* Itasca, IL: F. E. Peacock.

Meador, B. D., and Rogers, C. R. (1984). "Person-Centered Therapy." In R. J. Corsini, (Ed.). *Current Psychotherapies.* Itasca, IL: F. E. Peacock.

Mischel, W. (1973). "Towards a Cognitive Social Learning Reconceptualization of Personality." *Psychological Review, 80,* 252–283.

Mitchell, A. M., Jones, G. B., and Krumboltz, J. D. (Eds.). (1979). *Social Learning Theory and Career Decision-Making.* Cranston, RI: Carroll.

Mosak, H. (1984). Adlerian Psychotherapy. In R. J. Corsini (Ed.), *Current Psychotherapies* (3rd ed.). Itasca, IL: F. E. Peacock.

Munn, N. L. (1974). *The Growth of Human Behavior.* (3rd ed.). Boston: Houghton Mifflin.

Murray, H. A. (1938). *Explorations in Personality.* New York: Oxford University Press.

Napier, R. W., and Gershenfeld, M. K. (1985). *Groups, Theory and Experience.* (3rd ed.). Boston: Houghton Mifflin.

National Board for Certified Counselors. (1987). *Code of Ethics.* Alexandria, VA: Author.

National Counselor Certification, Information & Application. (1989). Alexandria, VA: Author.

Newman, B. M., and Newman, P. R. (1984). *Development through Life: A Psychosocial Approach.* (3rd ed.). Homewood, IL: Dorsey.

Neff, W. (1985). *Work and Human Behavior* (3rd ed.). New York: Aldine.

Nichols, M. P. (1984). *Family Therapy, Concepts and Methods.* New York: Gardner.

O'Connell, A., and O'Connell, V. F. (1980). *Choice and Chance: The Psychology of Adjustment, Growth, and Creativity.* Englewood Cliffs, NJ: Prentice-Hall.

Osipow, S. J. (1968). *Theories of Career Development.* New York: Appleton-Century-Crofts.

Parsons, F. (1909). *Choosing a Vocation.* Boston: Houghton Mifflin.

Patterson, C. H. (1980). *Theories of Counseling and Psychotherapy.* (3rd ed.). New York: Harper & Row.

Pavlov, I. (1927). *Conditioned Reflexes* (Vol.1) (W. H. Grant, trans.). New York: International.

Perls, F. S. (1969a). *Gestalt Therapy Verbatim.* Moab, UT: Real People Press.

Perls, F. S. (1969b). *In and Out of the Garbage Pail.* Lafayette, CA: Real People Press.

Perls, F. S. (1970). "Four Lectures." In J. Fagan and I. Shepherd (Ed.), *Gestalt Therapy Now.* New York: Harper & Row.

Perls, F. S. (1973). *The Gestalt Approach.* Ben Lomond, CA: Science and Behavior Books.

Perls, F. S., Hefferline, R. and Goodman, P. (1951). *Gestalt Therapy: Excitement and Growth in the Human Personality.* New York: Dell.

Piaget, J. (1926). *The Language and Thought of the Child.* New York: Harcourt & Brace.

Piaget, J. (1972). "Intellectual Evolution from Adolescence to Adult." *Human Development,* 15, 1–12.

Pietrofesa, J. J., Hoffman, A., and Splete, H. H. (1984). *Counseling: An Introduction* (2nd ed.). Boston: Houghton Mifflin.

Quey, R. L. (1968). "Toward a Definition of Work." *Personnel and Guidance Journal,* 47 (3), 223–227.

Roe, A. (1956). *The Psychology of Occupations.* New York: John Wiley & Sons.

Roethlisberger, F. J., and Dickson, W. J. (1939). *Management and the Worker.* Cambridge, MA: Harvard University Press.

Rogers, C. R. (1957). "The Necessary and Sufficient Conditions of Therapeutic Personality Changes." *Journal of Consulting Psychology,* 21, 95–103.

Rogers, C. R. (1961a). *On Becoming a Person.* Boston: Houghton Mifflin.

Rogers, C. R. (1961b). "The Characteristics of a Helping Relationship." In Stein, M. I. (Ed.), *Contemporary Psychotherapies.* New York: Free Press of Glencoe.

Rogers, C. R. (1962). "The Interpersonal Relationship, the Core of Guidance." *Harvard Education Review,* 416–429.

Rogers, C. R. (1970). *Carl Rogers on Encounter Groups,* New York: Harper & Row.

Rubin, S. E., and Roessler, R. T. (1987). *Foundations of the Vocational Rehabilitation Process.* Austin, TX: PRO-ED.

Salomone, P. R. (1971). "A Client-Centered Approach to Job Placement." *Vocational Guidance Quarterly*, 19, 266–270.

Sattler, J. M. (1982). *Assessment of Children's Intelligence and Special Abilities* (2nd ed.). Boston: Allyn & Bacon.

Shaffer, D. R. (1988). *Social and Personality Development* (2nd ed.). Pacific Grove, CA: Brooks/Cole.

Sheehy, G. (1976). *Passages: Predictable Crises of Adult Life*. New York: Dutton.

Shertzer, B. (1985). *Career Planning: Freedom to Choose*. (3rd ed.). Dallas: Houghton Mifflin.

Shertzer, B., and Stone, S. C. (1974). *Fundamentals of Counseling* (2nd ed.). Boston: Houghton Mifflin.

Sigelman, C. K., Miller, T. E., and Whitworth, L. A. (1986). "The Early Development of Stigmatizing Reactions to Physical Differences." *Journal of Applied Developmental Psychology*, 7, 17–32.

Skinner, B. F. (1938). *The Behavior of Organisms: An Experimental Analysis*. New York: Appleton-Century.

Skinner, B. F. (1970). *Science and Human Behavior*. New York: Macmillan.

Skinner, B. F. (1974). *About Behaviorism*. New York: Alfred A. Knopf.

Slimak, R. E., and Berkowitz, S. R. (1983). "The University and College Counseling Center and Malpractice Suits." *Personnel and Guidance Journal*, 61 (5), 291–294.

Smith, D. (1982). "Trends in Counseling and Psychotherapy." *American Psychologist*, 37, 802–809.

Staffieri, J. R. (1967). "A Study of Social Stereotypes of Body Image in Children." *Journal of Personality and Social Psychology*, 7, 101–104.

Stolov, W. C., and Clowers, M. R. (1981). *Handbook of Severe Disability*. Washington, D.C.: Rehabilitation Services Administration, U.S. Department of Education.

Stone, I. (1971). *Passions of the Mind*, New York: Doubleday.

Stone, G. L. (1980). *A Cognitive Behavioral Approach to Counseling Psychology*. New York: Praeger.

Super, D. E. (1957). *The Psychology of Careers*. New York: Harper & Row.

Szuhay, J. A. (1987). *Health and Medical Manual*. University of Scranton, Scranton, PA: Human Resources.

Thoresen, C. E. (1966). "Behavioral Counseling: An Introduction." *The School Counselor*, 14, 13–21.

Thorne, F. C. (1961). *Personality*. Brandon, VT: Psychology Publishing.

Tiedeman, D. V., and O'Hara, R. P. (1963). *Career Development: Choice and Adjustment*. New York: College Entrance Examination Board.

Truax, C. B., and Carkhuff, R. R. (1965). "Client and Therapist Transparency in the Psychotherapeutic Encounter." *Journal of Counseling Psychology*, 12, 3–9.

Truax, C. B., and Carkhuff, R. R. (1967). *Toward Effective Counseling and Psychotherapy: Training and Practice.* Chicago, IL: Aldine.

U.S. Department of Commerce, Office of Federal Statistical Policy and Standards. (1980). *Standard Occupational Classification Manual.* Washington, D.C.: U.S. Government Printing Office.

U.S. Department of Labor (1977). *Dictionary of Occupational Titles,* (4th ed.). Washington, D.C.: U.S. Government Printing Office.

_____ (1979). *Guide for Occupational Exploration.* Washington, D.C.: U.S. Government Printing Office.

_____ (1981). *Selected Characteristics of Occupations Defined in the Dictionary of Occupational Titles.* Washington, D.C.: U.S. Government Printing Office.

_____ (1982). *Dictionary of Occupational Titles, Fourth Edition Supplement.* Washington, D.C.: U.S. Government Printing Office.

U.S. Executive Office of the President, Office of Management and Budget. (1972). *Standard Industrial Classification Manual.* Washington, D.C.: U.S. Government Printing Office.

Walen, S. R., DiGiuseppe, R., and Wessler, R. L. (1980). *A Practitioner's Guide to Rational-Emotive Therapy.* New York: Oxford University Press.

Wallace, W. A. (1986). *Theories of Counseling and Psychotherapy: A Basic Issues Approach.* Boston: Allyn & Bacon.

Walsh, W. B., and Betz, N. E. (1985). *Tests and Assessment.* Englewood Cliffs, NJ: Prentice-Hall.

Ward, D. (1983). "The Trend toward Eclecticism and the Development of Comphrensive Models to Guide Counseling and Psychotherapy." *Personnel and Guidance Journal,* 62, 154–157.

Watson, J. B. (1924). *Behaviorism.* New York: W. W. Norton, 1970.

Watson, J. P., and Marks, J. M. (1971). "Relevant and Irrelevant Fears in Flooding: A Cross-Over Study of Phobic Patients." *Behavior Therapy,* 2, 275–293.

White, R. W., and Watt, N. F. (1973). *The Abnormal Personality,* (4th ed.). New York: Ronald Press.

Williamson, E. G. (1939). *How to Counsel Students.* New York: McGraw-Hill.

Wilson, G. T. (1984). "Behavior Therapy" in R. J. Corsini (Ed.), *Current Psychotherapies.* Itasca, IL: F. E. Peacock.

Wolfe, R. (NRCA Ed.). (1988). *Professional Report of the National Rehabilitation Counseling Association* (Vol. XXIX). Alexandria, VA: National Rehabilitation Counseling Association.

Wolpe, J. (1958). *Psychotherapy by Reciprocal Inhibition.* Stanford, CA: Stanford University Press.

Wolpe, J. (1973). *The Practice of Behavior Therapy.* New York: Pergamon Press.

Wright, B. A. (1983). *Physical Disability—A Psychosocial Approach* (2nd ed.). New York: Harper & Row.

Wright, G. N. (1980). *Total Rehabilitation.* Boston: Little, Brown.

Wubbolding, R. E. (1981). "Balancing the Chart: 'Do It Person' and 'Positive Symptom Person.'" *Journal of Reality Therapy.* 1, 4–7.

Yalom, I. D. (1985). *The Theory and Practice of Group Psychotherapy* (3rd ed.). New York: Basic Books.

Yuker, H. E., Block, J. R., and Younng, J. H. (1966). *The Measurement of Attitudes toward Disabled Persons.* Albertson, NY: Human Resources Center.